The Struggle to Serve

The Struggle to Serve
The Ordination of Women in the Roman Catholic Church

SIMONE M. ST. PIERRE

McFarland & Company, Inc., Publishers
Jefferson, North Carolina, and London

The present work is a reprint of the library bound edition of The Struggle to Serve: The Ordination of Women in the Roman Catholic Church, *first published in 1994 by McFarland.*

LIBRARY OF CONGRESS CATALOGUING-IN-PUBLICATION DATA

St. Pierre, Simone M., 1964–
    The struggle to serve : The ordination of women in the Roman Catholic Church / by Simone M. St. Pierre.
       p.   cm.
    Originally presented as the author's thesis (M.A.) — University of Manitoba.
    Includes bibliographical references and index.

    ISBN 978-0-7864-6716-7
    softcover : 50# alkaline paper ∞

    1. Ordination of women — Catholic Church.   2. Women in the Catholic Church.   3. Catholic Church — Canada — History.   I. Title.
BX1912.2.S7   2011
262'.142'082 — dc20   93-41758

BRITISH LIBRARY CATALOGUING DATA ARE AVAILABLE

© 1994 Simone M. St. Pierre. All rights reserved

No part of this book may be reproduced or transmitted in any form or by any means, electronic or mechanical, including photocopying or recording, or by any information storage and retrieval system, without permission in writing from the publisher.

Front cover image © 2011 Shutterstock

Manufactured in the United States of America

McFarland & Company, Inc., Publishers
  Box 611, Jefferson, North Carolina 28640
    www.mcfarlandpub.com

To my son Justice with love

Table of Contents

Acknowledgments	xi
Introduction	1

1. THE ORDINATION OF WOMEN — 7

The Conclusions of the Pontifical Biblical Commission	7
The Development of the Christian Priesthood	8
Tradition in the Church	10
The Church's Fidelity to Christ	12
The Argument in Terms of Male Representation	15
The Restriction of Women	16
The Use of Aquinas	16
Jesus' Maleness	18
Can Women Represent God?	20
Does the Priest Represent Jesus' Humanity or His Maleness?	21

2. WOMEN IN THE MINISTRY OF JESUS — 29

Jesus' Maleness	30
Jesus' Message	30
Jesus' Attitude Towards Women in the New Testament	31
The Women in Mark's Gospel	32
The Women in John's Gospel	33
The Women in Luke's Gospel	34
The Women in Matthew's Gospel	35
Women in Jesus' Ministry	36
Mary and Martha	36
The Unknown Woman	37
Mary Magdalene	40
Mary of Nazareth	42
The Twelve	45

Why "Twelve" Men?	46
Why Twelve "Men"?	47

3. THE ROLE OF WOMEN IN THE EARLY CHURCH — 51

Can Scripture Determine Appropriate Roles for Women?	51
Paul and Women	52
Towards a Biblical Methodology	53
A Feminist Historical Reconstruction	56
Women's Roles in Paul's Writings	56
Silence for Women in the Church	57
I Timothy 2.8–15	60
Roles for Women in the Pauline Tradition	62
Phoebe	62
Apostle	64
Prophet/Prophetess	66
The "House" Church	66
The Order of Widows	67
Searching for Historical Documentation	67

4. OVERCOMING THE LAY-CLERGY DUALISM — 71

The Lay-Clergy Distinction	72
The Laity in the Early Church	72
The Theological Implications	72
The Official Treatment of the Laity	74
Vatican II	74
The Implications of the Term "Laity"	74
The Problem	75
The Effects	75
The Code of Canon Law	78
The Bishops' Synods	80
The Bishops' Synod	81
The Canadian Interventions	82
Ministry in the Church	85
Lay-Clergy Tensions in the Early Christian Community	85
Jesus' Ministry	86
The Concept of Ministry in the Early Church	87

Table of Contents ix

    The Role of "Apostolic Succession" — 88
    The Council of Chalcedon — 89

5. **WOMEN IN THE CATHOLIC CHURCH** — 93
    The Problem — 94
        "No" to Women Priests — 97
        Ministry for Men and Women — 98
        The Structure of the Church — 99
        Women's Struggle for Equality — 102
        The Resistance to Change — 104
    Pastoral and Liturgical Roles for Catholic Women — 105
        The Bernier Case — 106
        Arguments Against the Promotion of Women — 107
        Arguments for the Promotion of Women — 112
        A Comparison — 114
    Women's Inequalities — 115

6. **A CONTEMPORARY UNDERSTANDING OF THE ORDINATION OF WOMEN** — 117
    "On the Dignity and Vocation of Women on the Occasion of the Marian Year" — 117
        Men and Women in the Created Order — 118
        Jesus' Attitude Towards Women — 118
        Equality versus Diversity — 119
        Bridal Imagery — 121
        What Does the Official Church Offer for Women? — 122
    The Theology of the Ordination of Women — 124
        Understanding How God Was Revealed — 124
        Understanding Tradition in the Early Church — 125
    The Church's Ministry of Service — 127
    A "Christian" Ministry of Service — 129
        Bernard Cooke — 129
        Denise Lardner-Carmody — 131
        Edward Schillebeeckx — 133
    The Official Teaching on Vocations — 134
        The "Vocations" Prayer — 135
        The Problem with the Lack of Vocations in the Roman Catholic Church — 136
        Towards a Renewal of the Hierarchy — 136
        The Legitimate Call to Vocation — 137

Equal But Different 137
The Spiritual Effects of Women's Exclusion from the
 Ministerial Priesthood 138
A Theology of Liberation from Clericalism 141

Conclusion 145

Chapter Notes 149

Appendix 173

Bibliography 177

Index 199

Acknowledgments

Without the wisdom, assistance and guidance of certain special people, this book would not have been realized. I wish to express sincere thanks to Archbishop Rembert G. Weakland, O.S.B. from Milwaukee, Wisconsin, for his permission to reprint the talk he gave at the Synod of Bishops in Rome in 1987. His comments in this talk as well as various recently published articles strongly promote the inclusion of women at every level of the hierarchy.

This work began as a thesis in partial fulfillment of my Master's degree at the University of Manitoba in Canada. As such, I remain deeply indebted to my thesis advisor, Dr. Egil Grislis, for his editorial assistance and constant attention throughout the initial writing of this work. I am also indebted to the members of my thesis committee: Dr. Larry Hurtado, Dr. Dawn McCance and Dr. Richard Lebrun. Their insights challenged me to clarify my own thought and focus on the main issues at hand.

I also wish to acknowledge Sr. Thérèse Dion from Lorette, Dr. Edmond Cormier from St. Boniface College, Dr. H. Gordon Harland, formerly from the Department of Religion at the University of Manitoba, Professor Michael Shute, formerly from St. Paul's College and Fr. Sam Argenziano, formerly from St. Edward's Church in Winnipeg, for their direction and friendship throughout my academic years. I must also mention Teresa Whalen, whose "joie de vivre" and special friendship helped me persevere through the academic treadmill.

From a practical standpoint, I must also thank various people who assisted me in my research: Bill Wsiaki and Father Drake from St. Paul's College library and John Adams from the Correspondence Service at the Dafoe Library for their promptness and assistance in locating sources for my work, Lynn Innerst and the staff at the public library in Dauphin, Manitoba, for their services and general assistance, Rosemary Murphy who is currently the Directrice of Communications for the Archdiocese of Milwaukee in Wisconsin for her researching of Archbishop Rembert G. Weakland's articles and talks which treat the role of women in the Church, Agostino Bono, a CNS reporter stationed in Rome who amazingly sent me information regarding Edward Schillebeeckx's latest published interview within a day as the conclusion of this work was quickly approaching, Matilde Magnifico for translating the Italian copy of the Schillebeeckx interview to English, and Helen M. Zuefle for her legal advice regarding the publication of this work.

On a more personal note, I wish to thank my sister, Janine Durand-Rondeau, for her diligence in typing out revision after revision, until the final copy was complete, as well as Kim McDonnell for typing out the index on her computer. Also, I am deeply indebted to my parents, Denis and Laurette Durand, for their love and nurturing over the years and for their constant concern for my well-being and that of my family. Having children of my own made me realize how much they love me. Lastly, to my husband, Jacques, to whom I am eternally committed: thank you for your love and strength and encouragement to finish this work.

Introduction

This work began as a master's thesis, and took the form of an academic inquiry into the role of women in the Roman Catholic Church. After the completion of my degree in 1991, I began revising the work for publication. At this time, my thought started to center on the "discipleship of equals" according to Rosemary Radford Ruether and Elisabeth Schüssler-Fiorenza. Ministry in this setting is understood in terms of a ministry of service—as Jesus initiated in the early Christian communities. The admission of women to the ministerial priesthood could not possibly be exercised within a power system such as the Catholic Church—unless the latter should undergo various modifications which would demand a de-clericalization of its organizational model.

The main preoccupation in this work is in calling attention to the injustices that women experience within the hierarchic and patriarchal confines of the Roman Catholic Church. It identifies the latter with a power structure which is self-serving and clerical in character. Its expression and unfolding of ministry could not be further away from Jesus' missionary activity here on earth. The identification of this reality is an attempt to examine the extent to which the current Church is an expression of Jesus' ministry of service and discipleship of equals.

It is important to note here that despite these practical concerns, affiliation to a specific community such as the Roman Catholic Church remains significant. It is after all, a Church initiated by Christ, and baptism as full members entails a membership in Christ's body—the Church. It is therefore not the intent of this work to do away with Roman Catholicism. Rather, the main intent of this work is to examine the exclusion of women from the ministerial priesthood in light of Schüssler-Fiorenza and Ruether's process of conversion to a self-awareness that men and women are the Church. Such a process demands a metanoïa from the understanding that God's salvific action is accomplished from above to a claiming of gifts among community members and the expression of God's salvific action through a ministry of service from below.

Therein lies the understanding behind my title: *The Struggle to Serve*. It is a variation of the phrase "the struggle to survive." I think that if the Roman Catholic Church survives, it will largely be because of women. Throughout Jesus' ministry and still today, women in the Church are the more active in comparison to men. That is not to say that men should be excluded and that women should take charge. Rather, the notion of service remains a struggle mainly for women and in part for men because women are not recognized in any official manner, nor are they included among the clergy or the decision-makers in the Church. It is a struggle for men "in part" because some men who sincerely and willingly dedicate themselves to Christ are officially acknowledged and recognized for their contributions. It remains an injustice, however, to men and women who possess the gifts by virtue of their baptism in Christ for the fulfillment of His Church on earth and yet are not given the opportunity or the vehicle to use these gifts creatively.

I entitled this work a struggle to "serve" because the concept of *ekklēsia* or women-church is one which is based on the "service" model of Jesus' ministry. He taught that "Whoever would be great among you must be your servant" (Matthew 20.26, RSV). The mutual empowerment to service is one which comes from the community. The Roman Catholic model for service comes from above and filters through the hierarchy. As such, this becomes a "power" system based on domination and authority. One of the ways in which this aspect of dominance is conveyed occurs in the exclusion of women from the ministerial priesthood. Therefore, my work begins with a discussion of the three main arguments presented in the *Declaration on the Question of the Admission of Women to the Ministerial Priesthood*. Issued in 1976, this document reinforces the Church's exclusion of women from the ministerial priesthood by presenting more innovative arguments to justify the current legislation. To assist the members of the Sacred Congregation for the Doctrine of the Faith, who were responsible for compiling the report, Pope Paul VI appointed the Pontifical Biblical Commission to examine the role of women in the Bible, and therefore provide some insight as to the roles that women can be accorded in a contemporary setting.

Although various conflicts occur when seeking to identify roles for women from a purely scriptural perspective, the Biblical Commission's three main findings concluded that the New Testament does not conclusively give enough evidence to settle the issue of women's ordination, that scripture alone does not justify the exclusion of women to the ministerial priesthood, and that Christ's will would not be disobeyed if the Roman Catholic Church decided to ordain women. Despite these findings, the Sacred Congregation clearly excludes women from the ministerial priesthood based on three main arguments that stem from the Church's constant tradition, fidelity to Christ's will, and sacramental-male representation, and neglects to mention or even acknowledge the Biblical Commission's report.

Despite this practical concern, I examine the *Declaration*'s arguments, and proceed to outline its strengths and weaknesses. Having completed this exercise, I found that the *Declaration* offered little new insight as the arguments presented made no use of contemporary feminist scholarship. I therefore found it essential to treat the role of women in the ministry of Jesus in such a manner that it would allow for contemporary insights from feminist biblical scholars. Here, various conflicts arose.

Although it is clearly attested among biblical scholars that the Bible was written against the backdrop of a patriarchal culture, the figure of Jesus is predominantly portrayed as a feminist, in terms of one who promotes the equality of women with men. Apart from the Twelve, Jesus does not restrict the ministry of women. Yet certain passages indicate that the role of women has been somewhat downplayed in comparison to that of the men in Roman Catholic tradition. For example, Peter's confession of faith after having denied Jesus three times is the foundation from which the Papacy was built, whereas Martha's confession of faith is overshadowed by the raising of Lazarus. Similarly, the "unknown" woman who anointed Jesus remains insignificant, while Peter, the disciple who denied Jesus, and Judas, the one who betrayed Jesus, figure prominently in the passion accounts. Further, although Mary Magdalene fulfills all the criteria for apostleship outlined by Paul and Luke, she remains insignificant because she was not included among the Twelve.

I devote a much longer section to Mary of Nazareth in comparison with the other women that figure prominently in Jesus' ministry. In the Roman Catholic Church, Mary is regarded as the "model" woman whose prominence and significance overshadow any other feminine figure in the Scriptures. Mary of Nazareth is submissive and obedient. My discussion of Ruether at this point is intended to demonstrate that it is not essential to prove that Mary was anything but faithful and serving in order to extract any positive role models for women. One can find very creative and active elements in Mary's ministry that can be applied to women in a contemporary setting.

On a whole, I observe that apart from Peter, James, John and Judas, none of the other apostles who are among the Twelve figure prominently in the gospels. The women, however, are almost always identified by name, along with the duties and functions they performed in Jesus' ministry.

This leads me to question the value of the Twelve in terms of their maleness. What was the eschatological significance of the Twelve? Was their significance *solely* eschatological? If it was, Jesus' choice of twelve men can hardly be seen as a prescription to be upheld for a long period of time. If Jesus willed that priestly ministry only be conferred upon men, why was he so inclusive of women throughout his ministry?

This brings me back to the Biblical Commission's report, whose findings indicated that, should the Church decide to ordain women, it would not be acting contrary to Christ's will. In terms of functions, if the apostles' main concern had to do with proclaiming the gospel message and administering new churches, women were not excluded from performing these roles. Further, it remains curious that although there is no clear evidence to support the idea that any of the Twelve ever presided at the Eucharist, women are to be excluded from Roman Catholic priestly orders based on the argument that the twelve male disciples set an unalterable pattern of male precedence at the Last Supper.

Chapter 3 searches for a biblical methodology that could assist in discovering women's strengths against the backdrop of a patriarchal culture. There follows a detailed discussion of Paul: Did he really silence women? What was Phoebe's role in the Church at Cenchreae? This leads me to a discussion of the term *apostle*. Paul includes himself as well as other disciples, yet women are not considered apostles in Roman Catholic tradition, even though they observe the same criteria as Paul. For example, there is some dispute over the name *Junias* in Romans 16.7. While some scholars have held that *Junias* was really a woman named *Junia,* others have held that *Junias* had to be a man, because he was given the title of apostle. Regardless of whether *Junias* was a man or a woman, the fact remains that there were other disciples who were noted as apostles, even though they were not among the Twelve.

Other roles discussed include that of house church leader, prophetess, and widow. In short, the *Declaration* appears to have been quite selective in choosing texts that restrict women's roles in the Church, and I observe that the Pauline writings bear witness to a community of believers in which ministries for women abound unconditionally.

In Chapter 4, I move towards a more contemporary understanding of the apparent dichotomy between lay and clerical roles. Not only is there an ongoing tension between the laity and the clergy in terms of their duties and functions, one can also observe a segregation among the laity themselves in which women are restricted in comparison to men. The Roman Catholic Church must overcome the segregation of lay women from lay men, if it will ever facilitate the ordination of women to the ministerial priesthood.

Chapter 5 begins by outlining the problems that continue to plague the Roman Catholic Church, which stem from the restriction imposed on women. On a practical level, the number of available candidates for the priesthood each year is declining. Seventy-three percent of priests in Canada are 50 years and older. By the second or third decade of the twenty-first century what will the Catholic Church experience? If the Roman Catholic Church continues to exclude women from the ministerial priesthood, the future Church will experience parishes without priests. That means parishes without sacraments, and parishes without pastoral care.

I observe that although the shortage of priests is of practical importance, there still remains a serious apparent injustice for women in the sense that women remain unequal to men. For example, several pastoral letters or papal pronouncements deal with the full equality of women and men. How can this ideal of full equality be truly accomplished if women are not permitted to fully respond to their baptismal calling? In short, while the Church is saying to women that on a theoretical level they are equal members of the Church, when it comes to the practical level men have certain rights and women, fewer.

In Chapter 6 I examine the theological impediments that need to be overcome when dealing with the ordination of women, in an attempt to show that, although the Church has become more inclusive of women since the *Declaration* was published, complete inclusion of women will be accomplished only when they are admitted to the ministerial priesthood. Roman Catholics must come to realize that women also have a vocation to fulfill in the Church — one that goes beyond their biological function as virgins and mothers. If the Roman Catholic Church continues to exclude women from the ministerial priesthood, not only are women being unjustly treated, I observe that their exclusion has dire implications for the Church's salvific mission. In short, when the Roman Catholic Church continues to exclude women from the ministerial priesthood on the basis that Jesus chose only men to be a part of his apostles, and that women were absent from the Last Supper, the Church is communicating that Jesus excluded women from the Eucharist. If Jesus excluded women from the Eucharist, it would logically follow that

He excluded women from salvation. I observe that if the Roman Catholic Church attempts to remain credible for its people, it cannot overlook these facts. The work that follows is my interpretation of where the conflicts lie and what needs to be readdressed when regarding the question of women's ordination in the Roman Catholic Church and the discipleship of equals.

CHAPTER 1

The Ordination of Women

In 1976, the Sacred Congregation for the Doctrine of the Faith issued a *Declaration on the Question of the Admission of Women to the Ministerial Priesthood* which concludes that for various reasons, the Church "...does not consider herself authorized to admit women to priestly ordination,"[1] despite the Biblical Commission's[2] report whose three main findings were, "that the New Testament does not settle in a clear way ... whether women can be ordained priests, [that] scriptural grounds alone are not enough to exclude the possibility of ordaining women, [and that] Christ's plan would not be transgressed by permitting the ordination of women."[3]

Although complete analysis of the *Declaration* would be quite beneficial, it would also be impossible to do so given the scope of the present work. Therefore, this chapter will address three main arguments presented in the *Declaration* for the exclusion of women to the ministerial priesthood: First, the Church's determination to remain faithful to its constant tradition, second, its fidelity to Christ's will, and third, the notion of male representation due to the "sacramental nature" of the priesthood.

It is therefore intended that, by examining and interpreting the main arguments presented in the *Declaration,* one can come to a better understanding of the reasoning used by the Roman Catholic Church to justify its exclusion of women from the ministerial priesthood. In this manner, it will be possible to identify the *Declaration*'s strengths and weaknesses and to invite further discussion as to possible roles for women in the future of the Roman Catholic Church.

The Conclusions of the Pontifical Biblical Commission

The *Declaration* concluded rather decisively that on the basis of the New Testament, Christ willed that women not be ordained. In other words, Christ established the practice of the early Church, whose tradition continued to exclude women from the priesthood. I observe very definite inconsistencies when comparing the *Declaration* to the Pontifical Biblical Commission's report. For example, the *Declaration* argues that Christ initiated the concept of priesthood by choosing twelve male apostles. Since women did not belong to this exclusively male group, it would then follow that Christ willed that only men be ordained. The Biblical Commission's report, however, maintains that

> According to the witness of the New Testament, especially the Pauline epistles, women are associated with the different charismatic ministries (diaconies) of the Church (1 Cor. 12.4; 1 Tim. 3.11, cf. 8): prophecy, service, probably even apostolate ... without, nevertheless, being of the Twelve.[4]

Another conflicting area has to do with tradition. While the *Declaration* maintains that Christ entrusted his ministry to the Twelve and not to his female disciples, the Biblical Commission's report stresses its eschatological symbolism in that the "... group of twelve men, ... after the fashion of the twelve patriarchs of the Old Testament, would be the leaders of the renewed people of God (Mk. 3.14–19)."[5] If the *Declaration* has attributed the Church's practice of maintaining an all-male priesthood to Jesus' will, I suggest that the eschatological significance has distinct implications. As John Donahue observes,

> If the choice of the Twelve is dictated by the eschatological consciousness of Jesus that the end is near, then his choice can scarcely be seen as prescriptive for a long period of Church history.[6]

By interpreting Christ's will as such, the *Declaration* has done precisely this. It states that the Church's constant tradition has been to exclude women from the priesthood in order to remain faithful to Christ, on the basis that Christ willed an all-male priesthood by excluding women from the circle of the Twelve.[7] Yet, there is no indication from the New Testament texts that the Twelve ever functioned as "ministerial" priests.[8]

The purpose of this section will be to discuss these inconsistencies in order to address the implications that result when the arguments presented in the *Declaration* are examined.

The Development of the Christian Priesthood. The *Declaration* assumes that Christ ordained twelve men at the time of the Last Supper, and concludes that, since women were not a part of this group, Christ willed that women be excluded from the priesthood.[9] Regarding the missions entrusted to the Twelve at the occasion of the Last Supper, Thomas P. Rausch has suggested that

... if by ordination is understood an authoritative appointment to an apostolic function, then all the elements are here: the command to the Twelve, phrased in established ritual language, to repeat the new covenant meal. The words of institution themselves are referred back to cultic and sacrificial formulae of the Old Testament.[10]

Similarly, the apostolic letter *On the Dignity and Vocation of Women on the Occasion of the Marian Year,* issued in 1988, confirms the argument presented in the *Declaration,*[11] where the calling of only twelve male apostles is directly linked with the institution of the Eucharist, for it is here that the Twelve are told, "...do this in remembrance of me" (Luke 22.19, RSV). This in turn is concretely linked to the redemption of man, for it is through the Eucharist that "...the redemptive act of Christ, who creates the Church, his body ... is made present and realized anew in a sacramental manner."[12] Therefore, since the Eucharist is the ultimate sign for the redemptive act of Christ (personified as the Bridegroom) towards the Church (his Bride), the apostolic letter concludes that the Bride-Bridegroom analogy was used to establish appropriate roles for men and women. Further, it is directly related to the exclusive male service of the Twelve in that the sacramental ministry of the Eucharist must be fulfilled by a man.[13]

Given this argument, one can say that the Roman Catholic Church has directly linked the Last Supper with the institution of an all-male Christian priesthood.[14] Various biblical scholars, however, have been quite reluctant to associate the institution of the priesthood with the Last Supper. Among them, Raymond Brown has noted that the concept of Christian priesthood as opposed to that in Jewish times (i.e., the Levitical priesthood) could not have been initiated by Christ. He argues that it had to undergo several modifications—ones that took time to develop. For example, he notes that the idea that Christianity was a distinct religion in itself as compared to Judaism did not develop as such until A.D. 70. Another consideration Brown notes is the idea that the development of the Eucharist (as a replacement for sacrifices previously offered in Judaism) did not occur until the second century. Further, there is no indication in the New Testament that Jesus instituted the priesthood. As Brown states:

> The term priest (hierus) is not used in the New Testament for any individual Christian, although it is used to describe the priesthood of all believers and the priesthood of Christ which replaces all human priesthoods.[15]

Although His own priesthood is solely mentioned in the Epistle to the Hebrews, it has been noted that

> ... nowhere does [the New Testament] ... connect the priesthood and sacrificial ministry of Jesus with any sort of priestly or sacrificial ministry on the part of Christians.[16]

Further, the Pontifical Biblical Commission's report suggests that the Bride-Bridegroom analogy pertains to Christ and the Church, and never enters the area of ministry.[17] Therefore, the *Declaration*'s treatment of the relationship between the calling of the Twelve and the development of the Christian priesthood appears problematic.

Tradition in the Church. The argument presented in the *Declaration* observes that the Roman Catholic Church's constant tradition has found it unacceptable to permit women's ordination, with the exception of a few "heretical sects."[18] It can therefore find no justification for breaking a 2000-year-old practice rooted in a tradition guided by the Holy Spirit.

Prior to undertaking any examination of this argument, a definition of the term "tradition" is in order. Francine Cardman has called attention to a noteworthy distinction. She states:

> Tradition [upper-case] is the Gospel itself, transmitted from generation in and by the Church. It is, in a sense, Christ himself present through the Holy Spirit in the life of the Church ... [whereas] tradition [lower-case] is often referred to as apostolic tradition — [the handing-on of the Christian message as exemplified by the first apostolic community].[19]

Although the history of the life and practice of the Church has been commonly referred to as "Catholic doctrine,"[20] I observe that the very life of the Church itself has witnessed significant transitions in certain practices due to varying historical and cultural considerations. For example, the continuing exclusion of women from priesthood has been associated with the Old Testament practice of "temple" priesthood. As Rosemary Radford Ruether notes,

> With this identification comes the revival of purity laws which strictly exclude women from priesthood that becomes most strictly exclusive of women.[21]

It is apparent that in New Testament times, women prominently exercised leadership roles characteristic of the duties performed later by priests.[22] Therefore, if women became excluded from the Christian priesthood in order to conform with the Old Testament practice and not from Christ's apparent exclusion of women from the Twelve, the Roman Catholic Church's statement that they have continued to exclude women from the priesthood due to the Church's constant tradition and as an attempt to conform with Christ's will cannot be maintained. Elizabeth

1. The Ordination of Women

Carroll has argued that the tradition of excluding women from the priesthood in the Roman Catholic Church remains inconsistent on the basis that the practice stems from two traditions:

> ... that of Jesus and the earliest Church, which had some partial echoes in history, and that of the institutionalizing period of the Church (about 60 to 100 A.D.), which limited women in ministry and excluded them from priesthood.[23]

In this sense, she maintains that the Church's exclusion of women from official roles stems from the restriction placed upon women from performing authoritative social roles. I observe that if the restriction placed upon women in the formation of an "institutionalized" Church was indeed due to the social restrictions placed upon women at that time, the Roman Catholic Church has absolutized these cultural considerations in an attempt to justify its exclusion of women from leadership positions.

Similarly, Ruether maintains that the *Declaration*'s argument which stems from the Church's "constant" tradition is based upon a tradition of women's subjection. Of course the *Declaration* fails to acknowledge this, and asserts that the exclusion of women to the ministerial priesthood has to do with Christ's maleness.[24]

The underlying motive for Vatican II can be interpreted as a study and reexamination of certain practices in the Church that no longer met the needs of the People of God. In doing so, Vatican II illustrated the Church's constant need to evaluate the signs of the times. It is only in this manner that the Church can truly continue to be relevant for its people. As Francine Cardman notes,

> Because the Tradition is conveyed in tradition, there must be a continual reinterpretation of this tradition in light of the present hermeneutical situation. The way in which tradition understands and expresses the Tradition must change with changing historical situations, or otherwise the same thing would not continue to be understood.[25]

For example, one can say that the liturgical modifications that emerged from the Second Vatican Council (i.e., having the celebrant face the people, the change from Latin to a language that people could understand, and the like) indicate a progression towards improving the Mass so that it can offer a better understanding about Christ's message for the People of God. If the Church can justify these changes, it is rather inconsistent that it would not consider the extension of women's roles in the Church to include priestly ordination—since it is apparent to many modern women that if they are truly to become full members of Christ's Church, they must be allowed to participate actively in the building of that Church, including leadership, as well as ordinary roles. What better way to make Christ's message truly relevant for today's Church? As we shall see in Chapter 2, it is apparent that Jesus did not generally exclude women from his ministry.[26] If the Roman Catholic Church is truly faithful in preserving Christ's message, it cannot overlook the guidance of the Spirit in this age. To use the words of Edward J. Kilmartin, S.J.:

> ... the tradition of almost 2000 years should not provide an obstacle to ordaining women if serious attention is paid to the dependence of religious structures on historical circumstances. Preference should be given to the creative role of the Spirit in the life of the Church rather than to a Latin-Stoic tradition ... the exclusion of women and married men from spiritual office does violence not only to the spiritual right of all baptized, but clashes with the freedom of the Spirit.[27]

The Spirit freely chooses to bestow gifts upon men and women alike. When men and women are given the opportunity to develop these gifts, they become "empowered" to benefit their Christian community. Ruether describes this action as "leadership from power over others to empowerment of others."[28] Therefore, the Spirit "empowers" men and women to serve their community without totally depending on the hierarchy for direct access to God.

Another consideration which flows from this argument has to do with scripture—as scripture is a fundamental element when dealing with Tradition. As we shall discuss in Chapter 2, various biblical scholars have argued that the New Testament was written against a patriarchal background.[29] The *Declaration* contends that

> ... if he [Jesus] acted in this way, it was not in order to conform to the customs of his time, for his attitude towards women was quite different from that of his milieu, and he deliberately and courageously broke with it.[30]

I maintain that it is quite impossible to deny that Jesus' calling of twelve male apostles reflects the influences of his cultural milieu.

The Church's Fidelity to Christ. In light of the Church's "constant" tradition, the *Declaration* maintains that in an attempt to remain faithful to Christ's will and to the practice of the apostles, the Church can justify the notion that only men be called to priestly orders. Regarding this matter, it seems that the *Declaration* has taken the liberty of making several assumptions. First, it assumes that gender was the most basic consideration to observe when Jesus chose the Twelve. Chapter 2 will examine the notion that, although Jesus' ministry was inclusive of women and Gentiles, he did not call any from these groups to be a part of the Twelve. Yet the *Declaration* insists that, since Jesus did not call any women to be a part of the Twelve, he therefore "...did not entrust the apostolic charge to women."[31] Does this mean that since he did not call any Gentiles to be a part of the Twelve, they should be excluded as well?[32] Further, Bernard Cooke claims that

> Apart from their presence at the Supper and at the post-Resurrection meals, there is practically nothing in the New Testament that might refer to a special role of the Twelve in early Christian worship.[33]

If the Apostles had no "special role" in early Christian worship, the selection of twelve male apostles should not hinder women's ability or calling to leadership roles in a liturgical setting.

Second, the *Declaration* states that, although women seem to have exercised prominent roles in Christ's ministry, in an attempt to remain faithful to Christ's will, the apostolic community did at no time confer ordination upon women, "...since the official and public proclamation of the message ... belonged exclusively to the apostolic mission."[34] Given this statement, one can say that the collaborators of the *Declaration* assume that ordination is directly associated with apostolic mission in that by choosing only twelve male apostles, Christ willed that apostolic mission only be conferred upon men. My concern is that this argument appears untenable. It seems that if the *Declaration* holds that apostolic mission was conferred only to men, it should follow that it only be conferred to these twelve men in particular. As Sandra M. Schneiders has argued,

> The Twelve are immortalized as the foundation of the Church. As such, they have no successors. And as disciples, apostles, teachers, early Church leaders, etc., in which capacities they do have successors, they are members of a wider group which was never all male.[35]

Raymond Brown has noted that members of the Twelve were not necessarily bishops or leaders in the Church. For example, James was the leader in the Jerusalem Church and he was not a member of the Twelve. Further, it seems that there were other leaders who simultaneously exercised prominent roles in the early Church. For example, Brown has argued that the bishops were not necessarily seen as successors to the apostles. He stresses that

> One may persuasively argue that the sacramental powers were given to the Christian community in the persons of the Twelve; and while the Twelve themselves may have been baptized, presided at the Eucharist and forgiven sins, the Church may also have recognized the sacramental

> authority of others who were not ordained by the Twelve. [That is to indicate that women may have exercised roles comparable to that of the priesthood in the early Church.][36]

Therefore, it remains questionable whether the *Declaration*'s argument, based on the assumption that women be excluded from the priesthood because the first apostolic community did not ordain women, can be maintained.

In terms of apostolic mission, however, the *Declaration* refers to Paul as one through whom women's "collaboration" was not extended to "the official and public proclamation of the message."[37] One therefore wonders where Paul's authority comes from. He was certainly not a member of the Twelve. However, it seems that the *Declaration* has accorded Paul's leadership greater significance than members of the Twelve. Yet Paul is commonly referred to as an "apostle." What distinguishes his apostleship from that of the Twelve? It seems rather evident that the collaborators of the *Declaration* see little or no distinction. Further, if one cannot distinguish between Paul's apostolic mission and that of the Twelve, it seems rather untenable that the *Declaration* would overlook Junia's apostolic mission—as Paul refers to her as "outstanding among the apostles" in Romans 16.7. However, Junia's name fails to appear in the arguments presented. As we have seen, James is highly regarded as a leader in the Church of Jerusalem, yet Junia is not mentioned. One therefore wonders how the Roman Catholic Church can justify the leadership of men and disregard the leadership of women.

In short, the argument that, in an attempt to remain faithful to Christ's will and attitude towards women, the apostolic community did not ordain any women, and therefore the Church "does not consider herself authorized to admit women to priestly ordination,"[38] seems untenable given the fact that the only decisive reason for reserving priestly ministry to men is their gender. Otherwise, the Church would have to insist on preserving a priesthood based upon other characteristics of the Twelve—a notion the Church seems to have overlooked in outlining criteria for the priesthood. For example we know that although wine is the official beverage used to designate Christ's blood, the Church has permitted the use of alcohol-free wine for alcoholic priests. What of women? It seems that if the Church has confidently modified several aspects from the Christian priesthood in order to suit the needs of its people, it cannot overlook the admission of women to the ministerial priesthood.

Further, it seems that women exercised prominent roles in Jesus' ministry, as well as leadership roles in the early Christian community. Although Jesus chose only men to be part of the Twelve—in accordance with Jewish social customs, as "positions of authority were reserved to men"[39]—there is no indication that Jesus willed to exclude women from the priesthood. In fact, Ruether claims that Jesus tried to transform God's image from a dominant male figure to a more egalitarian model. However, Paul's theology of women's spousal subordination led the Church back to the Old Testament image of a ruling Father.[40] The concept of the first Christian priesthood emerged in the second century. Although Jesus was given the title of priest (in Hebrews) he did not ordain any men or women to the priesthood. The mystery of Jesus' incarnation was realized through the faithfulness of a woman—Mary. Therefore, to use Pope John Paul II's words, "...in Christ the mutual opposition between man and woman ... is essentially overcome."[41]

The Argument in Terms of Male Representation

The third main consideration given in the *Declaration* has to do with the representation of the presider and the manner in which he is called to celebrate "in persona Christi."[42] The argument states that the priesthood is of a "sacramental nature, [therefore] the priest is a sign, ... that must be perceptible and which the faithful must be able to recognize with ease."[43] Of significance here are the words "in persona Christi." The Jerusalem Bible has interpreted the phrase to mean "in the presence of Christ."[44] Similarly, the *Declaration* states that "the bishop or the priest, in the exercise of his ministry, does not act in his own name, ... he represents Christ, who acts through him."[45]

Sonya A. Quitslund has noted that the priest represents Christ in a mystical and not a sexual sense—"as Christ, not the priest, is the real celebrant of the sacraments."[46] Given this notion, one can say that if the priest's representation is to be understood in a truly mystical sense, it would be irrelevant whether the celebrant be male or female.

Further, Sister Joan Chittister has noted that the *Declaration* stresses the terms *symbol*, *sign*, *representation*, and *image* as evidence supporting the emphasis placed on the maleness of priests. In doing so, Sister Joan points out that the *Declaration* fails to pay significant attention to the fact that even the historical Jesus in his incarnate form shared two natures—one human, the other divine.[47] The word "incarnation" itself is derived from the Latin *caro*, meaning "flesh."[48] Therefore, one must stress that Jesus' incarnation (i.e., taking on the form of a human body) is of primary significance. The fact that he took on a male body is secondary.

The Restriction of Women. In terms of women's leadership, Margaret Farley has offered that when understood in light of the patriarchally influenced cultures in the time of the early Church, it becomes quite apparent why women could not be ordained as priests. As she states,

> They could not govern nor administer; they could not be decision-makers nor public teachers; they could not even be servants in a way that implied an equal share of responsibility for the life of the community.[49]

Given these cultural considerations, it is curious that the Church has not reconsidered its position on the exclusion of women to the ministerial priesthood. As Rosemary Ruether has noted,

> ... the persons who hold power for change [in the Roman Catholic Church] are elderly Italian male celibates; in short, persons whose entire personal, social and cultural experience most totally removes them from understanding the issues of women or contact with changing cultures where women are playing different roles.[50]

The Use of Aquinas. The *Declaration* uses the words of Saint Thomas to ascribe meaning to the idea of representation, in that the Christian priesthood be seen as one of "sacramental nature," and therefore concludes, in Saint Thomas' words, that "sacramental signs ... represent what they signify by natural resemblance." Further, the footnote explains:

> For, since a sacrament is a sign, there is required in the things that are done in the sacraments not only the res but the signification of the res, recalls St. Thomas, precisely in order to reject the ordination of women....[51]

If the *Declaration* had completed the authoritative quote, however, as John R. Donahue has aptly pointed out, it would have read as follows:

> Since, therefore, it is not possible in the female sex that any eminence of degree be signified for a woman is in the state of subjection, she cannot receive the sacrament of orders.[52]

Therefore, for Aquinas, the argument used has to do with the illusion that women have a naturally subject state and are therefore subordinate to men—as though women were not created in the same image and likeness of God as men were. Says Madeleine I. Boucher:

In light of the empirical evidence of women's equality in so many areas of achievement, it is extremely doubtful that we can continue to take that view as "revelation"; the evidence fairly compels us to attribute it to the cultural limitations of the biblical writers [just as patriarchy is no longer a valid reason for which women's roles should be restricted in today's church].[53]

Further, it has been suggested by Dr. Ida Raming that

... all the arguments against the ordination of women are founded on the assumption that women are inferior to men and that consequently, they ought to — and in fact do — live in a state of subjection to men.[54]

Her work entitled, *The Exclusion of Women from the Priesthood: Divine Law or Sex Discrimination* strongly supports the idea that canon 968 §1, which excludes women from the ministerial priesthood, has no theological basis. In fact, her research has called attention to several important texts that deal with the exclusion of women in various liturgical roles, and has discredited them as being forgeries. Not only does her research prove that Gratian, a patriarch of canon law, used sources that had no legal or authoritative basis to compose the laws that restrict women's roles in the Church, she also contends that he "formulated a number of laws restrictive to women on the assumption that women as such were inferior human beings."[55]

Further, Margaret Farley has indicated that in the history of the Church's tradition, it seems that women were deemed inappropriate subjects when dealing with anything of a sacred nature. As she states,

Women could not be given the symbolic role of entering the holy of holies because they continued to be associated with images of pollution and sin ... and thence of women as temptress, as a symbol of evil.[56]

Similarly, Ruether maintains that

... the source of women's exclusion from Church leadership is simply that both Judaism and Christianity existed within a patriarchal society which rigidly excluded women from public professional life and justified through an ideology of woman's generic inferiority.[57]

In contrast, Thomas Hopko has argued that there are in fact, to use his words,

theological and spiritual reasons why only some male members of the Christian Church may be ordained to her sacramental priesthood.... It is the position that it is not weakness, inferiority or sin that prevents women from holding the episcopal and presbyteral sacramental offices of the Christian Church, but rather their unique mode of being human and action, which is incompatible with exercising these positions in the community.[58]

One can say that Hopko's reasoning here is rather vague. A brief look at his argument, however, clarifies his conclusion. In other words, he states that women were created to be men's "helpers" as men were created to serve Christ, and Christ to serve God. Therefore, women must be actively submissive to men, as the Holy Spirit is to Christ and Christ is to God.[59]

Further, he notes that this "ideal" vision (i.e., of a subordinate order of creation) is compatible with society in general. The example given relates to the manner in which the family can be patterned in the likeness of the Trinity and the kingdom of God.

The *Declaration* argues that the sacramental nature of the Church sets it apart from any social structure and therefore asserts that the Galatian text (3.28) does not concern ministries. "It only affirms the universal calling to divine filiation, which is the same for all."[60]

The reasoning given here is that the ministerial priesthood does not result from a human right. Rather, it "...stems from the economy of the mystery of Christ and the Church."[61]

As to the relevance of these arguments to our discussion of the *Declaration*'s use of Aquinas, it seems that the restriction placed upon women from performing certain liturgical roles was largely based on the subordination of women and the notion that women were not worthy to serve. As Madeleine I. Boucher has pointed out, the Church can no longer maintain this view of women being subordinate to men in the order of creation.[62] One therefore wonders as to the Church's use of Aquinas to support the argument for the exclusion of women from the ministerial priesthood, when his argument seems to have been based on women's inferior state and subject condition.

Jesus' Maleness. When reflecting upon the *Declaration*'s argument concerning Jesus' maleness, various issues come to mind. For example, the Church teaches:

> So it was that Christ sent the apostles just as he Himself had been sent by the Father. Through these same apostles He made their successors, the bishops, sharers in His consecration and mission.[63]

In other words, Jesus was made incarnate in a *male* flesh so that *He* could accomplish his *Father's* plan. In doing so, he chose twelve *male* apostles, who in turn became *His* successors, along with the bishops and priests. What of women? Truly if women can be baptized as full members of Christ's Church should they not be allowed to partake in its

1. The Ordination of Women

salvific mission? Why then, are women permitted to be baptized? The hierarchic and patriarchal structure has nothing to do with women. How can women be members of something they are not allowed to be a part of?

The problem with a male hierarchy is that it excludes women to the point where the Church's salvific mission comes into question. If women were absent among the apostles and the early Church's structure, how is it that Jesus included women among God's salvific plan? In other words if women are baptized and made full members of Christ's Church, how is it they cannot participate as full members? This bias is called sexism in modern day terms, and such discrimination is usually punishable by law.[64]

This whole argument calls to mind the issue of "natural resemblance." The *Declaration* argues that this would be lost if women were admitted to the Sacrament of Orders. The reasoning used is that Christ's sacrifice is made present in the Eucharist. In the same sense, the priest acts as a "sacramental representation"[65] of Christ. Since Jesus was a man, the role of the priest is reserved exclusively for a male hierarchy.

A noteworthy distinction should be made regarding whether the priest is said to represent Christ or God. If the priest is said to represent Christ, then maleness must become imperative for Christian priesthood, since Christ was a male. If the priest is said to represent God, one concern lies in the reasoning used to accord women the title of "imago dei."[66] Regardless of whether the priest is said to represent Christ or God, I argue that women can represent either God or Christ. My reasoning is as follows: I suggest that women can in fact represent Christ by virtue of their baptism, for the conferral of baptism upon any individual implies not only a removal of original sin: as R.A. Norris, Jr., has argued, it also entails that the recipient

> ... share the identity of Jesus as the Christ, that they are incorporated in him, the representative of the human race, and that in consequence Christ lives in them [regardless of their sex]. So it must be said that baptism establishes women, as it does men, in the role of representatives of Christ — persons in whom the reality of the Christ-life, of at-one-ment with God, is proleptically manifested.[67]

Further, he has argued that

> The fact that women are baptized; that baptized women are in Christ and share his identity; that in virtue of this identity they exercise a lay ministry which involves the imaging and representation of Christ and for the world.[68]

From this basis, he asserts that women are also capable of "representing" Christ in the role of the priest, since Christ dwells in them regardless of their sex. Bernard Cooke maintains that

> This relationship [i.e., distinctness and complementarity], which is but one particularly symbolic aspect of the more basic and richer dialectic of all personal relationships, is an intrinsic element in all Christian sacraments, especially in the Eucharist. And this dialectic is bound to have much fuller play as both men and women minister actively in sacramental liturgy.[69]

I maintain that Christ entrusted a ministry to men and women alike. He was very inclusive of women throughout his missionary years and his choice of twelve male apostles can be seen as an eschatological consideration. This aspect will be treated in Chapter 2 of this work. At this time, it will suffice to say that women are capable of representing Jesus by virtue of their baptism. To deny that they do not is to deny their full membership in Christ's Church — one which must go beyond passive and inactive roles.

Can Women Represent God? Women are also capable of representing God on the basis that every individual was created in the "image and likeness" of God, regardless of their sex. For example, it has been argued that the "Fatherhood" of God could not be represented by a woman.[70] The reasoning given here is that since Christ was made incarnate in the form of a male, his "maleness" was therefore "intrinsic to his redemptive role."[71] Joseph A. Komonchak has mentioned that a common argument insists that "a woman could not have said, 'he who sees me, sees the Father'."[72]

Given this statement, I argue that in referring to His Father, Jesus was appealing to God's divinity rather than His "maleness" — if one can in fact say that God is a male. Ruether suggests that Jesus' teaching in Matthew 23.8-11 refers to the rejection of a "Father" in terms of a hierarchical figure:

> The Fatherhood of God could not have been understood as establishing male ruling-class power over subjugated groups in the Church or Christian society, but as that equal Fatherhood that makes all Christians equals, brothers and sisters.[73]

The New Testament stresses Jesus' humanity rather than His "maleness." When speaking of God the Father one can say that to interpret this in terms of a physical representation would risk limiting God to a "human" form. Although the Roman Catholic Church maintains that through the Incarnation, Jesus took on a human male form, I observe that to limit God to this restriction is completely unacceptable. Further, Sidney Callahan suggests that

> ... if God is beyond sexuality, and Jesus transcends sexuality and the risen life transcends sex as we know it, how can male sexuality in the priesthood be a sacramental sign of the first born of the new humanity?[74]

Similarly, Arthur Vogel has argued that

> The Fatherhood of God does not seem to be an adequate basis upon which to exclude women from ordination to the priesthood because Fatherhood, when applied to God, itself transcends masculinity: God transcends sex in its entirety.... God's difference from us is always the first thing which must be stressed about him; only so we can begin to comprehend his love in coming to us.[75]

The Bible uses several metaphors and symbolic images to describe God. In doing so, it uses male as well as female characteristics, so that as members of the human race we can relate to the manner in which God cares for us. Similarly, Christian ministry has been exemplified as having male and female attributes. As Komonchak notes,

> Paul called himself a father, but he also did not hesitate to call himself a nurse taking care of her children (1 Thess. 2.7) or to compare himself to a woman suffering birth-pangs until Christ be formed in his people (Gal. 4.19).[76]

The problem with the concept of a male God also comes into question when the notion of redemption is examined. For example, Ruether maintains that a "redeemer" could not at the same time "sanction" female subordination.[77] Such a contention would define God as the creator of a male-dominated ruling class. It is untenable to suggest that God can be redeemer on the one hand and patriarchal on the other.

Does the Priest Represent Jesus' Humanity or His Maleness? To return to the argument of male representation, the *Declaration* further states that

> ... the priest, especially when he presides at the liturgical and sacramental functions, equally represents the Church: he acts in her name with the intention of doing what she does.[78]

One can say that this argument is equally confusing. Since it is generally acknowledged that female and male attributes are used to describe God as well as Christian ministry, it remains rather contradictory that the *Declaration* would insist that a woman could not be a priest because Christ was a man and the priest cannot be represented by a female—and yet indicate that the priest, in representing Christ (a male) equally represents the Church, when the Church here is personified as Christ's bride—a female image! Therefore, one wonders how the *Declaration* can justify using an argument that seems to contradict itself. In Komonchak's words:

> Christ represented these [i.e., roles of official Christian ministry which only feminine images can communicate] to the world, although He was a male; Paul represented them to the Church, although he was a male. If a male could represent such feminine dimensions of the divine love, it is difficult to see why a woman cannot in turn represent to the Church dimensions of God's love in Christ for which masculine images are used.[79]

It is interesting to note here that Sr. Joan Chittister has argued that a priest is incapable of completely representing Christ because of His two natures.[80] While a man can represent Christ's humanity, he cannot represent His divinity. If the argument were to be followed to its logical conclusion, one would be led to question the significance of the Mass itself.

Regarding this query, the Council of Trent outlines the Mass as being truly instituted by Christ, whereby He

> ... offered His Body and Blood under the species of bread and wine to God His father, and under the same species, allowed the Apostles whom He at that time constituted priests of the New Testament to partake thereof, commanding them and their successors in the priesthood to make the same offering with these words: Do this in memory of me.[81]

In this sense, the Eucharist signifies Christ's redemption for His Church. The *Declaration* and Pope John Paul II's apostolic letter *On the Dignity and Vocation of Women* (issued in 1988) both stress this aspect.

Sr. Joan, however, has argued that by maintaining an all male priesthood, the Roman Catholic Church

> ... seems to intend a historical description rather than the communication of the essential elements of sacrifice, re-creation, reconciliation and redemption.[82]

According to the Roman Catholic Church, these elements are strongly present—and they must be exercised by an all-male priesthood. Despite these contentions, one can say that the question remains: Can the elements present in sacrifice, reconciliation, re-creation and redemption be communicated by a woman?

Although the Roman Catholic Church maintains that "...the

ultimate basis for the sacrament of orders is Christ's own priestly ministry on earth,"[83] it also acknowledges that His ministry was in direct succession from the prophets, the priestly castes, and the family of David. In doing so, the Roman Catholic Church emphasizes the relationship between father and son. For example, "sacerdotal privileges" were passed on from father to son in Aaron's family, as well as in David's—the family from which Jesus was born. In this sense, the Roman Catholic Church stresses the idea of succession in that Jesus' choice of twelve male apostles was to conform directly with the strictly male heritage that had been handed down in previous generations,[84] and therefore, a woman could not possibly represent the sacrificial elements in Christ's ministry.

I argue that these elements can be and are communicated by men and women, not by virtue of their being specifically male or female, but by virtue of their participation in Christ's body as Christians. Although the Roman Catholic Church emphasizes that the sacrament of orders is of "divine origin," one can say that Christ's priesthood established one that had several modifications. For example, Christ's priesthood is described as being that of a new covenant[85]—one that will replace the Levitical priesthood, as in Jeremiah 3.16; 33.18–20, and whose kingdom would be eternal. In doing so, one is no longer "born" into a priestly family—one is called to serve by virtue of the sacrament of baptism through which one is united with Christ and made a part of His Church, regardless of whether one is male or female. In Sr. Joan's words: "To put on Christ is the right and responsibility of all of us, male and female. And if not the right, then it is not the responsibility either."[86]

A similar argument put forth by the hierarchy has to do with Christ's relationship to Adam. For example, Monsignor Desmond Connell argues that

> ... a woman cannot be the sacramental image of Christ in the act that is proper to him precisely as the new Adam—the symbolism of the new Adam and the new Eve expresses the relation between Christ and the Church which is profoundly involved in the Eucharistic celebration.[87]

Connell's argument has to do with a sexual representation. Because men differ from women, he suggests a woman cannot represent Christ. Again, this argument calls attention to a cultural tradition which served as a foundation for a patriarchal hierarchy that has sustained throughout the history of the Roman Catholic Church. It is based on the notion that men are supposedly the superior gender. I maintain that this view denies Christ's message. Throughout his ministry, Jesus' message was one of equality and justice for the oppressed. Connell's argument excludes women as full members of the Church, and the same difficulty arises as with the *Declaration*'s argument. That is, that a male priest can represent Christ or the Church, but women can only represent the Church as long as no specific symbolic function is involved. Such a contention not only denies Jesus' message, it also suggests that Christ's role was to redeem *man*kind and not *human*kind. In an age where women's equality has become socially accepted, a Church which continues to deny the access of women to the ministerial priest in Christ's name completely contradicts the basis for Jesus' death. In Bernard Cooke's words:

> Because the Church's fundamental role in human history is to be the sacrament of the redeeming presence of the risen Lord, the recognition of women's rights to full ministerial activity, by increasing the extent to which the Church can express sacramentally the saving action that Christ is carrying on through and in it, will permit the Church to realize its historical destiny more adequately.[88]

Given the treatment of the *Declaration*'s argument concerning male representation, several observations can be made which seem to stem from the notion that women are inferior to men.

Although the Church affirms the restriction of women to the ministerial priesthood, it has a very unrealistic approach in dealing with issues regarding women's roles. For example, although the *Declaration* attests that in Jesus' time women were deemed inferior to men,[89] it fails to recognize that this very notion has excluded women from positions of leadership in the Church. Rather, it stresses that since Jesus did not call any women to become part of the Twelve, in order to fully represent Christ's role, the priest must remain a man. Given the arguments presented, it is quite difficult to justify the *Declaration*'s position on male representation. As we have seen, it can be said that a woman can represent either Christ or God. Furthermore, it seems that the *Declaration*'s use of male and female representation is contradictory. On the one hand, it states that only a male priest can represent Christ because Christ was a male, yet the priest is said to represent equally the Church, which has been personified as Christ's bride, with female attributes. It remains rather unsettling therefore, that the *Declaration* would insist that only a male can represent Christ because Christ was a male and yet argue that a woman cannot represent the Church, given the characteristics presented.[90]

The *Declaration* states that since Christ "...was and remains a man" by reason of "natural resemblance," the role of the priest must be undertaken by a man.[91] One can say that several implications result from this argument. First, it seems to imply that Christ's heavenly body remains in the form of a man—complete with its physical characteristics. Second, it seems to emphasize Christ's "maleness" rather than His humanity, as the *Declaration* affirms that regardless of the Galatian text (3.28) one cannot overlook the fact that the Incarnation occurred in the form of the male sex.[92] Further, it notes that this fact,

> ... while not implying an alleged natural superiority of man over woman, cannot be disassociated from the economy of salvation: it is indeed, in harmony with the entirety of God's plan as God himself has revealed it, and of which the mystery of the covenant is the nucleus.[93]

Let us examine the first consideration in conjunction with the second as the two are directly related. As Komonchak notes, "...the New Testament does not seem to have any theological interest whatever in the maleness of Christ."[94] Further, he has indicated that when compared to Adam in Romans 5, the term used to describe both Christ and Adam is *anthropos*—a term that according to R.A. Norris, "signifies primarily, human person, rather than, male person."[95] Further, the official term used by the Roman Catholic Church to describe Christ's coming among us in a human form is derived from the Latin word *caro*, meaning "flesh."[96] Therefore, one must not overlook the biblical and doctrinal emphasis on Christ's "human" nature, rather than his "maleness." Further, I argue that in terms of Christ's mission, i.e., the salvation of God's people, one cannot logically argue that his "maleness" was a constitutive element in being the "Christ." Rather, in being the "Christ," one can say that emphasis must remain on Christ's humanity, rather than his "maleness." Arthur Vogel has written:

> Even though the word became flesh in the man Jesus, the human condition redeemed in Jesus contains within it the masculine and feminine polarities. There is no doubt that these polarities are found within the redeemed community the mystical body of Christ, and within the general royal priesthood of the Church.[97]

After having briefly examined the three main arguments presented in the *Declaration*, in summary, one can say that several areas lack clarification, and reasons used to justify the arguments appear contradictory and therefore remain invalid. For example, although the Biblical Commission's report found that the New Testament cannot clearly settle the issue of women's ordination, and that Christ's will would not be violated if the Church did decide to confer ordination upon women, the *Declaration* stresses Christ's attitude and the practice of the apostles as the grounds for which women are not accepted into priestly orders.⁹⁸ Further, the *Declaration* seems to imply certain assumptions that, when fully examined seem invalid. For example, it assumes that since Christ called only men to be a part of the Twelve, it was his will that women not be admitted to the priesthood. As we have seen, Christ did not ordain women *or* men. Given Raymond E. Brown's insights, it seems that the concept of the Christian priesthood did not develop as such until the second century A.D.⁹⁹ Therefore, it seems highly untenable that the *Declaration* can validly argue that since Christ only called men to be a part of the Twelve, He willed that only men be ordained.

Another aspect that appears contradictory is the notion with the Church's constant tradition. First, it denies that women exercised prominent roles of leadership in the early Church—ones comparable to that of Christian priesthood. Second, although it asserts that in order to remain truly relevant for its people, the Church must not remain stagnant but should continue to develop according to its people's needs, it seems to overlook the fact that the ordination of women is one of those "signs of the times" that needs to be readdressed. Rather, the *Declaration* states that, "...the practice has enjoyed peaceful and universal acceptance."¹⁰⁰

As we have seen, the argument presented based on tradition stems from the notion that women have a naturally subject state, and therefore, must remain subordinate to men. One can say that, given several considerations already expressed, this argument is not only invalid, it remains untenable as well.

I observe that the reasons presented in the *Declaration* to support the argument of male representation appear contradictory. Although women cannot represent Christ because Christ was a man, men are capable of representing not only Christ, but the Church as well. Thus, while a man can represent a male (in the person of Christ) as well as a female (the Church), women are incapable of representing either! As I have argued, women can and do represent Christ as well as the Church by virtue of their baptism. To deny that women do not is to deny the effects of the sacrament itself.

In conclusion, one can say that although the *Declaration* has acknowledged women's contribution to the life of the Church ¹⁰¹ and that Jesus' attitude towards them demonstrates a high regard for women, it nevertheless maintains that in an attempt to remain faithful to the Roman Catholic Church's constant tradition and to Christ's will, women are to be excluded from the Christian priesthood. Although the *Declaration*'s intent seems to validly address women's admission to the ministerial priesthood, in doing so, it offers little revision whatsoever on the issue. The arguments used do not stem from contemporary scholarship, nor do the collaborators of the *Declaration* include the findings of the Biblical Commission whose task was to examine the issue from a biblical perspective in the first place. Further, there seems to have been a widespread rejection of the document among leading Catholic theologians.[102]

In short, the *Declaration on the Question of the Admission of Women to the Ministerial Priesthood* offers little insight for women seeking extended roles of leadership in the Roman Catholic Church. Prior to undertaking a discussion surrounding the role of women in contemporary times, it seems essential to examine the role of women in the ministry of Jesus in order to come to terms with His attitude towards women and the functions He permitted them to undertake. This will be the main focus in Chapter 2.

CHAPTER 2

Women in the Ministry of Jesus

To undertake effectively a study of the role of women in the ministry of Jesus, one must seriously consider the canonical gospels. Despite the fact that the New Testament writers were influenced by their patriarchal culture,[1] it is apparent that women surrounded Jesus, accompanied Him on His journeys, and proved to be among His most courageous disciples.[2] The main focus of this chapter will be to examine the role and function of women in Jesus' ministry, particularly in the four canonical accounts, for it is here especially that Jesus encounters women. Although the arguments presented in Chapter 1 may resurface, their treatment here will come mainly from a biblical perspective. To do this, I will rely on modern feminist scholarship to assist in identifying the roles Jesus assigned to women, in order to assess His understanding of the ministry of women in relation to His father's will. This will allow for further assessment of the Sacred Congregation for the Doctrine of the Faith's *Declaration on the Question of the Admission of Women to the Ministerial Priesthood*, along with other statements expressed by Pope John Paul II at a later time, and therefore establish some ideas regarding women's ministry in the life of Jesus following the conclusion of this study.

To do this, it is essential to begin with some background on the person of Jesus himself. Although numerous attempts have been made to examine the man Jesus from various scientific perspectives (i.e., psychological, sociological, archeological and the like), my main focus here will be to look at Jesus from a cultural perspective. Three presuppositions are significant[3]:

    1. That patriarchy was a cultural influence on New Testament writers.[4]

    2. That although Jesus performed many miracles, he was nevertheless restricted to a human nature, with all its limitations (i.e., he felt pain, hunger and the like).[5]

3. That the "historical" Jesus died according to the laws observed by the natural sciences.[6]

A discussion of the "cultural" influences on the historical Jesus will prove helpful here as one would surmise that the results would directly relate to His message and ministry.

Jesus' Maleness

One of the leading arguments put forth in the *Declaration* has to do with Jesus' maleness.[7] The *Declaration* stresses that a woman could not represent the "male" Christ.[8] In terms of culture, various biblical scholars have argued that the leader of a Jewish religious movement had to be male. Letha Scanzoni and Nancy Hardesty stress several points; among them: That Jesus was heir to David's throne—one that was occupied by men only; that a female would have had little scriptural knowledge according to the restrictions imposed on women against reading Torah; and that a woman would have been unclean at least once a month and could not have taught in a synagogue.[9]

Despite these concerns, they also point out that the Bible stresses Jesus' humanness rather than his maleness when speaking of his incarnation [10] (cf. Philippians 2.7; Romans 5.12, 15, etc.). Nevertheless, coming from a patriarchal milieu, the very fact that Jesus was made incarnate in the image and likeness of a man is of significance. If a messiah in the image of a woman had been sent—even though she would have taught the same ideas that Christ did—she would probably have been totally rejected simply because she was a woman. At the same time Jesus was prepared to set himself apart from his cultural background. Hence, Jesus himself has been labeled a "feminist" (in terms of "...a person who is in favor of, and who promotes the equality of women with men; a person who advocates and practices treating women primarily as human persons and willingly contravenes social customs in so doing")[11] and rightly so, given his treatment of women in the gospels.[12]

Given these considerations, one would say that the fact that Jesus was a male was of significance to the Jewish people. To limit women's roles in contemporary Catholicism, however, is to misunderstand the essence of Jesus' "maleness"—one that obviously sought to transform a patriarchal culture.

Jesus' Message. Despite the *Declaration*'s emphasis on Jesus' maleness with all of its revelatory baggage, I argue that Jesus' maleness was central to his message. From a theological perspective, Bernard Cooke maintains that although Jesus referred to His father as "ABBA" His understanding of God could not have contained authoritative and dominating characteristics. For example, even though Jesus' initial understanding of God must have been shaped by the Old Testament "God of Israel" concept, His unique and intimate relationship with God would have permitted Him to break away from the "patriarchal" overtones associated with God "The Father." In this sense, Cooke maintains that Jesus' knowledge of God would have been rooted in the Father imagery of the Jewish faith, coupled with the reality of a nonpatriarchal God. In this setting, Cooke argues it was more appropriate that the divine incarnation be manifested in a "male" form because the centrality of God's revelation as such would have been more radical:

> Jesus' experience of God does not allow him to think of himself as masculine in patriarchal terms. Beginning with the challenge to Jesus' own culturally-acquired understandings, the God known by Jesus refuses any claims made upon him by the negativities of a patriarchy that seeks divine legitimation.[13]

In this setting, Cooke argues that the religious authorities' main objection to Jesus' teaching had to do with the nonhierarchic structure of God's kingdom. This aspect of Jesus' teaching also had social ramifications. He proposed a very radical approach to human relationships based on loving service, rather than servitude. Throughout the gospel accounts, Jesus seeks to abolish human and social inequalities. On the cross, Jesus bore human suffering. The canonical accounts bear witness to Jesus' egalitarian treatment of men and women on a social and religious scale. Let us now turn to scripture and Jesus' treatment of women as viewed by recent feminist scholarship.

Jesus' Attitude Towards Women in the New Testament. Elisabeth Schüssler-Fiorenza has argued that the New Testament authors sought to speak of Christ in terms acceptable to the Jewish people as well as the heathen of their time.[14] Her point is that living in a patriarchal culture directly affected their thought, as well as the manner in which Christ's message was presented. Further, she notes we must assume that the New Testament writings can only present a fraction of the roles women must have exercised as women were marginal figures in the Jewish culture.

Given these observations, several considerations come to mind. First, assuming that the New Testament authors were writing against the influences of a patriarchal culture, I would not be surprised if the gospels downplayed women's roles in the early Church in order to conform to the current ideas regarding women at that time. Second, if all we have today is in fact a "fraction" of the roles women exercised in Jesus' ministry—and there is considerable evidence to support the notion that they were quite numerous—imagine what perspective we would have today if the New Testament authors were not writing against the background of a patriarchal culture. In other words, women's roles are still identifiable despite the circumstances presented. I conclude that the roles women exercised in the early Christian churches must have been quite significant for the evidence to have managed to survive all these years.

As to what these roles were, and what Jesus' teaching was regarding these roles, careful study of the gospels is essential. Let us be guided by modern feminist scholarship in a brief overview of the four canonical accounts in order to extract their treatment of women, and then give a detailed study of those women who figured prominently in Jesus' ministry. In this manner, it will be possible to juxtapose Jesus' treatment of women alongside that of the *Declaration*, compare the two and determine whether the latter, along with Pope John Paul II, has justified the claim that women should be excluded from the ministerial priesthood.

The Women in Mark's Gospel. Let us begin with Mark's gospel, since it is commonly accepted among biblical scholars today that the evangelist "called" Mark wrote the earliest account.[15] Mark's gospel presents the Twelve as being continuously set against women of faith. For example, Ben Witherington has indicated that in 5.24-30, Jesus heals a woman because of her faith, and in 7.24-30 a woman is commended for her faith, while in 4.40 and 6.52 the Twelve are repeatedly being criticized for their lack of faith and understanding.[16] Further, it is interesting to note that in Mark's passion narrative, the women (and not the Twelve) figure prominently as witnesses to the resurrection.[17]

As to the importance of women in Mark's gospel, Elisabeth Moltmann-Wendel has observed:

> In Mark's theological perspective, women are the functional successors of Jesus and they represent the true intention of Jesus and his mission within the messianic people of God.[18]

Not only does Mark simply "include" women in Jesus' ministry, he also notes that these were people of faith—at times more so than the Twelve! This indicates Jesus' attitude towards them. In no way does he exclude them from his ministry, nor does he push them away, as we note especially in Mark 15.40-41, where women followed Jesus, and he seemed to be comfortable with them.

2. Women in the Ministry of Jesus

Further, Elisabeth Schüssler-Fiorenza notes that Mark's gospel gives specific instructions regarding discipleship in that a "true" disciple is one who literally follows Jesus' example.[19] Community leaders must also strive to serve. For example, Mark 10.43-44 stresses "... but whoever would be great among you must be your servant, and whoever would be first among you must be slave of all" (RSV). In this passage, Jesus teaches that leaders must serve others and become their equals.[20]

"True" discipleship, Schüssler-Fiorenza maintains, is exemplified by the women who accompany Jesus to His death. The discipleship of the Twelve is characterized by betrayal, denial and abandonment.[21] Therefore the women in Jesus' final days fulfill all the criteria for Mark's understanding of discipleship. That is not to say that only women are "true" disciples. My point here is that Jesus' entourage included other disciples who were not part of the Twelve and some of whom were women—ones who faithfully accompanied Jesus and proclaimed His resurrection.

If Jesus permitted women to follow Him and become involved in His ministry, certainly the type of discipleship He encouraged was one of equality based on service and love. Let us now turn to the women in John's gospel.

The Women in John's Gospel.[22] Similarly, the gospel of John tends to affirm women's roles in the early Church. Evelyn and Frank Stagg have emphasized that apart from the Twelve, there are no distinctions among those who surrounded Jesus. Women were among his closest companions. Further, John's gospel is inclusive of women and does not indicate the subordination of women that was so characteristic of the time.[23] For example, in John 12.2b, "Martha served, and Lazarus was one of those at table with him" (RSV). One can say that this text serves as an indication of women's roles. To quote Raymond Brown:

> The Evangelist is writing in the 90's, when the office of *diakonos* already existed in post-Pauline churches (see the Pastorals) and when the task of waiting on tables was a specific function to which the community or its leaders appointed individuals by laying on hands (Acts 6.1-6). In the Johannine community a woman could be described as exercising a function which in other churches was the function of an "ordained" person.[24]

Further, as Evelyn and Frank Stagg have noted, "...the Evangelists not only preserve Jesus' perspective on women, but they seem to be comfortable with it."[25] Given the fact that the New Testament writers were influenced by a patriarchal culture (as established at the outset of this chapter), the idea that "they seem to be comfortable" with Jesus' treatment of women comes as quite a surprise. If one examines their treatment of women however, this notion finds justification. Of particular importance in John's gospel is Jesus' washing of his disciples' feet. Based on service and love, each individual is invited to serve one another. The Twelve have no special function here, as Jesus appears to all the disciples in 20.19, breathes the Spirit upon them, and gives them the power to forgive sins. Perhaps this is an indication that all of Jesus' disciples are invited to serve one another, as long as it is done with love and in Christ's name.[26]

The Women in Luke's Gospel. In the gospel of Luke, many women are present.[27] As to the author's intent in mentioning so many women, Evelyn and Frank Stagg have noted that Luke was especially concerned with the disadvantaged. Since women were mostly part of this group, Luke's gospel mentions many women.[28]

Luke's gospel, however, seems to go one step further. In several accounts, Luke not only stresses women's dignity and importance — but seems to have an egalitarian approach regarding men and women. For example, scholars have identified a type of parallel in the parables. It seems that Luke's accounts relating Jesus' encounter with men are almost always paralleled with a similar account with a woman. For example, Constance F. Parvey has noted that

> ... in the description of Jesus' ministry of healing, Luke juxtaposes the healing of a man (the centurion's slave, in 7.2-10) with the healing of a woman (raising from dead of a widow's son in 7.11-12). Later on the parable of the Good Samaritan is directed toward men (in 10.29-37) and Martha, directed toward women (in 10.38-42). Also in the parables, Luke couples the parable of the man and the lost sheep (in 15.3-7) with that of the woman and the lost coin (in 15.8-10).[29]

Given these findings, one can say that Luke's understanding of Jesus' message was rather inclusive of women. Further, Luke's apparent concern for women demonstrates the nature of God's kingdom as being one that remained accessible to all. As Ben Witherington notes,

> ... Luke expresses by this arrangement that men and women stand together and side by side before God. They are equal in honour and grace; they are endowed with the same gifts and have the same responsibilities.[30]

One can say that this statement has very distinct implications. For example, if indeed they are "endowed" with the same gifts and have the same responsibilities as men do, it would be in keeping with the Church's perspective of fundamental equality for all its believers.[31] In short, I observe that according to scholars concerned with feminist issues, the women in Luke's gospel are presented in such a manner that their dignity and importance are upheld.

The Women in Matthew's Gospel. In the gospel of Matthew, as again stressed by scholars open to feminist issues, women appear significantly in the resurrection account—to a degree that one can identify an apparent distinction when comparing the women's reactions as opposed to the men's. To quote Ben Witherington:

> Their devotion is sincere, their joy great, their obedience perfect. They worship Jesus. By contrast, there is no such outward expression of devotion by the men, rather it is said that some of Jesus' chosen leaders doubted.[32]

Nevertheless, Jesus appears to his male and female followers. In Matthew 28.10, Jesus says to the women: "Do not be afraid; go and tell my brethren to go to Galilee, and there they will see me" (RSV). Similarly, in Matthew 28.18, Jesus appears to the Eleven—although his message is quite different. Jesus says to them:

> All authority in heaven and on earth has been given to me. Go therefore and make disciples of all nations, baptizing them in the name of the Father and of the Son and of the Holy Spirit, teaching them to observe all that I have commanded you; and lo, I am with you always, to the close of the age [Matt. 28.18–20, RSV].

Ben Witherington has noted that these passages reflect specific roles for women in the community and at the same time reaffirm the Eleven's "headship" role.[33] I argue that although Matthew 28.18–20 mentions only the Eleven, women disciples could have been present. Elisabeth Tetlow has held that Matthew condensed many of the Markan stories where women surround Jesus, on the basis that Matthew wrote, "...from within the traditions of rabbinic Judaism, which at the time totally excluded women from rabbinic schooling."[34] Such a restriction would account for the apparent "headship" role Jesus accorded to the Eleven in Matthew 28.18–20, as women held no leadership roles in the Jewish religious tradition.[35] Given Tetlow's argument, one can say that the fact that Matthew accorded women the role of proclamation in 28.10 bears witness to the discipleship of women and the roles Jesus prescribed for them. Regarding the commissioning of women, Evelyn and Frank Stagg have noted that this text affirms women's role of proclaiming the gospel message.[36]

After having briefly looked at the women in the canonical accounts,

I observe that the main criterion for discipleship has to do with imitating Christ's ministry and serving others. Men and women are invited to serve one another on an egalitarian plane. Church structure (if we can actually call it a "structure") revolves around the gift of serving one another. There is no hierarchy of service. In fact, leadership is nonpatriarchal and based on suffering. In this setting, the women disciples are as prominent as the men. Given the social restrictions upon women at that time, Jesus' message was so radical and so intrinsic to His Father's nature that all four evangelists recorded it. The fact that they all record Jesus' inclusiveness of women in the circle of disciples indicates that although Jesus was a male, the centrality of his message was nonpatriarchal and nonhierarchic. This notion remains central in the study of women in the canonical accounts.

Women in Jesus' Ministry

Although it is quite impossible to examine every reference to women that occurs in the New Testament given the scope of the present work, a study of the women who figure prominently in Jesus' ministry is helpful in order to establish certain attitudes that prove pertinent to this study.

Mary and Martha. The pair of Mary and Martha appear only in Luke and John. In Luke's gospel, Martha, who is preparing a meal for Jesus, rebukes Mary for idly sitting at his feet and listening to his teaching (10.39). Jesus says to Martha: "You are anxious and troubled about many things; one thing is needful. Mary has chosen the good portion, which shall not be taken away from her" (Luke 10.41-42, RSV). Barbara J. MacHaffie contends that this passage portrays Jesus' "...willingness to consider women as worthy students"[37] despite Judaic customs of the time that did not permit women to study scriptures with a rabbi.[38] Further, Jesus "reveals" himself to Martha who becomes a model for women's discipleship.[39]

Martha also appears in the gospel of John as proclaiming her faith. When Jesus asks her if she believes in him, she responds, "Yes, Lord; I believe that you are the Christ, the son of God, he who is coming into the world" (John 11.27, RSV). Regarding this text, Elisabeth Tetlow has noted:

> In this scene the most important role of discipleship according to Johannine theology, that of proclamation of Jesus' true identity, is given to a woman.[40]

The significance of this text has also been attributed to its parallel in Peter's confession of faith. As Elisabeth Moltmann-Wendel notes,

> This is a confession of Christ which takes similar form only once more in the other gospels, where it is uttered by Peter. For the early Church, to confess Christ in this way was the mark of an apostle. The Church was built up on Peter's confession, and to this day the Popes understand themselves as Peter's successors.[41]

Similarly, Schüssler-Fiorenza parallels Martha's discipleship with Peter's in that Martha "...represents the full apostolic faith of the Johannine community, just as Peter did for the Matthean community."[42] Not only is Martha's confession of faith as powerful as Peter's, she becomes a "true" disciple with whom women can identify. However, the very nature of this parallel in scripture is used to downplay Martha's role in comparison to that of Peter. For example, the heading for Peter's confession of faith in the *Holy Bible* (New Catholic Edition) reads "The Primacy of Peter" (John 21.15), whereas Martha's reads "The Raising of Lazarus" (John 11). Further, in asking her to proclaim her faith, Jesus accords Martha the role of proclamation—one that is characteristic of discipleship.

Therefore, the scriptural interpretation of Martha's significance has been reduced, whereas Peter's "primacy" stands over and above Martha's discipleship. Certainly Martha's treatment in scripture has been downplayed through androcentric translations which seek to reduce women's importance. Although Martha's story remains among the texts, she is not accorded an egalitarian role when compared to that of Peter. It is interesting to note here that although it is difficult to prove from an historical perspective, Schüssler-Fiorenza contends that perhaps Martha herself is the author of John's gospel. Her conjecture is based on Robert Fortna's work and indicates that perhaps Martha herself was Jesus' "beloved" disciple who placed her confession of faith on her own lips to identify herself with the author of the gospel. Although such a contention is difficult to prove, it has some plausibility. For example, the entire New Testament has been attributed to male authors. If women also accompanied Jesus, participated in his ministry and became His disciples, various women could have contributed to the compiling of New Testament texts.

The Unknown Woman. Next, let us look at the "unknown" woman who anointed Jesus. In the gospel of John, this woman is identified as Mary of Bethany, Martha's sister (12.1–8). If this is the case, her discipleship would have already been established (see John 11.45).

However, in Mark and in Matthew, she remains unidentified. Alicia Faxon has suggested that this woman was among the group of Jesus' disciples on the basis that this woman knew where to find Jesus and obviously understood his missionary role. In this sense, this woman must have been in Jesus' entourage, and therefore, among his disciples. It was also common for Jesus' followers to share their belongings with the poor. In the Markan passage, the unknown woman is rebuked for having wasted such costly ointment when it could have been sold and given to the poor. Faxon therefore contends that the unknown woman was among the group of disciples as her resources would have contributed to the community's funds, and therefore, would have been available to give to the poor.[43]

I observe that, regardless of who she was, of significance are her actions as well as Jesus' treatment of her. To set the scene, in Mark 14.3–9, Jesus is eating in the company of his disciples when an unknown woman comes in and anoints Jesus' head with a jar of very expensive perfume, for which she is strongly criticized. Jesus' response is that she is to be left alone, for "...she has done a beautiful thing to me. For you always have the poor with you, and whenever you will, you can do good to them; but you will not always have me" (Mark 14.6–7, RSV). Elizabeth E. Platt maintains that this passage gives significance to ministering to an individual facing death as opposed to devoting one's attention to works of charity:

> Jesus commends the woman who lavishes her service on the special friend in her midst at this particular time who must face death very soon. That specific ethical deed takes precedence over other forms of social service and other conditions of poverty.[44]

Further, Schüssler-Fiorenza argues that the disciples' objection (i.e., the "male" objection) to the unknown woman's prophetic action is withdrawn.[45] Here, the unknown woman's action is characterized as "prophetic" for it "...foreshadows Jesus' act of washing the disciples' feet at the Last Supper, signifying their new life to come from his servant-death."[46] Platt maintains that this act establishes a precedent for women's participation at the Eucharist:

> If in light of John's Gospel, Jesus' footwashing is to be instituted as part of the Christian Passover liturgy, it is an appropriate act for a woman to carry out in memory of Mary of Bethany from whom Jesus himself replicated the ritual. This affirms that woman in her ministry does have Biblical precedent for being associated with the key ritual of faith in the Sacrament of Holy Communion.[47]

If Jesus accorded the unknown woman (perhaps Mary of Bethany) such a role, it remains quite ambiguous why the *Declaration* (as well as the official Church) only recognizes the role of the Twelve when it comes to official functions. Although this notion will be treated later in this chapter, it is important to note here that the unknown woman was permitted several functions despite the disciples' objection. In John's version, it is Judas who objects to her actions. Given that Judas was one of the Twelve (Mark 14.10, RSV), and a male, Jesus' reaction tells us that a woman's role is as significant as a man's. Further, could this also demonstrate that other disciples' work (such as Mary or Martha) is as important as that of the Twelve? Such a contention could dissolve the significance of the Twelve and reduce their standing as an "elite" group. Hints of our present Church's hierarchalism and elitism among the clergy are present here. Maybe Jesus' words could be applied here: "Let her alone; why do you trouble her?" (Mark 14.6, RSV).

Elizabeth Tetlow suggests that the disciples would have identfied Jesus with a Messiah figure, as in the Old Testament, prophets anointed the head of Jewish kings. By anointing Jesus the woman's actions also represent a political risk, as she is proclaiming that Jesus is king.[48] To do so in such an unsettled time demanded great courage. Equally surprising is Jesus' attitude towards her. The rabbinic tradition held that women were to be excluded from learning Torah. Jesus appears as the new law from which women are no longer to be excluded. Jesus praises the woman for her actions. He therefore moves away from the patriarchal tradition of excluding women and reveals that his messianic ministry is unlike that of the Old Testament kings, as he is preparing for his death, and accords a woman the prophetic role of anointing him.

Mark 14.9 concludes: "And truly, I say to you ... what she has done will be told in memory of her" (RSV). Schüssler-Fiorenza has argued that despite Jesus' words, the unknown woman's story and her faithfulness to him have been forgotten in the gospel accounts of Jesus' last days; whereas Peter, the disciple who denied Jesus, and Judas, the disciple who betrayed him, stand at the center of the passion accounts.[49] Why is this so? Regardless of her actions, she remains insignificant in Catholic tradition because she is a woman. In patriarchal Judaism, she would have never been permitted the role of a witness. Rosemary Radford Ruether maintains that such a role accorded to a woman bears witness to the Christian message.[50] The irony of her marginalization lies in the fact that Jesus praised her for her actions and affirmed that she would not be forgotten.

Mary Magdalene. Another woman who figures prominently in Jesus' ministry is Mary Magdalene. She first appears in Luke 8.1-3 along with Joanna and Susanna. These women are mentioned along with the Twelve and accompany Jesus in his ministry. Mary Magdalene is characterized as a woman from whom "...seven demons had gone out" (Luke 8.2, RSV). Alicia Faxon has suggested that if Mary Magdalene was commonly associated with Magdala, a town famous for its harlotry, one may therefore assume that she was also a prostitute on the basis that "...the demons cast out were sins of evil living."[51] If in fact she was a former prostitute, as the medieval tradition assumed,[52] this would support the notion that the Jesus group was inclusive of women and of former prostitutes. It would also support the idea that Luke had a special interest in the poor and the disadvantaged. To quote Evelyn and Frank Stagg:

> What is significant is that women whose conditions were subject to scorn and penalty found in Jesus a liberator who not only enabled them to find health but whom he dignified as full persons by accepting their own ministries to himself and the Twelve.[53]

Perhaps it could also be attributed to Luke's general portrayal of women. For example, Elizabeth Tetlow notes that Luke always characterizes women as submissive: "This is a literary device used throughout the gospel of Luke to present women as both weak and sinful."[54] As to what these "ministries" were, Mark 15.40-41 states that

> ... there were also women looking from afar, among whom were Mary Magdalene, and Mary, the mother of James the younger and of Joses, and Salome, who, when he was in Galilee, followed him, and ministered to him; and also many other women who came up with him to Jerusalem [RSV].

Leonard Swidler has observed that the use of the verb *diakoneo*, meaning to minister or to serve, is common to all three synoptic gospels. Since the term is used to refer to men and women throughout the New Testament[55] he suggests that the service rendered by women deacons was comparable to that of the men. As to the nature of these services, Swidler contends that Stephen and Philip in Acts 6.3-6 were associated with a teaching function.[56] Therefore, when the use of the term "deacon" is so widely used to characterize the women who followed Jesus, Swidler argues that it implies a role beyond "cooking" for the Twelve.

As to Mary Magdalene's importance, Tetlow indicates that "...the fact that Mary Magdalene was mentioned by name in all four resurrection narratives suggests that she was recognized as the leader among the group of women witnesses."[57] Further, she stresses that her apostleship is in keeping with the criteria outlined by Paul and Luke.[58] Therefore Mary Magdalene's apostleship is difficult to refute.

Regarding her possible leadership as an apostle, it is interesting to note that her mission has been set against Peter's. Tetlow has argued that in the gospel of John (20.1f), it is Peter who reaches the tomb first. However, it is Mary who is charged with relating the news to Jesus' "brethren" (RSV). Therefore Tetlow stresses that Mary was really the first apostle — i.e., the first witness to the resurrection. Further, she stresses that the primacy of witness in John and Matthew is accorded to a woman.[59]

Perhaps the Roman Catholic tradition has difficulty according Mary Magdalene a leadership role because of the suspicion regarding her past. Certainly a prostitute could not be accorded such a role.[60] Schüssler-Fiorenza argues that the primacy of Mary Magdalene's role can be found in the resurrection account where Jesus appears to her in the "garden." Mary Magdalene is weeping near Jesus' tomb when He appears to her. He asks: "Whom do you seek?" (John 20.15, RSV). He then calls her by name and she responds "Rab-bo'ni!" (which means Teacher; John 20.16, RSV).

Schüssler-Fiorenza identifies these three elements as the root of Mary Magdalene's significance. The verb "to seek" in Greek refers, "to engage in the activities of a disciple." Further, Jesus calls her by name as the "Good shepherd" knows his flock. Here Mary can be characterized as a follower or a disciple — an interesting parallel with the Petrine command: "Tend my sheep" (John 21.16, RSV) on which the papacy is built. Lastly, Mary Magdalene calls Jesus "Rab-bo'ni" (teacher). She recognizes Jesus and becomes an eyewitness to the resurrection and fulfills the criteria for apostleship outlined by Paul and Luke.[61]

Given this treatment of Mary Magdalene, several observations come to mind. Not only did Jesus choose Mary Magdalene (perhaps a former prostitute) as one of his followers, but her leadership role indicates that Jesus did not distinguish between men's and women's roles. Further, there is evidence that not only Mary Magdalene but other women accompanied Jesus and ministered to him in various ways. There is therefore evidence that women were among the followers of Jesus (at least Mary Magdalene was), and that they were just as important as the men in Jesus' eyes.[62] Her apostleship has been denied, however, perhaps because of her uncertain past, or simply because she was a woman. Certainly these two factors alone carry much weight for exclusion. What is surprising today is the fact that Mary Magdalene's primacy in the gospel accounts has survived all the translations and the androcentrism which predominate our current scriptural interpretation, despite the historical debate regarding Mary Magdalene's apostleship over and against Peter's.[63] Given the *Declaration*'s contention that women are to be excluded from the ministerial priesthood on the basis that they were not among the apostles,[64] one can say that the collaborators have denied Mary Magdalene's leadership and importance as one of the primary witnesses to Jesus' resurrection. Certainly this denial cannot possibly legitimize the exclusion of women priests today.

Mary of Nazareth.[65] In the Roman Catholic tradition, Mary has been perceived as "...a model of the Church in the matter of faith, charity, and perfect union with Christ."[66] Various incidents throughout Mary's life have been highlighted and paralleled to Jesus' own life and ministry.[67] For example, Mary was faithful and obedient to God's will, as Jesus was. She endured much hardship throughout her pregnancy and birth—as Jesus undertook throughout his ministry. She witnessed and experienced the death of her son, at the foot of the cross (John 19.25-27). In short, the Catholic portrayal of Mary has been one of obedience and submissiveness. Therein lies the obstacle for most feminists, as Mary's characterization seems to indicate that she exercised a subordinate role.[68]

In contrast, Rosemary Ruether has characterized Mary as an "unbeliever"[69] who was absent from the crucifixion,[70] and whose devotion and strength were originally manifested by Mary Magdalene.[71] Although Ruether's insights regarding the interpretation of scripture from a feminist perspective have been helpful,[72] her characterization of Mary contradicts much of Catholic tradition. The latter has instead centered attention on Mary's song of faith:

> My soul magnifies the Lord, and my spirit rejoices in God my savior, for he has regarded the low estate of his handmaiden [Luke 1.46-48, RSV].

This text, expressing Mary's faith and undying love, has often been seen as a pivot that strengthened her servanthood in times of hardship and doubt.[73] Further, she is the first to receive the annunciation of Jesus' coming and she is the one who speaks for both parents when they visit the Temple in Luke 2.48.[74] In the gospel of John, Mary accompanies Jesus to a wedding and urges him to perform his first miracle.[75] This text also exemplifies Mary's discipleship. Despite Jesus' harsh comment: "O woman, what have you to do with me? My hour has not yet come" (John 2.4, RSV), she tells the servants: "Do whatever he tells you" (John 2.5, RSV). Schüssler-Fiorenza asserts that this text places Mary among Jesus' disciples, based on the notion that neither Jewish nor Greco-Roman tradition would allow for a mother to be called "woman" by her own son. In this sense, she claims Mary's discipleship does not stem from her motherhood, but from her authority when she tells the servants: "Do whatever he tells you."[76] Similarly, at the foot of the cross, Jesus provides for his mother by giving her a son (cf. John 19.25-27). Given Mary's new role, she becomes readily identifiable with Jesus' family of disciples (Acts 1.14). In this sense, Mary and John stand as "disciples" and as "equals."[77]

Ruether's criticism has to do with Mary's absence from the crucifixion scene. In the synoptic accounts, Ruether notes that Mary is not mentioned at the crucifixion.[78] In John's gospel (19.25-27), Mary is mentioned but does not appear as a central figure.[79] Other Catholic scholars, however, have used the same text to affirm Mary's faithfulness at the foot of the cross. Anthony Tambasco, for example, has argued that Mary has become so important for Christians because of her faith and therefore one can readily associate her with a believing community.[80]

In short, Ruether downplays Mary's significance at the crucifixion in order to show the centrality of Mary Magdalene. Ruether characterizes Mary Magdalene as an "unconventional" woman[81] who, despite her faith, remains inconceivable as a role model for Catholic women on account of her uncertain past. She attributes the "suppression" of Mary Magdalene's role to the "official" Church's emphasis on "subordinate" and "conventional" roles for women. In this sense, Ruether contends that the "official" Church substituted Mary Magdalene's significance with that of Mary of Nazareth in order to portray a suitable role model for women.[82]

Given the treatment of Mary Magdalene outlined in the previous section of this chapter, I observe that even though Mary of Nazareth has been the subject for Catholic devotion and meditation and has been exemplified as the "ideal" woman in the tradition of the Roman Catholic Church, this does not necessitate the downgrading of Mary Magdalene's (as well as other women's) leadership and significance for contemporary women. Ruether seems to imply that one must accept either Mary of Nazareth's obedience and submissiveness or Mary Magdalene's active leadership among the followers of Jesus. Must one choose?

I argue that in defining appropriate roles for women in the Catholic

Church, one should not be obliged to choose between Mary of Nazareth and Mary Magdalene. Both were women of faith, as others were, and each can contribute to our contemporary understanding of roles for women. In the case of Mary Magdalene, she is presented as a woman of faith who finds in Jesus a liberator whose acceptance serves as a pivot for her steadfastness and ministry of service and proclamation.

Similarly, as has been stressed in traditional Catholicism, Mary of Nazareth's role in Jesus' ministry has been quite prominent. First, being a virgin, not only did she faithfully accept her duty to carry and give birth to Jesus in order to fulfill God's will, but second, Mary is included in the circle of Jesus' disciples as she (along with other women) accompanied her son in his ministry, and was included among his family of disciples at Jesus' death. Third, Mary's faith and obedience to God distinguish her as a role model for all women. As opposed to Peter, we have no evidence to support the idea that Mary ever denied Jesus.

In this sense, Mary of Nazareth can also be seen as a role model for contemporary women. Where Ruether's argument stems from the traditional understanding of Mary as being passive and submissive, I observe that Mary's role can be interpreted as active and involved. She actively participated in Jesus' nurturing as a child. I would also contend that at times she actively participated in the unfolding of his ministry.[83] These were by no means passive roles. Similarly, Mary's faith can be seen as a strength in itself as she was free to love and to respond to God's will—she freely and faithfully accepted being a part of his plan.

Further, Tambasco has maintained that other characteristics used to qualify Mary need not be appropriated negatively. Her virginity, for example, can be used to emphasize

> ... that woman need not be identified totally with her sexuality, not because sex is evil, as was thought in the past, but because woman can have a self-directing autonomy which need not define her purely in relation to the male.[84]

Lastly, Mary can become a symbol of justice for the poor and the oppressed as she—a humble virgin—was chosen to carry out God's will.

After having briefly looked at the roles of women who figured prominently in Jesus' ministry along with his apparent attitude towards them, I observe that Jesus did not ordinarily distinguish between roles accorded to women and those accorded to men. In each case, Jesus commends women's faith and encourages them into performing active roles within his ministry. Although Jesus' treatment of women may have shocked people as his attitude towards women did not conform to current rabbinic traditions, the disciples seem to have recorded it. The canonical texts stress Jesus' egalitarian approach on a theological and social scale. He gave women in this setting a radical invitation to share his ministry and become His disciples. Schüssler-Fiorenza surmises that the Galilean women who were among Jesus' disciples gathered the "dispersed" disciples and kept Jesus' message "alive" on the basis that it would have been much easier for women to secretly carry on the gatherings perhaps because their actions were less noticeable than the men's. Given the fact that many women were present in Acts 1.14, this theory is certainly plausible.[85] In order to appreciate fully the arguments presented in the *Declaration*, it would be helpful at this time to examine the significance of the Twelve, as the Roman Catholic Church has regarded their maleness as the basis for an all-male priesthood.

The Twelve

The *Declaration* stresses that Jesus "...did not call any woman to become part of the Twelve,"[86] as one of its arguments for women's exclusion to the ministerial priesthood. Heinz Günther has made some noteworthy comments regarding the significance of the Twelve in terms of their function in early Christianity. Among them, he stresses scripture's lack of biographical information about the Twelve, as their names seem to appear in the form of a list without giving any prior details about them.[87] For example,

> ...apart from Peter, James, John and Judas Iscariot, none of them feature prominently in the gospels, and they are not mentioned at all in the rest of the New Testament.[88]

Further, Günther observes that Paul curiously had no personal contact with the Twelve, although they seem to have exercised a missionary function. What is even more curious is Matthias' function. In Acts, for example, he strangely appears as a replacement for Judas and is never again mentioned as fulfilling any specific function.[89]

Women, on the other hand, are almost always identified by name, along with the duties and functions they performed in Jesus' ministry. Further, it seems odd that the *Declaration* would interpret Jesus' calling of the Twelve as specifically "the" apostles when the evidence suggests that he appointed women to perform what in many ways were comparable tasks.[90] I think the ministry of Mary Magdalene can be regarded as apostleship, as she was the first witness to the resurrection and was given the task of proclaiming the risen Lord, even though she was not included on the list of Twelve men.

These contentions therefore raise some doubt as to the historical existence of Twelve specifically appointed men in Jesus' ministry.[91] Schüssler-Fiorenza observes that in the gospel attributed to John, the Last Supper includes "all the disciples" and not just the Twelve. Similarly, he appears to "all the disciples" who in turn receive the Spirit and the authority to forgive sins in John 20.21-23.[92] Therefore, one wonders about the authenticity of the Twelve, not to mention their significance to early Christianity.

Why "Twelve" Men? The previous contentions raise further ambiguities regarding the nature of the "Twelve." For example, the *Declaration* stresses Jesus' maleness and insists that the Twelve apostles were men in order to represent Christ's maleness.[93] Perhaps I should attempt to resolve a more pressing question and then return to the latter. That is, what was the relevance of the number 12, in the appointment of male apostles, to the gospel's authenticity as well as its acceptance, given the social, religious and political unrest that characterized early Christianity?

Let us turn our attention to the work of Heinz Günther as his research has made a significant contribution to our contemporary understanding of numerology and its function in the Greco-Roman world. According to Günther, astrological signs had become a part of the Eastern life and dominated religious and secular spheres, such that

> The number twelve had established its spiritual empire long before the ancient Israelites even began to move into the cultural land of Palestine.[94]

Thus we have a history full of symbolism relating to the number 12, which according to N. Gottwald refers to "totality and wholeness."[95] In this setting, the 12 tribes of Israel (Exodus 24.4), 12 leading priests (Ezra 8.24), 12 prophets (Sirach 49.10), and so on, come to be associated with prestige and divinity. Another example of this type appears in the Old Testament. The prophet states that "In the twelfth year, in the twelfth month, on the first day of the month, the word of the Lord came to me" (Ezekiel 32.1, RSV). Thus Günther claims:

> The figure of the twelve ... functioned in Israel's historiography as an effective vehicle enabling the biblical writers to understand their own past in terms of a divinely ordained history.[96]

Further, Günther's work carries into the Qumram texts which parallel the symbolism of 12 as portraying dominance and authority.[97]

2. Women in the Ministry of Jesus

Given Günther's numerological research, several observations come to mind. If the astrological concept of the number 12 carried through the scriptural texts, this raises serious doubt as to the authenticity of the function of the Twelve in Jesus' ministry. Further, Günther's and Schüssler-Fiorenza's insights regarding the absence of biographical information as well as lack of clarity regarding the role of the Twelve have raised serious contentions which call to mind the whole structure of the Church. If Jesus' message was so radical and the exercise of his ministry so egalitarian why would the gospel writers have inserted a list of "twelve" men? Certainly Jesus' resurrection would have formed a solid enough basis for the spreading of Christianity.

One aspect which Günther's work does not address is the reasoning behind the male character of the Twelve, perhaps because it is so obvious that divinity must take on a "male" symbol. Let us now turn to the ambiguity with which this section began.

Why Twelve "Men"? Frank and Evelyn Stagg have surmised that the Twelve were all men because Jesus' break with Jewish culture was so radical that his principles could not be immediately implemented. For example, he spoke to Samaritans, yet there are no Samaritans listed among the Twelve. Similarly, Jesus affirmed the dignity and freedom of women, yet he did not include them in the circle of the Twelve.[98]

Elizabeth Tetlow has suggested that the significance of the male character of the Twelve indicates a symbolic function.[99] Like Günther, she argues that the Twelve played a symbolic role in representing the twelve tribes of Israel, in order to portray the completeness of God's new people at Pentecost and at the eschaton. For this reason, she contends, in keeping with the Judaic tradition[100] the Twelve had to be men. She concludes, therefore, that

> ... the male character of the members of the Twelve had to do with the theological symbolism of that temporary institution, not with the ministry of the Church.[101]

Although the *Declaration* states that Christ entrusted a ministry to the Twelve,[102] scriptural evidence demonstrates that He did not ordain them, or anyone else for that matter.[103] Thus, the argument that priestly ordination must be restricted to men because Jesus entrusted his ministry only to men appears untenable. To quote Sandra M. Schneiders:

> There is simply no historical grounds for regarding the Twelve as the first priests, for maintaining that Jesus ordained them, or for considering them as the exclusive precursors of that role in the Christian community which is later filled by ordained priests.[104]

It is also curious that the *Declaration* fails to record or even acknowledge the Pontifical Biblical Commission's findings regarding the ordination of women in relation to Christ's will. One will recall that the Commission reported that, should the Church decide to ordain women, it would not be acting contrary to the will of Christ.[105] Regarding these observations, we can say that the evidence used to support the arguments presented in the *Declaration* appears selective, and has no scriptural warrant.

The roles and functions performed by the Twelve do not differ from the roles exercised by women in the ministry of Jesus. If the apostles' main concern had to do with proclaiming the gospel message and administering new churches,[106] one can say that women were not excluded from performing these roles. Given Mary Magdalene's function, it cannot be maintained that Christ conveyed different roles to men and women according to their sex.

Regarding the importance ascribed to the "maleness" of the Twelve, we can say that although certain scriptural texts exclude women from the Twelve, Jesus in no way seemed to limit their missionary activity. If we accept Tetlow's argument relating the symbolic significance of the Twelve, along with Günther's numerological research and the contention that the earthly Jesus did not institute this selective group of Twelve men, it seems rather evident that the "maleness" of the Twelve does not warrant the exclusion of women from the ministerial priesthood. Schneiders has written that

> We have no clear evidence that any of the Twelve ever presided at the Eucharist and it is relatively clear that others, notably prophets, [among whom were women] did so by some sort of official designation.[107]

Since the Jesus group included women who were actively engaged in his ministry,[108] and the Twelve were never ordained as presiders of the Eucharist, it remains somewhat quetionable whether the *Declaration* can justify the argument used to exclude women from the priesthood based on Christ's will.

Further, scriptural evidence demonstrates that the early Christian communities were structured on an egalitarian basis whose leadership functioned according to service and love.[109] Günther also observes that

> The overall purpose of Mark's composition makes it crystal-clear why the evangelist preferred to portray them as missionaries, and not, ... as the foundation of a new church organization.[110]

2. Women in the Ministry of Jesus

If Günther's assumption regarding the evangelists' insertion on the list of twelve men is correct, an interesting exercise could be to omit any mention of the Twelve throughout scripture, replace the term with "apostles" (men and women) and then proceed to derive the organizational character of Jesus' earthly ministry. Certainly this would give us a clear indication of the "type" of Church Jesus intended.

Regardless of the initial reasons for which women were gradually excluded from the ministerial priesthood, it seems that today's Roman Catholic understanding of the situation indicates a regress from Christ's message and ministry. Throughout Jesus' ministry, we can identify a new understanding of the Jewish customs. For example, Jesus reinterpreted the Mosaic law regarding divorce (see Mark 10.2f) and the "uncleanness" of a woman (as we have previously seen). Certainly this "new understanding" should include a reshaping of the concept of "twelve" dominating patriarchs. In short, Jesus' treatment of women in his ministry indicates a heightening of their status as human beings— they were to be treated as people.

As mentioned at the outset of this chapter, women's status at the time of Jesus' ministry was quite inferior to that of men. Jesus sought to transform their status by giving them a new sense of dignity and personal worth. In no way did he treat women any differently than he treated men. The Church in its tradition seems to have detracted from Christ's teaching in assuming that women (because of their gender) are to be abased and excluded when regarding matters of priestly functions; this practice is untenable. To quote Elizabeth Tetlow:

> The later exclusion of women from the official ministry of the Church raises serious questions about the authenticity of such a practice. According to the evidence of the New Testament, the exclusion of women from ecclesiastical ministry is neither in accord with the teaching or practice of Jesus nor with that of the First-century Church.[111]

Considering Jesus' attitude towards women and its implications regarding the ministry of women in the Roman Catholic Church today, one can say that a study of women's roles and functions in the early Christian Church would seem appropriate. Chapter 3 will examine these roles in light of the arguments presented in the *Declaration* that selectively deal with women in the early Christian community.

CHAPTER 3

The Role of Women in the Early Church

In the *Declaration*, the Roman Catholic Church has denied the access of women to priestly ordination, claiming an attempt to remain faithful to a constant tradition and the practice of the apostles. The purpose of this chapter is to survey modern feminist assessments of women's roles in the early Christian movement in light of the *Declaration*'s argument in order to gain new insight as to the development of women's roles within the Roman Catholic Church. To do this, I will attempt to apply Elisabeth Schüssler-Fiorenza's methodology. Her treatment of scripture offers a reconstruction of Christianity in relation to Vatican II's treatment of tradition in the Roman Catholic Church. I will attempt to outline the impact that scripture has had in the tradition of the Church and demonstrate the manner in which a feminist interpretation of scripture can shed new light on a contemporary understanding of the role of women in the Roman Catholic Church. This chapter will focus primarily on women's ministry and leadership as revealed in the writings of Paul. His works depict the early Christian mentality regarding women and their function in the community.[1]

Can Scripture Determine Appropriate Roles for Women?

While the use of scripture by Vatican II accents the transmission of the faith by the apostles,[2] "...the Bible can speak with full power only when its message is brought into correlation with present-day questions."[3] One such question has to do with the role of women in the Roman Catholic Church. Without attempting to rupture the relationship between scripture and tradition, as the two are virtually "one sacred deposit,"[4] one wonders as to the significance of the tradition in the first century Church and its impact on the development of roles for women in the history of the Church. The biblical texts that discuss the function of women in the early Church are therefore basic when addressing this issue.

In the study and interpretation of any biblical passage, one must take into account the authorship of the text, the context in which it was written and the author's intended audience. In doing so, feminist scholars such as Sandra M. Schneiders caution that one must not absolutize certain directives given within biblical texts if they deal with a specific situation. For example, she cites Paul's letter to Philemon. Is Paul trying to legitimize slavery or is he giving advice for a particular situation? Further, she contends that biblical texts can bear significance if appropriated in a contemporary setting. In this manner, the text can serve as a guideline for certain questions even though scripture may not address a specific modern dilemma. For example, she notes the New Testament cannot give certain directives when addressing a question such as nuclear war per se, but scripture does outline Christian behavior in light of comparable conflicts.[5] Brendan Byrne, S.J., has written:

> We should see in them [that is, scriptural texts] the ways in which the Church in its formative period adapted the values of Jesus to the circumstances, threats and opportunities of its time. We should find in this, not law, not imprisonment, but instruction—perhaps warning too—about what is incumbent upon believers in our time.[6]

A study of women's roles in the writings of Paul will be subject to these criteria. Prior to undertaking a study of the women in Paul's writings, a general description of the cultural situation surrounding women in his time will prove helpful as it will reflect the current mentality regarding women in the light of Paul's ministry, and therefore provide one manner of interpreting Paul.

Paul and Women. Although women's status varied from one area in the Roman empire to the next, the general underlying motif seems to be that of patriarchy.[7] Catholic scholars have argued that Paul's letters depict the situation of women in patriarchal Judaism, and that his thought must be understood in the light of women's status in the Old Testament.[8] Another consideration which Florence Gillman notes is that not only were most biblical texts written by men, they also reflect a man's perceptions regarding the situation which is being described. In this setting, the information given regarding women in Paul's letters (that is, letters attributed to Paul) is minute.[9] In Virginia Mollenkott's words:

3. The Role of Women in the Early Church

We cannot assume that because the Bible was written against the backdrop of a patriarchal social structure, patriarchy is the will of God for all people in all times and all places.[10]

In this sense, even though Paul refers to women in terms of their social status in patriarchal Judaism, one cannot absolutize the social and cultural conditions regarding women at that time. To do so would be to absolutize patriarchy. For example, I Corinthians 11.5 prescribes that a woman who prays should cover her head.[11] Does this mean that any woman today should veil herself when she participates in a prayer service? I argue that this prescription was a cultural consideration bound to a social tradition. Therefore, I observe that although the Bible is useful, one must nevertheless distinguish between the prescriptions that deal with a cultural consideration and those that specifically belong to the tradition of the Church. In other words, how can we interpret a biblical text if women's functions are determined by the cultural practices of a particular society?

Towards a Biblical Methodology. Although the biblical message addresses a patriarchal society, Elisabeth Schüssler-Fiorenza has aptly noted that androcentric language is the form and not the content of the message. Therefore, one cannot disown a biblical text on the basis that it addresses a patriarchal culture. Schüssler-Fiorenza proposes that these texts bear witness to women's presence in the heart of biblical revelation, even though that presence exists in an oppressed state. One must therefore seek to move away from the androcentrism and come to terms with their "social-historical" contexts[12]:

> A feminist hermeneutical understanding that is oriented not simply toward an actualizing continuation of biblical tradition but toward a critical evaluation of it must uncover and reject those elements within all biblical traditions and texts that perpetuate, in the name of God, violence, alienation, and patriarchal subordination, and eradicate women from historical-theological consciousness.[13]

In this sense, Schüssler-Fiorenza proposes that androcentric biblical texts should be understood in the light of their historical situation.[14] Then and only then can the Bible represent not only women's victimization, but also their strengths. In other words, one can uncover the prominence of women's leadership despite the androcentric injunctions placed upon women in the early Christian Church that were characteristic of a social structure in which women were subordinate.[15] Further, Schüssler-Fiorenza stresses that a feminist critical hermeneutic must attempt to come to terms with the dynamics involved when the body of theological texts and tradition are considered. Therefore, she proposes a methodology that would incorporate the biblical texts along with the history of its tradition:

> The history and theology of women's oppression perpetuated by patriarchal biblical texts and by a clerical patriarchy must not be allowed to cancel out the history and theology of the struggle, life, and leadership of Christian women who spoke and acted in the power of the Spirit.[16]

In this manner, Schüssler-Fiorenza asserts that one cannot simply "do away" with the texts in which women appear as marginal figures. Rather, a feminist critical hermeneutic must seek to "break" women's silence in much the same way as a detective pieces together bits of information. In this sense the Bible can be used as a source for women's presence in the early Christian communities, but cannot be relied upon as an absolute vehicle for historical facts. If biblical translations remain androcentric, such that women are mentioned only when they engender conflict, Schüssler-Fiorenza proposes one must "reconstruct" the text in order to recover the discipleship of equals.[17]

This method, of course, has been strongly criticized. William Oddie's work entitled *What Will Happen to God?* (a work which has a naked female Christ nailed to the crucifix on its cover), for example, rebukes Schüssler-Fiorenza's approach because it is not based on "historical facts."[18] Rather, he states, "the truth is what feminist consciousness says it ought to be."[19] First of all, I do not think the Bible can be solely read as an historical work. Further, Schüssler-Fiorenza's method does not originate *ex nihilo*. Her reconstruction of texts is based on the notion that women are present, but only as marginal figures, given the androcentrism of the text. In addition, Oddie assumes that Schüssler-Fiorenza's method proposes a "new theory of revelation" which is based on imagination and not fact.[20]

Here Oddie has clearly missed Schüssler-Fiorenza's point. For example, she cites the work of various contemporary scholars regarding the possibility that certain biblical texts were written by women. Her interest in this position is later qualified by the following contention:

> The suggestion of female authorship, however, has great imaginative-theological value because it opens up the possibility of attributing the authority of apostolic writings to women and of claiming theological authority for women.[21]

This is clearly Oddie's problem. Although Schüssler-Fiorenza examines the plausibility of female authorship, Oddie qualifies her research as "revolutionary" and concludes that such contentions can only foster more division in the Church.[22] Why such hostility towards Schüssler-Fiorenza's feminist hermeneutic? Because Oddie claims this approach threatens to redefine the Church's traditional understanding of revelation. As his book cover indicates, Oddie assumes that a feminist hermeneutic threatens to usurp the place of a male Christ with that of a woman. He cites a passage from Rosemary Radford Ruether's *Sexism and God-Talk* describing the Church's traditional perspective on marriage — one where a woman is completely subservient to her husband.[23] In this setting, a woman has a certain place, at the bottom of the pyramidal and hierarchic structure of Christ's Church. Certainly this is the "rightful" place for women according to Oddie. In an age where women are capable of managing careers as well as continuing to care for their families, Oddie's perspective entertains a sexist philosophy — one, nevertheless, that continues to plague Christ's Church.

The *Declaration,* for example, continues to absorb this attitude towards women:

> That is why we can never ignore the fact that Christ is a *man*. And therefore, unless one is to disregard the importance of this symbolism for the economy of Revelation, it must be admitted that, in actions which demand the character of ordination and in which Christ himself, the author of the Covenant, the Bridegroom and Head of the Church, is represented, exercising *his* ministry of salvation — which is in the highest degree the case of the Eucharist — *his* role must be taken by a *man*.[24]

Again, this understanding is full of essentially "male" overtones. Where is the problem? First of all, I argue that Jesus was made incarnate in the form of a "human" flesh. His maleness was secondary. Second, although it is true that Jesus was a man, he ceased being a "man" when he became a Savior — the "Christ." To argue that Christ in his divine state continued to possess a "male" body with physical characteristics is to completely miss the point of his coming. Christ's Spirit dwells in each of us. Male and female make up Christ's body — which is the Church.

The feminist rejection of an all-male framework has to do with the economy of salvation. If Jesus was made incarnate in the form of a "human" flesh, it was to redeem humanity. To emphasize Jesus' maleness is to ultimately contend that Jesus came to redeem men. Such a contention remains unacceptable to Christian tradition. Therefore, a feminist hermeneutic seeks to re-discover the discipleship of equals that Jesus' ministry established.

A Feminist Historical Reconstruction. Bernadette Brooten has established a similar "reconstructive" approach, although she employs a different structure. She claims that a feminist hermeneutic must move beyond the canonized literature because women in this setting are qualified by male attitudes and male understandings. For example, if the literature we have on women today was written by men, it originates from a male perspective. Such a perspective could not accurately describe a woman's thought, nor her struggles pertaining to certain events, laws or cultural considerations. Thus Brooten argues one cannot simply "deposit" women into a male philosophy, a male perspective — in essence, a male world. This could not possibly give a reasonable account of women's lives.

Brooten's reconstruction involves a search for nonliterary papers, letters, legal documents, business papers, archaeological remains, inscriptions, and the like. Her work in this field is quite remarkable, and has endless possibilities.[25] It will be fascinating to see where her work leads her as this will require much time to complete. It would also be interesting to pursue her methodology regarding a study of women in Christian tradition. Since such a study would demand researching noncanonical works, it is beyond the scope of the present work. Perhaps this could be undertaken at a later time. The value of Brooten's work and the significance it bears to my discussion of a biblical methodology are quite relevant. At this time, the hierarchy has denied the access of women to leadership positions based in part upon its understanding of canonical works. Perhaps Brooten and other scholars working within her field could eventually influence enough theologians to persuade the hierarchy to broaden their perspectives. Certainly this would demand a reshaping of attitudes, but if there was enough pressure from theologians and clergy to promote more inclusion for women, the hierarchy would eventually have to come to terms with this issue.

Although Brooten's work and Schüssler-Fiorenza's methodology are very enlightening, my discussion of women must be limited to the canonical texts at this time, for it is these texts which the *Declaration* cites as plausible arguments for the hierarchy's exclusion of women to the ministerial priesthood. I argue that such texts can provide enough evidence to discredit the *Declaration*'s contentions when interpreted in the light of modern feminist scholarship.

Women's Roles in Paul's Writings

In dealing with Paul's statements that directly concern women, one must remember that one purpose of Paul's letters is to respond to certain needs or questions arising in a specific community.[26] Therefore, one must seek to comprehend the context in which Paul addresses women when regarding appropriate roles for women in the early Church. For example, several texts that the Roman Catholic Church has attributed to Paul appear contradictory. For the purposes of this study, I will focus on certain texts that the *Declaration* has used as a basis for the exclusion of women from the ministerial priesthood.

Although the *Declaration* acknowledges the difficulties involved when interpreting Paul, it nevertheless attempts to classify Paul's prescriptions regarding women. For example, the veiling of women in I Corinthians 11.2-16 is regarded as a cultural concern, while the restriction imposed upon women from teaching in I Corinthians 14.34-35 and in I Timothy 2.12 is regarded as a prohibition of women's exercising an "official function" of teaching in a public worship gathering.[27] Further, the *Declaration* states that this restriction is directly based on the orders of creation, as in I Corinthians 11.7. Given the implications that flow from this argument, it may be helpful at this time to treat each text separately and then proceed to examine them in relation to one another.

Silence for Women in the Church.

> The women should keep silent in the churches. For they are not permitted to speak, but should be subordinate, as even the law says. If there is anything they desire to know, let them ask their husbands at home. For it is shameful for a woman to speak in Church [I Corinthians 14.34-35, RSV].

Taken literally, this text can be interpreted as an injunction against women from speaking in church assemblies with particular attention placed on teaching. In contrast, various feminist scholars have argued that women exercised prominent roles in places of worship.[28] For example, in Romans 16.4, Paul sends greetings to Prisca and Aquila, ". . . who risked their necks for my life, to whom not only I but also all the churches of the Gentiles give thanks" (RSV). Regarding Prisca's importance, Schüssler-Fiorenza has theorized that she is addressed first because she is the more significant of the two,[29] while other scholars have deduced that she taught the "learned" Apollos and that she and Aquila worked independently from Paul, by virtue of their own authority.[30] Further, Florence Gillman contends that Prisca and Aquila's description in Romans 16.3 bears witness to the "mutual solidarity" with which the early churches functioned.[31] Such a setting would account for Paul's greeting in I Corinthians 16.19 to the church in "their" house.[32]

If this is so, it would seem rather curious that Paul would restrict women from speaking at public assemblies, or even suggest that Prisca consult her husband at home, since she seems to have been the more dominant of the two. According to the *Declaration*, the restriction has to do with the "official function" of teaching in the Christian community.[33] It is interesting to note that the New Testament in its entirety only contains two passages that impede women's ministry.[34] On the basis of these passages alone, the *Declaration* attempts to exclude women in an absolute manner. Arlene Swidler maintains that this passage deals with women "speaking out" in public assemblies. If women are permitted to function as lectors and commentators, she maintains that this restriction has already been challenged.[35] In light of these arguments, it is therefore necessary to appeal to the wisdom of recent feminist scholarship.

Regarding the authorship of the text, Joan Morris has argued that in various Greek and Latin manuscripts, verses 34–35 are placed at the end of the chapter and appear as verses 39–40, and therefore she raises some doubt as to whether verses 34–35 were part of the original letter.[36] Brendan Byrne, S.J., maintains that verses 34 and 35 seem to interrupt Paul's argument. In this sense, he claims if verses 34–35 were extracted, the letter would regain its continuity.[37] Other scholars have argued that verses 34–35 were a later interpolation based on the contrasting tone found in these lines.[38] For example, I Corinthians 14.34–35 seems to contradict what was previously stated in the same letter:

> ... but any woman who prays or prophesies with her head unveiled dishonours her head—it is the same as if her head were shaven [I Corinthians 11.5, RSV].

In light of such contradictions it is even doubtful that Paul was the author of verses 34–35.

I suggest that, in light of the teaching put forth in Galatians 3.28, it would be difficult to attribute the Corinthian text to Paul: "There is neither Jew nor Greek, there is neither slave nor free, there is neither male nor female; for you are all one in Christ Jesus [RSV]."[39]

Moreover, Ben Witherington has argued that the restrictions prescribed in I Corinthians 14.34–35 reflect Paul's advice regarding a specific problem that arose in the Corinthian community.[40] As to the nature of the problem, Randy Peterson has argued that

> ... women and men probably sat, synagogue style, in separate sections of the Church. When women had questions about the preaching (as they often would since they were generally untrained in the scriptures), they would call to their husbands. In the interest of orderly worship, Paul forbids this.[41]

Schüssler-Fiorenza prefers to accept verses 34-35 as Pauline because they cannot be withdrawn on "textual-critical grounds." In this sense, she discards the problem of authorship and goes on to explain the context of this passage. She assigns most of this Corinthian chapter to Church order and discipline and resolves the ambiguity that arises when one compares the apparent contradiction in 11.2-16 which assumes that women already prophesy in the Church alongside the latter injunction against women in 14.35-36, by qualifying that the restriction pertains to Christian wives and not to all women. Her reasoning is that Paul prefers celibacy as opposed to marriage in I Corinthians 7.38. Schüssler-Fiorenza claims that Paul's preference for celibacy is reflected in his theological argument regarding the prophecy of women in I Corinthians 11.5. In the Greco-Roman tradition, the subordination of women to their husbands was part of the "law." Paul therefore denies married women such active participation in a public sphere. He does appeal however to married women to wait until they get home to ask their husbands about certain questions. This, Schüssler-Fiorenza maintains, is done to promote order in the Christian worship service.[42]

Regardless of such problems as already mentioned, the *Declaration* holds that I Corinthians 14.34-35 is authentically Pauline, and resolves the ambiguity which occurs when examining I Corinthians 11.5 alongside I Corinthians 14.34-35. The *Declaration* argues that the former text recognizes women's right to prophesy whereas the latter text imposes a restriction against women teaching in the community, based on the order of creation.[43] In light of the insights provided by recent feminist scholarship, I suggest that the *Declaration*'s use of the Corinthian text to justify women's exclusion from teaching in a public assembly is ambiguous as the text itself appeals to maintaining proper conduct during worship services and not to a revelatory tradition.

Regarding the *Declaration*'s interpretation, Robert Karris has offered that the verb *lalein*, meaning "to speak," is usually accompanied by an object as in I Corinthians 14.2, where speaking "in tongues" is discussed. Since the object that specifies the "teaching" function is absent from I Corinthians 14.34-35, Karris maintains that this text does not in any way prohibit women from teaching in the Christian assembly.[44]

Further, the injunctions placed upon women in I Corinthians 11.2-16 give evidence to support the notion that women prophesied in the early Church. Schüssler-Fiorenza notes that women commonly offered their homes for oriental cults and ecstatic worship celebrations that included unbound hair.[45] In I Corinthians 11.5, Paul states: "but any woman who prays or prophesies with her head unveiled dishonours her head" [RSV]. This statement could serve as an example of Schüssler-Fiorenza's claim that one can uncover roles for women in the early Church if one moves beyond the language and analyzes the context. In subsequent verses of the same chapter, Paul outlines the order of creation where man is "the image and glory of God, and woman is the glory of man" (verse 7). Although this text could be interpreted to designate woman's subordination to man, in the order of creation, I observe that it gives specific directions as to the manner in which a woman should pray. To do so with uncovered or unbound hair may have given the appearance of an orgiastic worship service. As Schüssler-Fiorenza stresses:

> It is important to note, that woman is not said to be the image of man. Thus the statement does not deny woman the "image of God" status, but explains why man is the glory of God.[46]

ALTHOUGH THE *Declaration* uses the Corinthian text to justify the restriction of women to official roles in the Roman Catholic Church, various areas remain problematic. For example, I Corinthians 11.5 already establishes that women prophesy in the Church. Further, the evidence from Romans 16.4 acknowledges Prisca's significance to Paul's ministry and it is apparent from I Corinthians 16.19 that she and Aquila established a church in their house. Given these facts which are documented throughout Paul's letters, it is hardly likely that he would silence women from speaking in a public worship service. I have raised certain difficulties that emerge when regarding the *Declaration*'s fixation with the I Corinthian 14.35-36 text. If Paul really meant to silence women, certainly this restriction would appear in other letters as well. Rather, the earlier Corinthian passage (section 11.5) establishes that women already prophesy. I Corinthians 14.35-36 maintains this practice as long as it is done with grace and propriety. Certainly the *Declaration*'s use of this text to justify women's exclusion from public ministry is untenable.

I Timothy 2.8-5. The *Declaration* cites this text alongside the Corinthian text as a basis for the exclusion of women from official teaching functions,[47] although contemporary feminist scholarship has viewed this text as non-Pauline.[48] However, it is important to consider the text as it has been included in the New Testament canon. Let us therefore proceed to examine the text itself, in order to determine what is prescribed for women. Although the *Declaration* has focused its main attention on verse 12, I observe that some additional insight may be gained from the comments of David Scholer. Verses 8–10 seemingly deal with propriety in grooming and attire for men and women. The verses that follow, however, introduce what might seem to be a different note:

> Let a woman learn in silence with all submissiveness. I permit no woman to teach or to have authority over men; she is to keep silent [RSV].

Yet, when understood in the context of the letter as a whole, as David Scholer has argued, this passage also deals with maintaining cultural standards. Given Paul's encounter with false teachers in Ephesus (I Timothy 1.3–7), Scholer holds that the remainder of the letter exemplifies Paul's attempt to maintain proper order and conduct in the Church communities. In this sense, I Timothy 2.8–15 focuses on women and reminds them of the standards proper to their culture so that their teaching authority would not be abused as it had been by the women in Ephesus. Scholer describes the discussion as follows:

> Thus, the progression of thought in I Tim. 2.9–15 moves from concern for women's adornment (v. 9–10) to concern for women's submission and silence in public worship (v. 11–12). These are two sides of the same coin in the cultural settings of the first century A.D., which assumed male dominance and a belief in women's subordination and inferiority.[49]

Further, Schüssler-Fiorenza observes that the teaching in Titus 2.3–5 gives specific instructions for women who teach (presbyters?) and therefore maintains that women were permitted to teach as long as they taught other women.[50] In this sense, the restriction for women in I Timothy 2.12 can be seen as a code of conduct for women. They are to be submissive, therefore nonauthoritative, and observe the patriarchal order in which women and slaves are to be completely subordinate to their masters.

Although the *Declaration*'s use of this text appears to have merit, I argue that the choice of texts here is selective, and does not treat the restrictive verses in the context of the letter as a whole. Based on Scholer's observations, I argue that I Timothy 2.8–15 deals with a specific problem that arose in the Ephesian community. In an attempt to restrain women from abusing their teaching authority, the writer appeals to local social customs that restricted women based on their subordination to men.

When discussing appropriate roles for women, I argue that several Pauline texts promote the equality of women and demonstrate that women in the early Church functioned in positions of authority and leadership. In order to exemplify the manner in which roles for women can be found, let us now turn to certain Pauline texts that describe women in authoritative roles.

Roles for Women in the Pauline Tradition

Despite the apparent conflicts in dealing with contrasting texts, various texts attributed to Paul outline women exercising prominent leadership roles in the early Christian community. The purpose of this section is to discuss the modern feminist evaluation of these roles in order to gain some insight as to the *Declaration*'s exclusion from the ministerial priesthood based on the Church's constant tradition.

Phoebe. In Romans 16.1-2, Paul states:

> I commend to you our sister Phoebe, a deaconess of the Church at Cenchreae, that you may receive her in the Lord as befits the saints, and help her in whatever she may require from you, for she has been a helper of many and of myself as well [RSV].

The three words used to characterize Phoebe are: sister, deaconess and helper. The term "sister" is commonly used to signify a "coworker."[51] Paul uses the term *diakonos* in I Corinthians 3.5 and II Corinthians 3.1-11 to refer to himself or other male leaders.[52] When referring to Phoebe however, the translation used in the RSV is "deaconess."[53] Why is this distinction made?

Although some scholars have downplayed Phoebe's role as simply being that of a hospitable woman,[54] others have associated the term with a teaching and preaching function.[55] As to the deacon/deaconess distinction, scholars such as Letha Scanzoni and Nancy Hardesty have argued that the deaconess ministered mainly to women and tended to needs that would have been inappropriate for men to carry out, such as bathing women recovering from sickness and anointing in baptism. Therefore, the distinction has been regarded as qualifying ministering roles to men as opposed to those of women.[56] I must caution however that this distinction appears among the *Didaskalia* and the *Apostolic Constitutions*—works that date back to the third and fourth centuries.[57] Although certain restrictions occur when regarding functions of women compared to those of men "deacons" at that time, these restrictions shed no light whatsoever on Phoebe's role.[58]

Schüssler-Fiorenza for example has noted that the term *diakonos* is used elsewhere to denote preaching and teaching functions, and has characterized Phoebe's role as an "official" designation. In this sense,

Phoebe's recommendation indicates that her ministry was already established and that its duration was long-term. Further, she notes that Paul's use of the term *diakonos* as opposed to the term *apostle* may have been used so that Phoebe would not be mistaken for one who was commissioned for a shorter period of time. As she explains, "The apostles of the churches were commissioned only for a definite and limited function."[59]

Based on Schüssler-Fiorenza's observations, I argue that deacons in the Church at the time of Paul (both male and female) exercised more of a leadership role than the third and fourth century distinction suggests. Is it clear from the context that Paul makes no distinction when referring to Phoebe in Romans. He states she is a deacon of the Church at Cenchreae. Is it possible she held a leadership role in that community? Although Klauck has suggested that Phoebe's ministry had to do with being a hostess for the Church at Cenchreae, Schüssler-Fiorenza has argued that Phoebe ministered to the whole Church and not just to women.[60]

Further, the term *prostatis* is translated as "helper" in the RSV, or "patroness" in others.[61] In the literature of the time, however, Schüssler-Fiorenza notes that the term has the connotation of "leading officer," "president," "governor," or "superintendent."[62] Suzanne Heine has indicated that the use of the same verb elsewhere (in Romans 12.8 and I Thessalonians 5.12) suggests that Phoebe functioned as a leader in the community.[63] Further, Catherine Kroeger maintains that the masculine form for the term *prostatis* was later used to characterize one who presided over the Eucharist.[64] Therefore, I observe that Phoebe's role reached beyond that of a "hospitable" woman. Paul clearly makes no deacon/deaconess distinction when speaking of Phoebe — and he associates her ministry with that of a particular Church community.

Robert Jewett has even suggested that Phoebe's role extended beyond that of Church presider. He postulates that Phoebe figured prominently in Paul's attempt to evangelize Spain based on the notion that he planned to go there in Romans 15.24. In this setting, there were fewer Jews to evangelize there and no synagogue to establish contacts. Further, the language impediment would have also created a barrier, as Latin was the main language in use there. Jewett speculates that her position was undeniably that of Church leader and translates the second verse as "provide her whatsoever she needs from you in the matter."[65]

According to Jewett, this "matter" has to do with Phoebe's evangelizing role in Spain. In this sense, Jewett outlines three tasks. First, Phoebe was to act as a trustworthy letter-bearer and unify the Roman house churches. This would involve political skills on Phoebe's part. Second, she would have to assure the churches of Paul's sincerity, given his controversial past. Third, she would need to find suitable resources, lodgings and the like. Further Jewett speculates that it was Phoebe who provided the financial support Paul needed to survive another two years under house arrest.[66] Whether Jewett's theory is correct, it is certainly plausible. Further, his work demonstrates the ambiguities that lie when a text such as Romans 16.1-2 undergoes one translation after another. Not only can valuable information be lost, the whole meaning of the text can be altered to suit one's purpose. Since most of the New Testament's translators have been men, one can only speculate as to the androcentrism that has prevailed among the texts.

Apostle. Although the term "apostle" commonly refers, in Catholic circles,[67] to the Twelve, it was used by Paul to include other members as well. Paul's criteria for apostleship have to do with witnessing the resurrection and being commissioned by the resurrected Lord to missionary work (I Corinthians 9.4).[68] Although Luke's requirements differ somewhat (i.e., when finding a replacement for Judas, only those who had also witnessed the resurrection in Acts 1.21 could be considered as worthy candidates), one finds that women qualify under either criterion.[69] In contrast, Bernard Cooke maintains that a reading of the New Testament texts demonstrates that one cannot simply equate the term "apostle" with the Twelve. Rather, Cooke dates the Twelve's apostolic journeys to a much later time. In this setting, he notes that numerous members in the early church became "apostles"—such as Paul.[70] For example, Paul clearly saw himself as an apostle—and yet he was not one of the Twelve. The *Declaration* argues that "...priestly ministry ensures the continuity of the functions entrusted by Christ to the Apostles."[71] Here, the collaborators have clearly included Paul in the group of the apostles as his ministry is characterized as an "apostolate."[72]

If Paul is included as an apostle and he was clearly not one of the Twelve, on what grounds has the *Declaration* excluded women from priestly service? It seems quite evident that although apostleship has been commonly associated with the Twelve in the Roman Catholic Church, the *Declaration* includes Paul in the circle of the apostles.[73] If Paul's apostleship can be recognized, what of others?

Further, scriptural evidence indicates that women were considered apostles in the early Church. In Romans 16.7, Paul states:

3. The Role of Women in the Early Church 65

> Greet Andronicus and Junias, my fellow kinsmen and my fellow prisoners; they are men of note among the apostles and they were in Christ before me [RSV].

The translation seems to indicate that "Junias" was a man. Bernadette Brooten, however, has argued that the name "Junias" was originally *Junia*—a woman, based on the notion that the feminine form was later reported as a man's.[74] Similarly, Catherine Kroeger has argued that the name "Junias" is "...unknown in antiquity; and there is absolutely no literary, epigraphical or papyrological evidence for it."[75] As to the context of this passage, Brooten has observed that both John Chrysostom and the Pontifical Biblical Commission place *Junia* "in the rank of the apostles,"[76] and therefore maintains that *Junia* was one of the apostles. I argue that, given the apparent dispute among biblical commentators over the centuries, the possibility that *Junia* was one of the apostles has always been considered.[77]

As noted earlier, various biblical scholars have held that the Twelve were not alone among those designated as "apostles." Bernard Cooke has argued that many apostles were sent as emissaries to help form new communities as the good news spread from one territory to another.[78] They traveled in pairs and often women served as comissionaries.[79] In this setting, the women who accompanied the men were also actively committed in the missionary movement. For example, perhaps Prisca is mentioned first because she was the more important of the pair. It is plausible to suggest that Andronicus and *Junia* were a missionary couple, much like Prisca and Aquila were, and that *Junia* was as involved as Andronicus was. Further, Schüssler-Fiorenza surmises that Andronicus and *Junia* were among the apostles in I Corinthians 15.7 when Jesus appeared to "all the apostles," based on the evidence which suggests that they had become Christians prior to Paul's conversion.[80] In such a setting, perhaps *Junia* and Andronicus had already established a Christian community and functioned independently from Paul.[81]

As to the apostle's role, Cooke has argued that, although Paul's intent was not to baptize merely, it would be tenable to suggest that Christian missionaries baptized and acted as eucharistic celebrants, given the context of the New Testament writings.[82]

Therefore, *Junia* was a woman much like Prisca who accompanied Aquila on a missionary journey, as the "partnership" or "couple-mission" seems to have been the form undertaken in the early Christian missionary journeys.[83] In this sense, the women would have exercised comparable roles to those of the men. If Prisca is mentioned first because of her importance, it would then follow that she was not excluded from performing any duties as a missionary. If *Junia* accompanied Andronicus, much as Prisca accompanied Aquila and was considered an apostle of note, it is plausible to suggest that *Junia* probably performed comparable roles as well. Given Cooke's insights, this could include baptizing and presiding, as well as teaching and preaching.

Prophet/Prophetess. In Acts 21.8-9, the four daughters of Philip are characterized as ones who prophesied. According to Schüssler-Fiorenza, Eusebius acknowledges these women prophets as "transmitters of apostolic tradition."[84] Lesly F. Massey has argued that the function of the prophetess should be understood in the light of the Old and New Testaments' concept of prophecy.[85] In the Old Testament, a prophet was one who announced, proclaimed the word of the Lord, or sought to interpret the meaning of dreams and visions. Although men seem to dominate the scene, women were not excluded. Such was the situation with Miriam, Deborah, Huldah, Noadiah and Isaiah's wife. In the New Testament, the prophet was more of an "inspired preacher or teacher and an organ of special revelation from God, functioning under the guidance of the Holy Spirit."[86] (Massey even contends that the women in I Corinthians 14 were inspired prophetesses who ministered for the building up of the Christian community by official designation.[87]) Further, Cooke has argued that

> ... since the prophetic role is essentially that of bearing witness to the word of God revealed in Jesus' death and resurrection, and since the eucharistic gathering is seen as an action of proclaiming the death of the Lord until he comes, the prophet seems a logical person to exercise liturgical leadership, roughly equivalent to what we would call the eucharistic celebrant.[88]

If the Roman Catholic Church has acknowledged that prophetesses carried on the same functions as New Testament prophets[89] (i.e., that of teaching), and if Cooke's observation was applied to the prophetess as well, it remains likely that women acted as eucharistic celebrants in the early Church. Given the treatment of prophetess in this section, as well as Massey's insights regarding the concept of prophecy in the Old and New Testament, it seems quite evident that women were officially recognized and exercised a special prophetic ministry in the early Church.

The "House" Church. Another aspect which bears significance in the study of women's roles in early Christianity is the nature of the early Church. Here two related patterns may be noted. Paul speaks of moving from one missionary center to another,[90] and several communities begin to meet in homes. For example, Paul mentions Prisca and Aquila supporting a "Church in their house."[91] Similarly, Nympha of Laodicea (Colossians 4.15) and Lydia of Thyatria (Acts 16.15) offered their homes where first century Christians shared the Lord's Supper and taught the good news.[92] Since wealthy women exercised authoritative roles in Greco-Roman households, Catherine Kroeger maintains that it would have been normal for such women to assume leadership roles in the house church.[93] As the Church gradually evolved into the public arena, she argues, women's roles would have become extinguished, for "...Hellenistic women were not allowed to exercise authority in the public sphere."[94] Further, Kroeger claims that the injunctions placed on women in the *Statute of Apostles* indicate that women performed various leadership roles including that of eucharistic ministry.[95] In this sense, it is probable that women acted as eucharistic celebrants as long as the Church community remained in their homes, given the egalitarian nature of Christian ministries in the early Church gatherings.[96]

The Order of Widows. Sister Mary McKenna has argued that the group of disadvantaged women who surrounded Jesus in Luke 8.2-3 formed an official body that came to be known as the "order of widows" based on the independence with which they followed Jesus and the fact that they were able to "provide" for Jesus and the Twelve (Luke 8.3, RSV).[97] The criteria for belonging to such a group are set out in I Timothy 5.3-16. In short, an authentic widow is one who has no family left to support her, is at least sixty years old, has raised children with one husband and is known for having performed good deeds in the community. The congregation financially supported these widows, who in turn prayed for members of the Church community.

The notion that widows led a passive role in the community, however, has been widely disputed. For example, Massey has suggested that the woman whom Peter raised from the dead in Acts 9.39 was a member of the order of widows who "...had abounded in deeds of charity and kindness."[98] Although the Interpreter's Bible suggests that the widows were present "...as Dorcas' beneficiaries,"[99] Massey notes that the text indicates that they stood displaying garments she had made "...while she was with them" (verse 39, RSV), and not "for them." Further, she highlights Peter's appeal to the saints and widows in an attempt to prove that widows were a distinct group in the Christian community.[100]

In I Timothy 5.11, younger widows are refused "enrollment"[101] on the basis that they still desire marriage and therefore lack the maturity that an elder widow has. Verse 13 reads:

> Besides that, they learn to be idlers, gadding about from house to house and not only idlers but gossips and busybodies, saying what they should not [RSV].

Massey has argued that the restrictions placed on younger widows in this verse suggests that authentic widows, those who were "enrolled," were given visitation duties whose purpose was to instruct the younger women in terms of domestic duties and responsibilities.[102] Further he calls attention to the *Apostolic Constitutions* which describe the duties of widows as caring for the sick, instructing younger women and teaching Christianity to "heathen" women.[103] This same work, however, restricts women from teaching in an official manner. Roger Gryson in his work entitled *The Ministry of Women in the Early Church* calls attention to this impediment:

> He sent us the Twelve to make disciples of the people and of the nations, did nowhere send out women to preach.... For had it been necessary for women to teach, He Himself (Jesus) would have commanded these to instruct the people with us. For "if the head of the woman is the man," it is not reasonable that the rest of the body should govern the head.[104]

Given the fact that this work dates back to the end of the fourth century, I argue that by this time, the Church had become "institutionalized" and excluded women on the basis that they should be subordinate to men. The text itself suggests a submissive tone. Such a contention remains unacceptable in the face of the treatment of women's roles in the early Church that I have outlined. I established earlier that the Twelve represented a symbolic function, and that most of the "evangelizing" was done by other "apostles." Further, it is quite evident that numerous women functioned in official roles which is documented throughout the New Testament. Given Paul's praise towards such women, it is unlikely that the teaching put forth in the *Apostolic Constitutions* reflects Paul's attitude towards women, nor the ministries accorded women in the early Christian communities. Further evidence indicates that widows were part of the ordained clergy. Catherine Kroeger calls attention to the description of widows documented in the *Testament of Our Lord Jesus Christ*[105]:

> During communion, they stood by the altar, close to the bishops, presbyters and deacons, and within the veil that screened off the laity.[106]

Although the details in her argument appear quite sketchy, she contends that widows exercised an official function in the early centuries of the Church.

Bonnie Thurston also maintains that widows were among the early Church leaders on the basis that I Timothy includes widows in the discussion regarding Church leaders. She holds that certain widows made up an "order" who served as Church officials.[107] For example, I Timothy 3 describes the office of a bishop and gives detailed criteria for deacons; I Timothy 5.17 treats widows and elders, who "labour in teaching and preaching" (RSV).

Although it is difficult to specify the exact role of widows in the early Church, I argue that there is enough scriptural evidence to support the idea that widows were an official group who exercised a leadership role in the community. The criteria outlined for widows in I Timothy acknowledge that certain widows belonged to a recognized caste as opposed to other widows, and given their inclusion in the discussion of Church leaders, it would be difficult to refute that these widows did not serve as official leaders—as did bishops, deacons and elders. Whether widows' service extended to the altar however, it is difficult to assess. Rather than emphasize the information that is lacking, I argue that we can establish a role for widows that paralleled that of deacons and elders based on the fact that criteria for widows are treated alongside those for deacons and elders.

Searching for Historical Documentation. A recent work which bears significance to this whole discussion is that of Mary Ann Rossi. In 1991, she translated an Italian work written in 1982 by Georgia Otranto which was apparently "unnoticed" until Dr. Rossi discovered it in the Vatican library.[108] Basically, Otranto's original work calls attention to letters and terminology which refer to women priests. For example, Gelasius, bishop of Rome, in 494 sent an epistle to Church leaders. Among 27 decrees, apparently four of these deal with a concern which had emerged because women were serving at the altar in an official manner.[109] Such a contention threatens the *Declaration*'s insistence that the ordination of man "is a question of unbroken tradition throughout the history of the Church,"[110] and the notion that "the practice [of women's restriction] has enjoyed peaceful and universal acceptance."[111] Otranto's work also calls attention to numerous inscriptions dating back to the fifth century which document the deaths of women presbyters—women who exercised "sacerdotal ministry" in certain Church communities.[112] Further, a letter from Atto, bishop of Vercelli, dating back to the ninth and tenth centuries, documents that women were ordained as community leaders and functioned as sacramental presiders.[113]

Given the insights documented in Otranto's work as translated by Mary Ann Rossi, it is quite evident that women were sacramental priests and leaders of Christian communities. The fact that Otranto's work was buried somewhere in the Vatican library bears witness to the fact that the hierarchy has suppressed women's roles throughout the history of the Roman Catholic Church. Such measures cannot justify women's exclusion from the priesthood, nor can they continue to be tolerated.

After having briefly discussed the roles of women in the Pauline tradition, I observe that women in the early Church exercised prominent roles of leadership: as deaconess, apostle, prophetess, presider, widow and the like. The fact that women's roles were gradually eliminated does not alter this fact. Nor can we say that the Church has had a "constant" tradition. The Church's tradition has been anything but constant — works such as Otranto's and Brooten's are indicative of this fact.

In this chapter, I have attempted to apply Elisabeth Schüssler-Fiorenza's theory that a feminist reconstruction of scripture can offer new insights in terms of affirming prominent leadership roles for women. In doing so, I have sought to interpret selected passages from Paul, along with other material pertinent to this study that appears contradictory. In this sense, I have demonstrated the manner in which scripture can be used to justify the exclusion of women from various liturgical roles. Given Schüssler-Fiorenza's insights, I observe that scripture must be interpreted in the light of its context and can become meaningless if it is taken at face value. I am not saying that the Roman Catholic Church has done this. It has, however, used scripture and tradition to justify its exclusion of women from the ministerial priesthood. In doing so, it has not only preserved the androcentrism that predominates in the literature of the early Church, but has also absolutized patriarchy and regarded it as God's will in that the sacramental ministry be conferred upon men only.

I observe that scripture and tradition in the early Church bear witness to a community of believers (men and women) continuing Christ's example. The fact that scripture addresses a patriarchal audience and places limitations upon women that reflect their cultural situation does not logically absolutize the role of context over that of content. This is what the Roman Catholic Church has done.

CHAPTER 4

Overcoming the Lay-Clergy Dualism

In the present-day Roman Catholic Church, it is apparent that the laity (in comparison to the clergy) are given very specific and restrictive roles in terms of their active contribution towards the fulfillment of the Church's mission in the world. Further, one can clearly identify a segregation of roles among the laity themselves. Where laymen are restricted to nonclerical duties, laywomen are excluded from certain duties that involve leadership roles, as well as service at the altar.

In coming to terms with the lay-clergy distinction, a study of the distinction between laymen and laywomen will prove helpful. My reasoning here is as follows: If the Roman Catholic Church could overcome the exclusion of laywomen from certain liturgical roles, this would definitely affect their exclusion from the ministerial priesthood. I argue that we must seek to overcome the injustices that women encounter at the lay level, in order to facilitate women's ordination.

Prior to undertaking a study of the layman-laywoman dualism, however, I observe that the lay-clergy distinction should be examined first as it proves helpful when attempting to single out the elements that contribute to the segregation of classes at each level.

The purpose of this chapter is therefore twofold: to trace the emergence and development of the lay-clergy distinction, in order to gain some insight as to the implications resulting from the manner in which these groups have been segregated, and to seek to interpret these implications from a Catholic perspective in order to identify the tensions involved. To do this, I will make use of various papal pronouncements and theological studies that directly treat these issues along with reports that discuss lay involvement and clergy relations in the Canadian Catholic Church. Further, I will give a brief study regarding the concept of ministry in the early Church along with a detailed section on the ministry of service. This study will permit a helpful comparison of the concept of ministry as it was understood in the early Church alongside the current position regarding ministries in the Roman Catholic Church. In this manner, it will be possible to outline various problems affecting laywomen in the Catholic Church, and from there the focus will turn to laywomen's roles, and particularly to their exclusion from the priesthood (in chapters 5 and 6).

The Lay-Clergy Distinction

Given the fact that an exhaustive study of the emergence and development of the distinction between lay and clerical roles in the two-thousand-year history of the Church would require a thesis itself, it will suffice here to highlight some contributing factors that led to the segregation of the laity and clergy. To do this, it will prove helpful to return to the practice of the early Christian community.

The Laity in the Early Church. As noted at the close of Chapter 2, the first-century Church seemed to be moving towards a segregation of classes among the people of God. As a result, the structure of the household church gatherings became more hierarchical in organization, and the role of women was restricted, because of a willingness to conform to the cultural practices of the Roman empire. In this sense, the shift from house-church to public worship services would have limited the role of women as the social practices of the Roman empire did not permit women to hold positions of leadership and authority.[1] Further, Edward Schillebeeckx maintains that the lay-clergy distinction was also due in part to a segregation of social classes in the Roman empire. The government, for example, was structured such that anyone belonging to the group of senators formed the upper class in comparison to the ordinary people. Accordingly, the Church patterned its hierarchic structure to model the class distinctions in the social setting. Thus the clergy became part of the higher class, and the faithful remained at the bottom of the social scale. Schillebeeckx refers to this transition as the "clericalization" of church ministry.[2]

By the Middle Ages, the term *laos* officially represents one who is unholy, subjected to authority from a hierarchic order and regarded as a member of the lower class.[3] Therefore, for the laity, salvation was available through the authoritative leadership of the Church.[4] Thus began the understanding that laity were to exercise a passive role—leaving all activity and authority to the clergy.

The Theological Implications. At this point, let us briefly attempt to define a contemporary understanding of the term "laity," using various sources in order to identify the implications involved when addressing the ministry of the laity in the Roman Catholic Church. In traditional terms, the layperson was defined negatively—as one who has no position,[5] does not participate in the hierarchy, and is therefore not given clerical status. In contemporary terms, however, being a Christian has been seen to encompass the whole people of God—lay and clerical. The distinction has to do with the function each undertakes. Each Christian is incorporated into Christ's body in the same manner, regardless of his or her function.[6]

From a clerical perspective, Bishop James L. Doyle has argued that one must not view the Church entirely as an organization. To do so would depersonalize the men and women who value the gospel and have dedicated themselves to God's work through service and love.[7] Although I agree with the notion that one must not perceive the Church in terms of an organization, I argue that it is difficult to imagine the true essence of the Church when the one encountered is hierarchic in nature. Further, this hierarchy is such that laity and clergy are called upon to achieve one common goal, while exercising segregated roles that often produce conflict and disagreement.

From a lay woman's perspective, Mary Matthews has indicated that prior to Vatican II, lay people were not consciously aware of being a lay Church. Those who faithfully attended Mass every Sunday associated the Church with a building, personified by the priests and bishops. Although men and women were actively involved in sustaining their Church community, the priests always made the decisions.[8] In terms of the lay-clergy relationship the priests were associated with God, and therefore were never questioned and always obeyed. There was never any question of being a lay apostolate, as everything revolved around the clergy.[9]

Given Mary Matthews' observations, I note that there seems to have been a lack of communication between laity and clergy. Lay people perceived themselves as part of a pyramidal structure, where the Pope and the bishops were at the top and they were at the bottom somewhere beneath the priests. In short, lay people experienced clericalism, in terms of an "elitism" among classes where clergy have all the authority to make the decisions that affect any given community.[10] Although this type of "elitism" among the clergy still exists in part, Vatican II viewed the laity as belonging to the one family of God and sharing common responsibilities. In this sense, Vatican II's treatment of the laity was long overdue.

The Official Treatment of the Laity

At this point, let us first look at Vatican II's treatment of the term "laity" along with the treatment of the term in the *New Code of Canon Law*. I will conclude with a study of the *Lineamenta* provided in preparation for the 1987 Bishop's Synod, whose subject was the vocation and mission of the laity in the Church and in the world twenty years after the second Vatican council.[11]

Vatican II. In the documents of Vatican II, references to the laity abound. For the purposes of this study, I shall focus mainly on those which give definition to the laity, along with a detailed description as to what their roles and functions are in comparison to those of the clergy in the Church's mission as a whole.

The definition by Vatican II of the term "laity" refers to all the faithful, with the exception of those in holy and religious orders. Through baptism, one is incorporated into Christ's body and therefore becomes a part of God's people.[12] The Council's reference to the laity as the People of God was used in order to stress the membership and personal qualities of the Church as opposed to the hierarchic aspects that usually overshadowed the personal side of the Church. In this sense, the emphasis on Church shifted to the people—the faithful and their membership in Christ through baptism and their active participation as community members for the building up of Christ's Church.[13]

By returning to what Vatican II described as the biblical notion of People of God, the Council sought to restore the laity's function in terms of a sharing of missionary roles vis-à-vis the clergy. In doing so, the Council emphasized the egalitarian nature of the People of God—where laity, religious and clergy are equal.[14] Where they differ, however, is in the manner that each is called to carry out the missionary work of the Church in the world.[15]

The Implications of the Term "Laity." Regarding the nature of the term "laity," Pope Paul VI referred to the structure of the Church in terms of an expectation that the laity be completely loyal to the Church authorities.[16] Further, in 1976, the Pope affirmed that the clergy's task was to establish and develop the community, whereas the laity's task specifically had to do with an active role in the secular sphere.[17]

Given these perspectives, one can say that the impression made is that although laity and clergy make up the People of God, and both are called to exercise the Church's mission in the world, the laity remain somewhat subordinate to the hierarchic structure of the Church—and therefore seem subservient to a higher order. It is interesting to note here

4. Overcoming the Lay-Clergy Dualism

that the role of the laity is described in terms of their membership and participation in their Church communities, their parish and their daily lives in general:

> It is amid the surroundings of their work that they are best qualified to be of help to their brothers, in the surroundings of their profession, of their study, residence, leisure or local group.[18]

The Problem. In contrast, the role of the pastor is described as being one of "shepherding":

> To the degree of their authority and in the name of their bishop, priests exercise the office of Christ the Head and the Shepherd. Thus they gather God's family together as a brotherhood of living unity, and lead it through Christ and in the Spirit to God the Father. For the exercise of this ministry, as for other priestly duties, spiritual power is conferred upon them for the upbuilding of the Church.[19]

Although these roles were previously described as a sharing of responsibilities within the Church, one can detect a note of subordination in terms of lay-clergy duties. For example, clergy are charged with matters of a salvific nature, whereas laity are left to deal with matters of everyday life. The analogy is one of clergy having the vertical responsibilities whereas laity share the horizontal duties in the Church. I observe that the laity's duties are equally significant, but are downplayed, because of the hierarchical structure in the Church.

Although the Council did affirm the role of the laity in the Church (as we have seen, prior to Vatican II, lay people were not consciously aware of their apostolate), one cay say that by segregating lay and clerical functions, the Church established another barricade in that the laity were left to matters of a secular nature, whereas the clergy were left to the more "holy" tasks.[20]

The Effects. As to the effect Vatican II's treatment of the laity has brought about, Alan F. Blakley has indicated that lay participation has greatly increased, as well as the opportunities for lay involvement in parish communities, for both the professional and nonprofessional members.[21] From a clerical perspective, Cardinal Carter has stated that among the major positive developments in the life of the laity since Vatican II, of significance is the more active participation of the lay faithful. For example, lay people now share the duties of proclamation as they are currently being invited to deliver the word of God.[22]

Similarly, Bishop Bernard Hubert has noted that we must all be allowed responsibility, not so much in the sense of power as in the sense of "quality service." In this sense, he argues that the increase in lay participation in the Mass is directly related to their sense of duty and vocation, and not so much to the shortage of priests.[23]

Given these observations, I argue that although Vatican II's redefinition of the Catholic lay individual germinated a new awareness of the laity's mission in the Church, one cannot overlook the fact that there is an international problem with the shortage of priests. In this setting, the laity are not only becoming "aware" of their missionary roles in the Church on a cognitive level, but also on a practical level, as they are being called upon to serve in various ways. From a Canadian perspective, the ministries of lector, eucharistic minister and lay presider come to mind—to mention only a few.

As a result of this shortage, what has emerged is a sense of co-responsibility among laity and clergy. Historically, one was always told that as a lay person, one could not do without the clergy. What the clergy are presently finding is that they cannot do without the laity either. And the shortage of priests seems to have contributed significantly to this phenomenon. If there existed an abundance of priests, for example, one wonders about the effects this would have on the nature of the roles now (in the decades of the nineteen seventies, eighties and nineties) accorded to lay people. With this practical incentive in the background, laity and clergy must continue to work more and more closely together in the building up of Christ's Church. This can be manifested in various forms. For example, lay people are being invited more and more to participate in conferences and study sessions from which they had previously been excluded. The Bishops' Synod in 1987 invited active lay participation in the sense that laity were allowed to present briefs and participate in the study groups immediately following the bishops' interventions.

Another example that may be easier to relate to arose in Canada. Rosemary Haughton has identified a group of lay people (of which she is a part) who came to terms with their call to service by establishing housing facilities for people in crisis. Here, I must explain her use of the term "lay." Rather than operating from a hierarchical structure, Rosemary Haughton's use of the term is rooted in a self-awareness of people who discover themselves as "God's" people with a specific calling to fulfill the gospel in their community.[24] In this sense, she explains the group shares a "communal" vision that is being expressed through a "consensus model of organization and decision-making, and an awareness that real change for the poor [in this case, women], requires that people learn to share and act together."[25]

As a result, Haughton has identified various benefits. She notes:

4. Overcoming the Lay-Clergy Dualism

It has brought people together, deepened their knowledge of scripture and of each other, vitalized some parishes, and led to a new social consciousness among many Catholics.[26]

Such lay ministry seems encouraging. I must indicate, however, that in the Canadian setting there have also been and continue to be negative experiences. Although lay leadership has seen the implementation of parish councils, lay ministries in liturgy, and other developments, it has been argued that the benefits affect only those who are comfortable within the hierarchic structure of the Church and who regularly associate with their respective communities.[27] Further, many of the baptized have been so "out-of-touch" with changes in the life of the Church, that they remain unaware of its growth and challenges as a faithful community. There are also many who have left the Church for reasons varying from lack of interest to marriage breakdown, loss of dignity, and others. One can say that it is to these people that the Church as a whole must strive to minister. In this sense, I observe that ministry could be exercised at every level of the Church.

It has also been noted that among the clergy, many have refused to share their responsibilities with lay people. Roger Haight observes:

> Laity in such a situation is "merely laity," ministered to but having no or only subordinate officially sanctioned offices of ministry to exercise their responsibility for the well-being of the whole community.[28]

There have also been various complaints from women who have suffered very painful experiences due to the ever-infectious sin of sexism. I think this is a recurring problem that needs to be resolved at every level of the hierarchy — particularly at a time when the Church is coming to terms with the "fundamental" equality of its baptized members.[29]

After having briefly identified the Church's "official" position on the laity, one can say that although Vatican II's treatment of the term initiated a step forward in terms of a self-awareness that produced a more active participation on the part of the lay faithful, its treatment also preserved the existing barrier in the sense that laity and clergy must still operate within separate frameworks. Where the clergy function mainly in terms of one's spiritual needs, the laity are said to cater to one's secular and temporal needs. While several perspectives previously cited outlined a coresponsibility among clergy and lay faithful, the hierarchical structure through which the "official" Church operates leaves no authority or administrative concerns to its laity. Further, women have experienced rejection when it comes to leadership roles in their respective communities.

Prior to a study of women's issues, though, one can say that it would seem essential to identify the various forms of ministries for the laity as expressed in *The New Code of Canon Law*, issued in 1983.

The Code of Canon Law

On a general note, it is apparent that the laity have a fundamental right and duty to participate actively in the Church's mission. For example, roles that previously excluded the laity are now being opened to men and women.[30] John Martin feels that this notion can be attributed in part to the reworking of the code, based on Vatican II's redefinition of the laity as the People of God.[31]

In the previous code, dated 1917, the laity were perceived in a negative and passive way. They were simply among the baptized who were not clerics, and the lay-clergy distinction was presented in such a manner that it gave the impression that it was of a divine origin.[32] The new code defines the laity as follows:

> The Christian faithful are those who, inasmuch as they have been incorporated in Christ through baptism, have been constituted as the People of God; for this reason, since they have become sharers in Christ's priestly, prophetic and royal office in their own manner, they are called to exercise the mission which God has entrusted to the Church to fulfill in the world, in accord with the condition proper to each one [canon 204 §1].

This statement is therefore in keeping with Vatican II's treatment of the laity, in the sense that they are referred to as the "People of God," and that baptism is at the root of one's incorporation into the Church.

According to the commentary that accompanies the code, baptism produces a personal effect, in the sense that one participates in Christ's body, and a social effect, in that one becomes a member of God's people. These effects, in turn, have two consequences:

> One is that the baptized are made participants in the priestly, prophetic and kingly functions that Christ continues to exercise in the world. The second consequence is to be called to the mission that the People of God carry out as the Church of Christ, a mission God has given the Church to fulfill in this world until the end of time.[33]

It is therefore a two-fold mission which seems to be divinely instituted—one by Christ, the other by God. It is interesting to note that although canon 208 stresses the "fundamental equality" of all Christians,[34] in canon 207 the People of God appear in two segregated classes. The canon reads:

4. Overcoming the Lay-Clergy Dualism

> Among the Christian faithful by divine institution there exist in the Church sacred ministers, who are also called clerics in law, and other Christian faithful, who are also called laity.[35]

One can therefore say that although the code stresses a "fundamental equality" for all, the exclusion of women from performing certain liturgical roles remains. In the commentary that accompanies the code, however, James Coriden maintains that

> ... the question can be raised whether discrimination based on sex is justified within the Church because of the need for the Church to be consistent in practicing what it preaches if it is to be credible in its social magisterium.[36]

Although this issue will be examined when looking at women's roles as a whole, it is interesting to note here that Coriden observes that the main discrimination in the code appears to be between clergy and laity, rather than between men and women.[37] This statement appears untenable if one regards the exclusion of women from the ministries of lector and acolyte. The code clearly states in canon 230 §1 that

> ... lay*men* [italics mine] who possess the age and qualifications determined by decree of the conference of bishops can be installed on a stable basis in the ministries of lector and acolyte in accord with the prescribed liturgical rite.[38]

Regarding this notion, one can say that careful interpretation of the text is in order, and that one's understanding of the passage would have to take into account one's cultural environment. For example, John Huels has suggested that the new code reserves the use of altar servers as an option, and therefore is not restricted to male or female.[39] I argue that since canon 208 §1 uses the term lay*men* and not lay people or lay faithful, the distinction does not explicitly include women although, of course, it applies to them. Other areas of the code pertaining to women's functions, however, appear quite positive. For example, canon 546 (relating to the appointment of parochial vicars) states that

> When there is a dearth of priests in a given diocese, the pastoral care of a parish may be exercised by a man or woman who is not a priest under the direction of a priest-supervisor.[40]

In terms of the functions which women are permitted to exercise, however, the notion of "pastoral care" can entail a variety of tasks.[41]

After having briefly looked at the treatment of the laity by *The New Code of Canon Law,* I think that although one can identify the progress made since the former code, dated 1917, the new code lacks clarification in some areas — ones that would leave much to the individual to interpret. For example, as we have seen, although canon 230 §1 has excluded women from performing roles of lector and acolyte, the commentary accompanying the code maintains that

> ... although a subsequent instruction indicated that women are not allowed to serve as altar servers, the code no longer states this prohibition and the force of this later instruction ceases.[42]

Therefore, the intention of canon 230 seems quite puzzling and has various implications. For example, in interpreting canon 230 §1, one parish priest may find that it excludes women, and does so in his parish, while another may find that it does not, and permits women to serve. The scenario could prove quite devastating, as the practice of allowing women to serve may be permitted in one parish and yet restricted in another.

While parish priests differ in their interpretation, one wonders how lay people are to react to this disparity in leadership. For example, John Martin observes:

> The advance made by Vatican II and reflected in the new code will not necessarily lead to expanding opportunities for laypeople in the Church. Rights, even those stated in law, still must be respected in fact, and there must be concrete means provided to protect and vindicate them. In these areas, the task is only beginning.[43]

I observe that although the code settles the issue from a legal perspective, based on the examples stated above, the conflict remains unresolved on a practical level.

The Bishops' Synods

Avery Dulles has made valuable comments regarding the manner in which Bishops' Synods proceed and it may prove helpful to enumerate a few at this time. First, he notes that the Synod documents never contain the entire discussions that take place. Rather, opinions that meet strong opposition are often omitted. Second, even if some themes are strongly emphasized, the documents may exclude them if the official Church decides it will not deal with certain issues at specific times. For example, Dulles notes that:

4. Overcoming the Lay-Clergy Dualism

Although they state that the talents of women should be more effectively used in the Apostolate, the [1985] Synod documents do not tackle the question whether women should be installed in official, nonordained ministries (such as lector and acolyte) or whether they might be ordained, at least to the diaconate. Yet these suggestions had been made at the Synod.[44]

Given Dulles' comments, several observations come to mind. For example, it is understandable that on a practical level, the Synod documents could not possibly contain everything that is discussed in its entirety. I cannot agree, however, that opinions that entail conflict or opposition should be omitted. Does the hierarchy think that problems that are not discussed will simply go away? The imagery that readily comes to mind here is that of dealing with a problem child. The issue in question does not simply disappear if it is not discussed and if constructive steps are not undertaken to resolve the problem. Similarly, the Church cannot simply "do away" with pressing issues. The case I quoted earlier that Dulles raised is a perfect example. Although the issue of allowing women to undertake official ministerial roles was raised in 1985, the question currently remains unresolved.

Dulles later comments that the collaborators of the Synod documents showed "good" judgment as such issues cannot be resolved within a two-week span.[45] Of course, he is right. I fail to acknowledge the Church's initiative, however, when eight years have passed since these talks, and the magisterium is even further away from dealing with issues such as these. I argue that the issue of according women official ministerial functions is not going to go away. The current shortage of priests is a sign of the times that the hierarchy will have to deal with. It is only a matter of time. For the purposes of the present work, it will suffice to carry on with a discussion of the Bishops' Synod in 1987, and come to terms with its treatment of the laity.

The Bishops' Synod. In 1987, the Bishops' Synod of the laity identified

> ... the necessity for a resumption of the Church's reflection on the vocation and the mission of the laity in the context of the plan of salvation which God in Jesus Christ fulfills in history.[46]

Further, it not only sought to reaffirm the lay person's identity and importance within the Church, it also sought to define the lay person's role and function in the schema of the Church.

In likeness to the statements of Vatican II, the *Lineamenta* stresses the notion that as People of God, lay people share a common mission rooted in baptism. Further, the *Lineamenta* emphasizes:

> ... from the fact of their union with Christ, the head, flows the layperson's right and duty to be apostles. Inserted as they are into the Mystical Body of Christ by baptism and strengthened by the power of the Holy Spirit in confirmation, it is by the Lord himself that they are assigned to the apostolate.[47]

One can say that this statement seems rather ambiguous when regarding the role of women in the Church. It clearly states that the "layperson" has a right and duty to be an apostle. The term "lay-person" seems to indicate that it is inclusive of women. The ambiguity lies in the fact that the *Declaration* argues that since Jesus did not call any women to become part of his twelve apostles, it would therefore follow that women be excluded from ordination and the ministerial priesthood. Further, the *Declaration* stresses men's roles whereas the *Lineamenta* treats lay people's (men and women) participation in the apostolate through baptism as one People of God—making no distinctions between men and women:

> Just as baptism forms the basis of the common vocation and Christian dignity, so also it lies at the origin of the common mission entrusted to each and every baptised person in the Church and in the world: becoming part of the one body of Christ forms the basis which makes possible and responsible demands of each and every baptised person, participation in the salvific mission of the Church in history.[48]

The Synod itself presented various implications for all the lay faithful. Although it is not my intention here to analyze the Synod in depth, it may be helpful to examine the Canadian bishops' interventions presented at the Bishops' Synod in 1987. By examining their statements regarding lay people as well as the manner in which these statements were received on the Canadian scene, one will gain insight as to the Synod's value as well as some understanding of the propositions cited in the concluding documents of the synodal message. I will focus on how the Synod treated the role of lay women in the Canadian Catholic Church in order to provide further insights for future reference.

The Canadian Interventions. Archbishop Hermaniuk stressed the positive element within the "secular" character of the laity in that it

> ... enables them to accomplish in a special way this salvific mission of the Church in the world, giving them the possibility of bringing Christ to everyday life.[49]

Further, he notes that "the laity can achieve this goal by an active participation in political, social, economic, cultural and artistic life on the national and international level."[50]

4. Overcoming the Lay-Clergy Dualism

Regarding this passage, one can say that the "secular character of the laity" has contributed to a lay-clergy dichotomy. My point is that more and more, as clergy are getting involved in political, social and economic structures, they are undertaking roles of a "secular" character. After all, they are of this world too! They are also the victims of political and economic restraints, and more and more are becoming challenged to express themselves regarding these social factors. It therefore appears untenable to insist that clergy are somehow segregated from the laity in terms of the latter's "secular" character. My argument is that priests are just as much a part of our secular world as lay people are. One has only to look at the manner in which clergy have become involved in the political scene. On a social level, priests have been involved in teaching in schools and antiabortion rallies. How can the Church attest to the clergy's antisecular character? I argue that this concept is one of the past, and therefore no longer has value in today's society.

Archbishop Hayes stressed the coresponsibility of laity and clergy, in the sense that they should be working together as one people, striving to achieve the same goal.[51] In this sense, the emphasis on coresponsibility of all of God's people seems to imply a sharing of responsibilities, rather than a delegating assignment of tasks by a hierarchic structure. Therefore, Archbishop Hayes' intervention is much more relevant to contemporary lay-clergy relationships as he reflects on the roles of lay men and women. In doing so, he is placing laywomen at the same level as laymen. His description also attempts to bridge the gap that exists when defining appropriate roles for laymen as opposed to those for laywomen as expressed in the code.

Similarly, Archbishop Chiasson's intervention stressed a rediscovery of the Church as communion rooted in baptism:

> This means that this people born of baptism is, in the world and for the world, the first bearer of the word, the first agent of reconciliation, the first builder of that communion that looks to the kingdom of God.[52]

Further, he indicates that the Church should come to terms with the lay-clergy distinction. The fact that laity and clergy are part of the same family should help renew the distinction that has placed one in opposition of the other for so long. Chiasson contends that this will not devaluate the contribution that each group makes.[53]

In this sense, one can attempt to classify all forms of ministry, whether performed by lay people or clergy, as part of the fulfillment of one's mission as God's people. Bishop Hamelin's intervention dealt specifically with roles for lay women and will therefore be treated at a later time (specifically in Chapter 5).

Lastly, Bishop Sherlock's intervention dealt with the role of evangelization in the context of one's cultural situation.[54] In an attempt to reconcile faith and culture, he stressed that faith must encompass the culture in which we find ourselves. To do this, he urged the laity to come to terms with their mission in the secular world, even though one may encounter frustration and become discouraged, as Christ also experienced these feelings, yet persevered through the worst conditions.[55]

Bishop Sherlock's intervention appeals to an active participation for lay people. In this sense, their call to evangelize is paralleled with that of the clergy. On a whole, the Synod seemed to stress the notion of coresponsibility regarding the mission of laity and clergy. Although this emphasis suggests a "sharing" of roles exercised among laity and clergy, the "distinction of ministries" remains an ever-present reality. To quote Michael McAteer (religion editor of the *Toronto Star*):

> It's the distinction that is causing the tension within the Church. And it's a growing tension, caused partly because coresponsibility has yet to be defined adequately and partly because, while there may be equality when it comes to spreading the message, some Catholics are more *equal* than others when it comes to making decisions.[56]

In this sense, the appeal to greater lay participation also has to do with decision making. Romeo Maione, a Canadian lay delegate to the 1987 Synod, has suggested that much work remains to be done, as the Church is discussing shared responsibility among the clergy.[57] His appeal calls not only for coresponsibility in terms of "working together" — but as a People of God, lay, ordained and religious members of the Church must consult together.

From the Canadian bishops' perspective, Archbishop Chiasson noted several disappointments. For example, he noted that the official report given did not seem to treat the material presented in the interventions and therefore gave the impression that the report had been compiled prior to the Synod.[58] In this sense, the report given to the Pope did not contain the information presented by the bishops.[59] Given Dulles' observations regarding Bishops' Synods at the outset of this section, this comes as no surprise.

From a lay perspective, Mary Ann Molinari also noted several disappointments. Among them, she states that although 32 bishops expressed the affirmation of women in liturgical functions, the question was never seriously undertaken. Further, the fact that lay men and women were not allowed to fully participate in the Synod, not to mention the language impediment (i.e., Latin's being the language of the "official documentation" left lay delegates at a disadvantage) created much frustration.

Ministry in the Church

Up to this point, I have determined (by use of various sources) that the ministry of the People of God, whether lay or religious, stems from one's baptism and is exemplified by a life of service that laity and clergy share coresponsibly. Richard McBrien has identified four levels of ministry based on the assertion that the call to ministry is rooted in one's baptism. They are as follows:

> General/universal ministry [which] is any service rendered to another person or group of people who happen to be in need of that service, general/specific ministry [which] is any special service rendered by people specifically called to serve others in the so-called helping professions, such as nursing, social work, and legal aid; ... Christian/universal ministry [which] is any general service rendered to others in Christ and because of Christ; and lastly, Christian/specific ministry [which] is any general service rendered to others in Christ and because of Christ in the name of the Church and for the sake of helping the Church fulfill its mission.[60]

Of significance here is his assertion that "...every level of ministry in turn is oriented to the same reality—namely, the coming kingdom of God, a kingdom not only of holiness and grace, but of justice, love and peace."[61]

In applying McBrien's treatment of the term "ministry" in relation to laity and clergy, I observe that regardless of the roles performed, as one People of God, working towards a common mission, clergy and laity should function on an egalitarian level. However, such is not the case. In order to resolve this notion I think it would be essential to trace the concept of ministry in apostolic and postapostolic times as the *Declaration* has clearly emphasized that the Church's current attitude towards the ordination of women is historically rooted in Jesus' attitude and the practice of the early Church.[62] In this manner, I will seek to clarify the apparent distinction between the ministry of the clergy as opposed to that of the laity.

Lay-Clergy Tensions in the Early Christian Community. It has been previously determined that although Christ was given the title of priest, he did not ordain anyone—nor did he distinguish between male and female roles. Second, apart from the Twelve[63] there were also other apostles who performed similar duties—among whom were men and women alike. Third, certain prophets contributed to the establishment of various Christian communities.

Edward Schillebeeckx has noted that, on an historical level, certain conflicts arising in Jerusalem about three years after Jesus' death gave birth to the installation (in Acts 6.2) of seven "deacons" to communicate with the Greek-speaking Jewish Christians in Jerusalem.[64] Further, these Greek-speaking Jewish Christians were later persecuted and fled to various parts of the country and continued to evangelize other communities as well. Therefore, "...the second generation of Christians ... began to call themselves apostolic."[65]

In this manner, leaders emerged who in turn went on to evangelize other communities, and their duties were then exercised by other leaders in that specific community from which they had come. It is interesting to note here that the emergence of leadership in New Testament times evolved as directly related to a certain need arising in the community. Therefore, leaders emerged from within their own communities and did not train elsewhere in order to be placed in some other community of believers—as is the case with present-day priests. In the early Christian Church, priestly ministry was directly related to the needs of a specific community.[66]

Jesus' Ministry. Bernard Cooke has observed that any study of Christian ministry must involve the examination and analysis of Jesus' ministry.[67] In this sense, he describes Jesus' public ministry as the preparation for the fulfillment of a new covenant with God's people represented in the emergence of early Christianity—through Jesus' death and resurrection. As he states:

> It is then that he becomes fully the Christ, gives the supreme prophetic witness, is enabled as Servant-Lord to give himself fully in love for the forgiveness of sin, functions as head of the community which is his body.[68]

Therefore, Cooke concludes that the first Christian community was dedicated to the continuation of Christ's ministry—one that the community as a whole shared:

> The principal ministry of the community was exercised by being precisely a community of faith and love, and as such bearing witness to the presence of God's saving action in Christ and the Spirit.[69]

4. Overcoming the Lay-Clergy Dualism 87

Given Cooke's treatment of Jesus' ministry and the continued work by the first Christian community, several observations come to mind. First, Jesus' formation of a community of followers or disciples was basic to the development and formation of the first Christian community, in the sense that it served as a medium through which Jesus' work could be continued. Second, given the treatment of women in Jesus' ministry in relation to Cooke's emphasis on community, I argue that the original community Jesus established had no hierarchical order,[70] nor was it exclusive of any unfortunate group. Third, it would naturally follow from the two previous observations, that the group Jesus established to carry on his work was nonhierarchical and inclusive. Therefore, one can say that the first Christian community, as formed by Jesus himself, carried on His work in an egalitarian way and was strengthened by the witness of their communal faith as a whole.

The Concept of Ministry in the Early Church. As to the nature of the early Christians, Cooke has argued that they formed communities, shared their goods, worshipped together, were strengthened by their continuous faith and strove to exemplify the gospel in their daily lives.[71] It is significant to note here that Cooke's description is in keeping with Elizabeth Tetlow's argument (as seen in Chapter 2) which leaned towards the active participation of women in the first Christian community.[72]

As to the influence of Jewish culture on the first Christian community, Cooke notes that although in Old Testament Israel

> Religious life not only depended upon the external structures of social and political life, the early Christian communities were based almost exclusively on faith in Jesus as Lord and Messiah ... [and although] Old Testament religion ... was marked by a high degree of institutionalization and by a somewhat narrow nationalism that stood in contrast to the broader viewpoint of some of the prophets, Christianity accepted neither of these, in large part because of the strong stand taken by Paul in defense of his apostolate among the Gentiles.[73]

Nevertheless, there seem to have been two distinct factors that strongly influenced the first Christian community's social structure—the role of elders and that of teachers in Israel's tradition.[74]

As to the role of elders, it seems that early communities that emerged from a Palestinian background gave authoritative responsibilities to the elders.[75] Cooke argues that their roles evolved from the practical needs of the community, and not from any office of divine institution, nor as direct successors of the Twelve.[76] In likeness to the role of elders, the teaching function seems to have resulted from the practical needs of the community, as teachers saw themselves as continuing agents of Christ's work rather than a role of succession.

Given these statements, several observations come to mind. First, it is important to stress that the first Christian community operated through nonrestrictive and nonhierarchical structures. Second, the fact that members of the community saw themselves as sharing in Christ's ministry indicates that the nature of that community was structured such that it was dedicated to the idea of service—one that was independent of any official leadership. To quote Cooke:

> There is every indication that the remarkable spread of Christianity during the early centuries of the Church's existence was the result of widespread unofficial activity on the part of laity as well as clergy.[77]

Further, Richard McBrien has argued that there is no evidence that the hierarchic structure of the Roman Catholic Church existed in the New Testament period, nor that the concept of such a structure was intended by Christ.[78]

The Role of "Apostolic Succession." Schillebeeckx dates the conflicts that arise surrounding the question of ministries about A.D. 80.[79] By this time, those who had founded the first Christian communities had died, and leaders were needed to continue their work. Although the end of the first century witnessed a more "formalized" Church order, Schillebeeckx maintains that the "ministerial charisma" was the responsibility of the whole community and not just its leaders.[80] The term "ministerial charisma" is used here to denote a ministry which is based upon service and which functions according to the various gifts possessed by community members. It is the service which stems from the notion of being apostolic—that is, carrying on the content of Jesus' "Good News" and modeling one's life according to his own discipleship. What does apostolicity have to do with a book about the ordination of women? The "official" Catholic Church defines apostolicity as

> ... an unbroken continuity with the original apostles in doctrine, tradition, and church order, a continuity preserved by an unbroken succession of bishops.[81]

In my treatment of the *Declaration*'s arguments used to deny women access to the sacrament of orders, one of the arguments stems from the practice of the apostles. The *Declaration* states that "The apostolic community remained faithful to the attitude of Jesus towards women."[82]

4. Overcoming the Lay-Clergy Dualism

To which "apostolic community" does this refer? The argument suggests that since Jesus did not ordain any women, neither did the apostles. Therefore the official Church must remain true to this practice. The discussion in Chapter 1 of this work demonstrates that Jesus did not ordain any men either. Further, the Biblical Commission which examined the question of women's ordination from a scriptural perspective concluded that Christ's will would not be transgressed if the Roman Catholic Church decided to ordain women.

I argue that the "continuity preserved by the bishops" should concern Jesus' life and ministry. If Jesus did not ordain any men or women the hierarchy has preserved a bias against women which denies them access to leadership roles in the Roman Catholic Church. If apostolicity has to do with living out Jesus' discipleship, the question of women's ordination also has to do with justice and the right to serve. In Schillebeeckx's words:

> The community has a right to a minister or ministers and to the celebration of the eucharist. This apostolic right has priority over the criteria for admission which the Church can and may impose on its ministers.[83]

As to the dynamics of leadership in the early Church, one finds a serious disparity with the current hierarchy.

The Council of Chalcedon. In his work entitled *Ministry: Leadership in the Community of Jesus Christ*, Schillebeeckx's treatment of the early centuries of Church ministry begins with the Council of Chalcedon. Dating back to A.D. 451,[84] the sixth canon verifies the practice of the early Church and documents the type of ministries performed. By that time, communities began choosing their leaders from among the various charisms. In this sense valid leadership occurred when a particular individual was called to lead a specific community. No leader was appointed unless the community had called upon a certain individual to lead them. Schillebeeckx stresses the relationship between community and ministry, because at that time the leader did not preside over the community but was empowered by the community to celebrate the Eucharist. Therefore, the authority required for an individual to lead a community and preside at the Eucharist did not stem from the bishop or a hierarchical order. It came from the community itself.[85]

Given Schillebeeckx's treatment of ministries in the early Church, several observations come to mind. First, the structure of the early Church communities had no hierarchic order and ministry developed within the Church communities. This ministry was based on the discipleship of Jesus. Second, the leader was empowered by the community to function within that same community. Third, ministry in the early communities was not based on status but rather on the idea of service which stems from the gifts that were bestowed by the Holy Spirit upon the community members. What implications do these observations reveal in regard to the issue of women's ordination? It calls into question the Church's understanding of ministry and service, as well as the notion that the exclusion of women from the ministerial priesthood is based on tradition, Jesus' will and the practice of the apostles.

After having briefly examined the emergence and development of the lay-clergy distinction with special emphasis placed on the apparent exclusion of laywomen from certain liturgical roles in particular, one can say that there seems to have been an increased awareness of coresponsibility among the People of God. Although *The New Code of Canon Law* assigns all the lay faithful the right and duty to participate actively in the Church's mission as a whole, there does remain a lack of clarification regarding women's roles. Further, the interpretation regarding the admission of women to certain liturgical roles remains ambiguous at times. For example, although *The New Code of Canon Law* stresses a sharing of duties by all of God's people, the *Declaration* emphasizes the distinction between men's and women's roles. Where the Synod of Bishops stressed the coresponsibility of all of God's People, there remains an apparent inequality among clergy and lay people when it comes to decision making. On a whole, the Church seems to lack initiative that would lead to a serious undertaking and discussion of issues that concern women in general.

Given the treatment of ministry in this chapter, it becomes apparent that the first Christian community was dedicated to the preservation of Christ's message. This task was shared by the whole community—one that was nonhierarchical and fairly inclusive in nature. Its main emphasis was the idea of service independent from any form of official leadership. "Apostolic succession" has to do with preserving Jesus' message and the tradition of the early communities. The structure of the early communities as well as the treatment of women in this latter setting remains incongruous with the current hierarchy. Although a treatment of the "service" model in the Roman Catholic Church will appear at a later time (see Chapter 6), I argue that the Church in its struggle to preserve roles for men and women as willed by Christ cannot overlook these facts. It is very unfortunate that the current hierarchy does not function on a more egalitarian basis. Such a structure

4. Overcoming the Lay-Clergy Dualism

would be more accessible for women. Since the current structure functions as it does, women are restricted to operating within certain parameters. Given this framework women must seek equality and justice above all. Maybe once this is accomplished other barriers may be overcome.

Lastly, if the Roman Catholic Church can move beyond the injustices that prevent laywomen from performing the same duties as laymen, I think it would help facilitate the inclusion of women to the ministerial priesthood. Chapter 5 will examine the nature of these injustices and will demonstrate the manner in which the ordination of women would prove advantageous, given the current shortage of priests in the Church.

CHAPTER 5

Women in the Catholic Church

Given the observations noted at the close of Chapter 4, it seems imperative that a discussion regarding women's roles in the Roman Catholic Church be pursued. (This discussion has, as its focal point, the experience of women in the Canadian Catholic Church.) Despite the fact that the *Declaration* as well as other papal statements[1] has excluded women from the priesthood, from a Canadian perspective, reports have indicated that by the year 2000, the number of available candidates for the priesthood will have decreased by 25 percent.[2] In Canada, sixty to seventy men are being ordained per year. Unfortunately, the number of deaths among the ordained clergy is greater than this.[3] While these statistics have promoted the notion among Catholics that women will eventually be admitted to the ministerial priesthood, one should realize that regardless of what the statistics indicate, women should be recognized for their gifts — including those that would enable them to perform duties comparable to those of priests, despite the apparent shortage of priests.[4] According to Mary Matthews:

> These opportunities should not exist only because there is a shortage of priests; it should be a right and an obligation for the laity to take on these ministries in the Church.[5]

Furthermore, it has been noted that women who seek leadership roles in the Roman Catholic Church would not favor ordination in a Church whose current hierarchic and pyramidal structure typifies a quest for power and domination.[6] Still, there are some women who feel that those who are being called to ministry and belong to a Church that has denied women access to specialized theological training and to fulfillment of their talents should take their gifts elsewhere and serve in a Church which accepts women in leadership positions.[7] Others feel it is necessary to remain within the structure in order to make an effective contribution towards the promotion of leadership roles for women in the Roman Catholic Church. Certainly, these elements all come into play in women's struggle for equality in the Roman Catholic Church.

The purpose of this chapter is to examine the main tensions that women encounter when conflicts of leadership within the Church arise. Given the scope of this work, this section will primarily focus on Canadian women. To do this, some attention will be placed on the restrictions imposed in liturgical functions, as well as proper vocations for women given the nature of Roman Catholicism. In short, without attempting to resolve the question of the ordination of women, this chapter will examine the nature of the tensions women encounter when dealing with authoritative positions in the Church and seek to outline some practical steps that have been suggested in order to come to terms with the issues involved.

The Problem

Vatican II outlined several modifications in our understanding of the Church. Lay people began to realize that the Church was not just a building or the priests or the bishops. It was all of Christ's members, joined together in His body. Through baptism, each individual is charged with the duty of proclaiming Christ's message, and active participation in the Church's mission as a whole.

> It is not only through the sacraments and Church ministries that the same Holy Spirit sanctifies and leads the People of God and enriches it with virtues. Allotting His gifts to everyone according as He will, He distributes special graces among the faithful of every rank. By these gifts He makes them fit and ready to undertake the various tasks or offices advantageous for the renewal and upbuilding of the Church.[8]

In this sense, women felt that they were also part of the Church and that they too were to be actively involved in ministries that they felt they were being called to perform. This new situation presented the opportunity for women to surface and grow in their commitment and service to the Church. The contradiction lies in the fact that despite the Church's call for true equality among all of God's people,[9] women are still being limited in that they are being excluded from liturgical installation in the ministries of lector and acolyte at the lay level, and from the ministerial priesthood at the clerical level. If the number of available priests continues to decline, women's exclusion also presents a practical problem—especially when parishes are growing and ministerial needs are being ignored.[10]

Women who are employed by the Church are frequently underpaid and have very little authority when it comes to making decisions regarding the duties they were hired to perform. For example, Mary Ellen Sheehan has observed that women who enter into pastoral ministries as a profession are

> ... most often not paid living wages and, further, easily fired because of a pastor's power to dismiss or replace them with another priest or a religious order woman because they cost less.[11]

Arlene Swidler attributes this bias against women to clericalism. In this setting, she notes that women are not included among the people who make decisions in the Church:

> All functions of the organization — executive, judicial, and legislative, as well as the allotment of monies and official theorizing — are done almost exclusively by priests and bishops.[12]

Recruitment procedures have also been altered which benefit male candidates over and against women. For example, colleges usually go through an institute called the Placement Bureau of the College Theology Society (in the U.S.). Swidler observes that more and more, colleges and universities seeking to hire teachers do not advertise positions, do not consult with the Placement Bureau, and operate on a "grapevine system" where candidates are selected on the basis of how well they are acquainted with other faculty members. Certainly this arrangement does not give women equal opportunities in a professional field.[13] Further, women are excluded from Catholic seminaries and as a result are not given proper training for the ministries they are permitted to exercise.

Funding is also a problem. In Canada, there is a diocesan fund available to young men studying to be priests — while there is no comparable funding available to women who wish to educate themselves for the purposes of serving their parish communities.[14] Women experience friction, competition and division when actively engaged in a professional ministry. Of course, these conflicts are not occurring in every parish, but they do occur more often than not.[15] Priests are being trained by other priests — not by professional lay individuals or married couples — and they are educated alongside other men. The women they come into contact with are librarians, cooks, housekeepers and the like. The whole seminarian environment encourages the subservience of women to men. Young men studying to be priests do not engage in dialogue with young females. It is no wonder that most priests feel uneasy and threatened by women seeking leadership roles in the Church.

An experience of mine in 1987 upon the occasion of a Canadian theological students' conference (C.T.S.C.) accurately demonstrates the seminarian mindset. This conference included students from theological and religious institutes across Canada. It also included seminarians. Various workshops were offered throughout the week, including one entitled "Patriarchy." As the workshop unfolded, a senior seminarian readily confessed he thought that a workshop entitled "Patriarchy" was going to talk about the "twelve" patriarchs. This was a young man who was preparing for ordination later that same year, and yet he remained completely oblivious to the term.

Can this be considered accurate preparation for the priesthood? Certainly the concept of patriarchy has been around for a number of years. Obviously, the term had never been mentioned with the exception of patriarchy relating to Abraham's clan. This was also a resourceful young man. Could his ignorance serve as an indication that the seminary library as well as his professors was also void of any knowledge regarding the subject? My main concern here lies in the fact that he, along with other "fellow"-candidates, was not given proper guidance or instruction regarding the dignity or respect with which women should be treated. These men are being ordained into "our" parishes. It is no wonder that so many priests today are uncomfortable with the notion of women undertaking responsible leadership roles.

This type of clericalism is demonstrated throughout the hierarchy. Recently, the American bishops were called together to draft a pastoral on women. "After nine years of consultations and four revisions," the U.S. bishops remain undecided as to the contents of the letter.[16] Apparently, some "secret communication" had been circulated from the Vatican which seemed to gain influence with the writing committee. As a result, the final draft excludes

> ... references to the sin of sexism within the Church, focusing instead on a broad list of societal problems affecting women ... Another deletion was a statement questioning the ordination of seminarians who could not treat women as equals.[17]

Although Church officials rave about the dignity now accorded women in the Church, such a contention remains in theory only. The latter quote demonstrates that the Vatican officials hold all of the power. Until women become members of the C.C.C.B., the United States Catholic Conference, the National Conference of Catholic Bishops and the like, change will not occur—and we are kidding ourselves if we think change can occur within the current clericalism.

Amidst the smoke, there is some glimmer of hope. Archbishop Rembert G. Weakland, Archbishop of Milwaukee in Wisconsin, for example, is among the bishops who are responsible for the pastoral draft on women and has been quite verbal about promoting leadership positions for women in the Church — including the Vatican. In a recent interview he stated:

> The bishop's failure to make progress on the issue undermines the Church's credibility and jeopardizes its ability to attract the next generation of worshippers. Significant redress could be made by installing women in the top three positions of prefect, secretary and undersecretary in each of the 21 bureaucratic departments of the Vatican. Those positions currently are held by cardinals, archbishops and monsignors.[18]

Such inclusion appears quite promising. Of course, not all priests or archbishops share this attitude but several priests and bishops have strongly encouraged a more active participation for lay women in their parishes and deaneries. It is therefore the purpose of this section to outline the conflicts that have surfaced regarding lay women's pursuit of leadership roles in the Canadian Catholic Church, in order to come to terms with the areas that need to be readdressed and reaffirmed.

"No" to Women Priests. Although Vatican II stressed that the gifts bestowed upon God's people "...are to be received with thanksgiving and consolation, for they are exceedingly suitable and useful for the needs of the Church,"[19] the *Declaration on the Question of the Admission of Women to the Ministerial Priesthood* issued in 1976 and commented on in Chapter 4 of the present work concluded that women were not to be admitted to the ministerial priesthood. The emphasis I wish to pursue concerns the consequences which result from the exclusion of women from the ministerial priesthood.

First, given our situation in Canada, that is, that there are considerably fewer candidates each year who are studying for the priesthood, in rural communities especially, women minister to otherwise neglected parishes. They minister to the physically ill, the disadvantaged, the spiritually weak — yet they cannot minister sacramentally. Mary Malone aptly notes that this area of ministry is self-initiated because of the needs that arise in parishes which have no priests or in a situation where the priest arrives to celebrate the Mass once a week or perhaps only once a month and neglects the parish's spiritual and temporal needs. Yet it remains unrecognized and irrelevant in the "official" Church's eyes because these ministries are exercised by nonclerical women. Malone maintains that women should be permitted ordination by virtue of their baptism but remain excluded because of authority. The restriction of women from official preaching roles also prevents a woman's experience or point of view from being expressed in the Church.[20] This remains a serious injustice and negates Christ's teaching on equality and respect for women.

Women cannot fully represent the Church and therefore only "distribute" communion which is the very life of the Church—because of the one very basic consideration—their gender. As Jean Forest states:

> Their frustration is not a sign of ambition for power that ritual confers on its leaders, [as the areas they minister in are so remote, there is no male competitor to compete against for power] but a result of the desire to meet the needs of suffering, neglected people within the Church.[21]

I observe that as a member of Christ's Church, the exclusion of women from the ministerial priesthood on the basis of their gender remains a discriminatory practice in the Roman Catholic Church. Everyone has gifts and talents that can be used to serve Christ's Church. Must these gifts be restricted on the basis of the sex of the individual who has been granted the gift? Is the sex of an individual more important than bringing the sacraments to God's people? What about women who prepare candidates for baptism or marriage, who journey together with these individuals—only to be replaced by a "stranger" who comes to administer the sacrament in Christ's name?[22]

Ministry for Men and Women.[23] In 1971, Cardinal George B. Flahiff, Archbishop of Winnipeg at the time, outlined the argument that excluded women from performing the same roles as men. It goes as follows:

> ... Christ was a man, not a woman; he chose twelve men as his first ministers; St. Paul has clearly said that women must keep silent in the Church; therefore, they cannot be ministers of the word ... Paul equally said that woman ... can have no authority on man. [Therefore], ministry is a man's work.[24]

His conclusion was thus: "As all of you know, this historical argument cannot be considered valid today."[25] This proposal was presented in 1971. Since that time, despite his appeal that the Church permit women to perform ministries that complement their gifts, little change has occurred. After twenty years, women are further away from having a chance at leadership roles in the Church than they were in New Testament times where, one will recall, women exercised prominent leadership roles quite successfully. Of course, some ground has been gained. Western Canada, for example, has initiated a "Lay-Ministries

Formation Program," which is a three-year undertaking that includes women as well. Since the diaconate program figures, however, as a step towards ordained ministries, women who complete the three-year program are "permitted" to lay-preside, whereas the men can be ordained as deacons. Although the value of such a program can be seen in that it gives specialized training for certain ministries, its aftermath is indicative of the Church's attitude of inferiority towards women.

Grace M. Anderson and Juanne Nancarrow Clarke, in their work *God Calls: Man Chooses—A Study of Women in Ministry*, have documented special concerns that women share regarding ministries in the Church. They note that women lack legitimate opportunities to respond to God's call, whereas men experience a range of opportunities, when they share the same qualifications. The contribution that recent biblical scholarship has made in our current understanding of the dynamics involved in the function of the early Church is also noted by Anderson and Nancarrow Clarke: Archaeological findings have disclosed certain information that documents the existence of women bishops in the early Church. In light of this evidence, as well as other historical scholarly findings, the restriction of women from sacramental roles can be viewed as a cultural consideration. Modern feminist scholarship calls into question the Church's practice of excluding women from liturgical and sacramental positions.

The area of "true" participation is also noted among the concerns of women. Women want to perform "real" tasks with viable implications. The value of placing a few "token" women on a parish council team, for example, only emphasizes the Church's organizational character.[26]

The Structure of the Church. This point brings our direct attention to the structure of the Roman Catholic Church. It has been frequently noted that women are not often consulted when it comes to issues that directly concern them. For example, Lise Baroni has noted the types of contributions women could make to the Church documents regarding issues such as rape, abortion, unwed mothers and the like, issues that have to do with women and that priests can discuss only from second-hand knowledge. As she notes:

> But instead of listening to them and of treating them as partners at the level of the content of these documents and of their first formulation, the only thing that is done is the setting up of some small information rather than real and true participation committees.[27]

In this sense, women become very frustrated as they are not permitted to voice their opinions when it comes to the official preparation of Church documents. Regarding this situation, one can say that the Church is somewhat behind the times. In an age where women are heading corporations and holding advanced positions in government and professional careers, and basically choosing whatever function they wish to perform in society given their talents and gifts, the Church must recognize that women have just as much to contribute to the Church as they do on a social scale. To quote Lise Baroni:

> We all, men and women, are the Church according to God's design, not only as private persons, but also in the essential services of its government. What Jesus intended is communion, not dispersion throughout closed hierarchical categories. Building the ecclesial community will always be an on-going task. When will women be allowed to work at it along with men, at the foundation as well as at the summit levels?[28]

In the view of numerous modern Catholics the Church should promote dialogue between men and women, lay and religious. Women must find

> ... a setting in which they can exercise their spiritual, political and intellectual talents, as well as their pastoral and theological gifts, while respecting their personal vocations as women.[29]

Elisabeth Schüssler-Fiorenza argues that the Roman Catholic Church's structural and organizational character has become more "Roman" than "Christian." In this setting, she identifies two frameworks, both of which perpetuate patriarchy: the "male" system, which is based upon obedience and clerical celibacy (i.e., a ruling system that is devoid of women), and the "female" system, which is economically dependent and subordinate to a "male" caste. Women figure at the bottom of the pyramidal structure. Such a hierarchy is self-serving and formulates its policies according to its own needs.

Schüssler-Fiorenza calls for a "restructuring" of the hierarchy which would include women at every level — from preaching the gospel to decision making and implementing new forms of ministry. The ordination of women in other Christian churches demonstrates that the inclusion of some "token" women has not resolved the patriarchalism that predominates most Christian churches. Schüssler-Fiorenza maintains that we must strive to transform the hierarchic structure of the Roman Catholic Church and reappropriate the Christian message to promote the "true" dignity of women which Christ intended.[30]

Schüssler-Fiorenza's theory is somewhat in keeping with Archbishop Rembert Weakland's call for installing women into certain Vatican positions. One wonders what type of environment would surround these women if such a reshaping should occur. I think it is important to emphasize here that a "reshaping" of clerical minds would also be in order. The entire (official) tradition of the Roman Catholic Church has been exclusive of women in any official, much less sacramental role. The inclusion of women to priestly orders would definitely call for a transformation of ideals and a revamping of Catholic seminaries. Needless to say, such a development would require a complete renewal of the entire Church. Schüssler-Fiorenza is quite adept at articulating the dynamics involved. Similarly, Rosemary Radford Ruether has also shed some light on women's liberation from patriarchal structures. This concept will be treated near the end of this chapter.

At this point, it may be appropriate to comment on the plight of women religious, as their struggles are quite similar to lay women's and it seems to me that the patriarchal character of the hierarchy is at the root of their exclusion as well. Here, one example will suffice as it demonstrates that their situation finds solidarity with the tensions that are experienced by all Christian women and Catholics in particular.

We have all heard of the "infamous" Bishops' Synod. Religious life is the topic for the 1994 synod. However, women religious are excluded from participating as full members—just as the Synod of the Laity in 1987 was exclusive of lay members. Apparently the synod "rules," which are no doubt made up by men, permit only "selected" bishops and some priests to be recognized as voting delegates. Women religious are permitted to attend, but are not allowed any formal input that would contribute significantly.[31] Based on the outcome of the Synod of the Laity in 1987 (treated at length in Chapter 4—one will recall the final draft did not contain the proposals dealing with women and therefore gave the impression of having been written prior to the Synod itself). I have seriously come to question the value of Bishops' Synods. Certainly the Vatican's constant interference with the bishops' deliberations serves as an indication that synods are not the proper vehicle for innovation and implementation of ideas that accurately relate to the needs of Christ's Church.

Another example of this type occurred in May of 1993 when the Quebec bishops met with the Pope in Rome. Although Bishop Bernard Hubert stressed that

> The North American culture gives so much attention to the rights of the person and to the equality of men and women in society that what the Church says about the place and role of women in the Christian community appears to be out of touch in relation to *real* life....[32]

the Pope responded by reiterating almost the exact same words as the *Declaration* used in 1976—as if he had memorized them in case the issue of women's ordination surfaced amidst the discussion.

This situation clearly articulates the hierarchy's resistance to change. It also indicates that the bishops have a clear understanding of the suffering that exists within their own parishes as well as in women's hearts. More and more, churches are being closed, and priests are asked to take on yet another parish. This really makes me wonder to what extent the papacy will go in order to "remain faithful to the Church's" constant tradition.

Women's Struggle for Equality. Archbishop Vachon's intervention at the Bishops' Synod in 1983 outlined that the major cause for the lack of dialogue between laity and hierarchy has to do with the fact that women are still being associated with "the occasion of sin."[33] In this sense, although the United Nations convention on the elimination of all forms of discrimination against women promoted the influence of women in society,[34] there is still a dire need for reconciliation between men and women in the Church. Archbishop Vachon's intervention stressed that Jesus abolished all forms of discrimination. If the Church is to remain faithful to Christ's teaching it cannot overlook the notion that Christ created a new humanity in which "...man and woman come into being and recognize each other on a basis of equality and destiny, and equality in mission and involvement."[35] In this sense, the place of women in the salvific mission of the Church must be affirmed. As members of Christ's body, women have a necessary function to carry out the building up of Church communities.

To do so, women should have access to specialized training that would assist them in their area of ministry. Diocesan funding should be made available for those women who are in need. Women who exercise formal ministries in their communities should be recognized. If the Church is truly concerned with

> ... the fundamental rights of the person, [such that] every type of discrimination, whether social or cultural, whether based on sex, race, colour, social condition, language or religion, is to be overcome and eradicated as contrary to God's intent.[36]

The fact that a permanent diaconate remains to be established for women can be perceived as an injustice when it clearly exists for men.

Although some priests have favored the promotion of women's participation in liturgical roles,[37] this is not often the case. When women express the need and desire to serve, the result is a major power struggle. As Lise Baroni explains:

> The women in pastoral ministry are no longer simply asking permission to serve the Church, they are demanding that they be free to think, to create, to be coresponsible, to share on equal terms in the process of important decision-making.[38]

Recently, over 100 women gathered outside a Catholic cathedral in Brooklyn, New York, to make a public outcry for justice and equality for women in the Church. Although most of the women present remain pillars of faith and donors of their gifts in their own parishes, they joined other women to protest the exclusion of women from priestly service. In Sidney Callahan's words:

> Nothing Christ does to save us depends upon his masculinity. To sacrifice one's body, to give one's life and one's will to God is an equal-opportunity response.[39]

In short, women are protesting for the right to serve in a sacramental manner. Christ's sacrifice has nothing to do with his masculinity. Discipleship is a call to be Christlike to one another — regardless of one's gender. Callahan stresses that the Church's exclusion of women is based upon the "sex" taboo in which women are considered "unclean" and unworthy to serve at the altar.

Although the purity regulations are documented in scripture, the United States bishop's committee banned the use of scripture to promote abusive behavior towards women:

> Even where the Bible uses traditional language to support the social order common in the day, the image presented is never one that condones the use of abuse to control another person.[40]

I argue that this resolution should be applied to the purity laws as well as the exclusion of women from the ministerial priesthood based upon scripture and the will of Christ.

Dolores Leckey has recently outlined the dynamics of power sharing and its role towards the equality of men and women in a marital and family relationship. Marriage is a "partnership" which calls for "mutual submission." Otherwise the relationship can become oppressive and self-serving. Further, she states that by practicing equality techniques at home, this will eventually blend into one's social practices.[41]

Given Leckey's treatment of power sharing among men and women, two observations readily come to mind. First, the marital relationship which she describes can be made applicable to the role of men and women in the Church. Women's state has become oppressed, and the Vatican's concerns have become self-serving. Leckey states that "mutual submission" is the key to an equal sharing of power. Women share no power in the Church because the hierarchy has become male-dominated and has stripped women from the freedom to serve Christ's Church. Second, Leckey's comment on practicing equality techniques at home would have no chance at blending into the clerical model because women are not permitted such a role. It is very ironical that women are more "equal" on a social scale than in the Roman Catholic setting — one that maintains fidelity to "Christian" values.

The *Revised Code of Canon Law*, for example, permits only lay men to be permanently installed as lectors and acolytes[42]; *The Declaration on the Question of the Admission of Women to the Ministerial Priesthood* says "no" to women's ordination; and the apostolic letter entitled *On the Dignity and Vocation of Women on the Occasion of the Marian Year* affirms women's responsibility in the life of the Church (page 5) but draws the same conclusions as the *Declaration* did regarding the exclusion of women in liturgical roles.

The Resistance to Change. Given these observations, one can say that if women are to be accepted in various leadership positions, the change of attitude has to come from within the structure itself. Regarding this apparent resistance, Lise Baroni has suggested that in an institution where pastoral roles have been reserved traditionally to priests, clergy have identified men's roles as being the norm. Therefore, women in these roles present a problem.[43]

Bishop Lebel of Quebec has expressed the opinion that although in theory the Church has recently promoted women's advancement, in practice the Church has not communicated to women that their talents and gifts are welcome. For example, he notes that the prohibition against women's serving at the altar ". . . has every appearance of a sexist attitude."[44]

Although many parishes are promoting more roles for women within their Church communities — the problem is that they lack an entree into the roles which bear significance in terms of authority and decision making. I am in no way saying that education and liturgy are not important. They become gender-specific roles, however, because women in this setting are subordinate to the clerical authorities, and often have to do things the priest's way, instead of being allowed innovative and practical input. Further, their duties are labeled as "work," whereas clerical functions are deemed "ministerial."

Another indication of women's subordination on a practical level has to do with remuneration. Professional women who have as much training in administrative duties as priests do are offered less remuneration—if they are paid at all—than priests, who have no family to help support and whose lodgings are often supplied by the parish. Therefore, one can say that if the Church wants to remain faithful to Christ's model, its practices must complement its theories. Given its all-male hierarchic structure, the resistance to change is rooted in a struggle to remain faithful to traditional practices. One must remember, however, that complying with active roles for women in the Church does not necessitate replacing male priests with female ones. Total inclusion and the sharing of ministries mean sharing authority and decision making.[45] This means that women are invited (not "told") to head programs and lead groups based on a mutual solidarity with clergy. In this setting women are free to act autonomously in Christ's name, and are given significant responsibilities that are recognized within their parish communities. To use Kaye Ashe's words:

> We [i.e., women] want to share power as we help invent new ways of exercising it and of empowering others. We want to create new kinds of relationships, those of partnership, in a Church where the line between governing and governed is crossed with relative ease. We want, in other words, to work with those who envision church as community rather than church as chain-of-command.[46]

There are so many areas (liturgical as well as geographical) in which women could give so much—not only of themselves but of Christ in them. Although the argument which stems from the apparent shortage of priests is of practical importance, women should be permitted to perform comparable roles in the Church by virtue of their incorporation into Christ's body through baptism, regardless of the number of candidates who are currently studying for the priesthood. In this sense, there is a dire need for reconciliation within the Church, not only between men and women but between lay and clergy as well. All gifts should be permitted actualization whatever one's gender or clerical status.

Pastoral and Liturgical Roles for Catholic Women

One such conflict continues to recur regarding the exclusion of women serving at the altar. Although canon 208 of the *Revised Code of Canon Law* issued in 1983 stresses that

... in virtue of their rebirth in Christ there exists among all the Christian faithful a true equality with regard to dignity and the activity whereby all co-operate in the building up of the Body of Christ in accord with each one's own condition and function.[47]

Canon 230 of the same Code maintains that only "...lay men who possess the age of qualifications ... can be installed on a stable basis in the ministries of lector and acolyte."[48] If taken at face value, one can say that these texts appear contradictory. When examined at length, however, these texts may not at all appear to convey two different meanings. For example, upon the occasion of the Bishops' Synod in 1987, Father Joseph Fessio circulated a paper entitled *Reasons Given Against Women Acolytes and Lectors*,[49] in which he presents the theological and pastoral reasons behind the exclusion of women from nonordained ministries such as those of lector and acolyte. In contrast, Bishop Hamelin's intervention at the 1987 Synod, entitled *Access of Women to Church Positions*, stresses that women should be permitted to perform liturgical functions that do not require ordination—such as those of lector and acolyte.

The purpose of this section is to examine the arguments presented in the light of a situation that occurred in Toronto in 1987 involving a young girl who regularly served Mass—until a special Mass celebrating her parish's 100th anniversary was scheduled. Shortly before the celebration, Sandra Bernier, 11 at the time, was informed that she and her "fellow" altar girls would not be permitted to serve because of the restriction outlined in the code. This section will seek to outline the tensions involved and present each argument logically in order to expose the implications and consequences that emerge directly from the reasoning used.

The Bernier Case. Needless to say, the Bernier case received various controversial news releases as well as negative publicity for the Roman Catholic Church. Although the question regarding female altar servers was formally raised at the Bishops' Synod in 1987, the proposal containing the request to reconsider the code's exclusion of women from the roles of lector and acolyte was omitted from the final draft that was later voted on because the issue was considered too specific and therefore irrelevant for matters concerning the "whole" Church.[50] According to the Rev. Francis Morrisey, professor of canon law at St. Paul University in Ottawa, "the matter was referred to the Sacred Congregation for Divine Worship and the Discipline of the Sacraments—a Vatican office responsible for such questions." The Congregation's task was to review the whole question and issue a new document on the subject. To date, however, "there has been no document."[51]

5. Women in the Catholic Church

Given the recent pressure for the ordination of women in the Catholic Church, it has been said that the Synod was merely a "sounding board"[52] that simply revoiced the official position regarding the exclusion of women and that Rome will keep silent on the issue. What follows is a detailed discussion of contrasting arguments presented for and against the promotion of women's roles in the Roman Catholic Church.

Arguments Against the Promotion of Women. Father Fessio's argument is twofold: theological and pastoral. To summarize, Father Fessio maintains that although there is no distinction between the dignity of men and women insofar as they are "creatures" of God,[53] there is a fundamental difference regarding their roles, as there is in the reproductive act, which is characterized by an active participation by two individuals who share a common goal achieved through diverse roles. In this sense, the symbol of creation becomes a symbol of the Church as Christ's bride. God became human through the incarnation and because he chose to be specifically male, Christ represents God the Father.

Father Fessio's theology exclusively equates the incarnation with "man"-kind. He links Christ's maleness with divine overtones which lead to the maleness of the priest. Grace is made present through the priest which symbolically represents Christ. My problem with this scenario is that the "male" character becomes a symbol for salvation. In this setting, clerical ministry becomes masculine and paternal. All of this is linked with a "profound spiritual complementarity between men and women."[54] I observe that "complementarity" refers to compatibility. How can something complete another if it is subordinate to the latter? My point here is that there is no complementarity between men and women if one begins with the supposition that man is superior to woman. Certainly Father Fessio has done this by equating man with the "exalted" order of the Divine. He rationalizes this notion by suggesting it is all part of the "mystery" of God. If God revealed himself through a "human" form, it was to redeem "human"-kind. To suggest that only a man can represent Christ's redemption is to suggest that Christ came to redeem "men" and not "humans." It is to suggest that only men can be Christlike and that women are not capable of representing Christ. Such a contention contradicts Christ's teaching on equality and justice for the oppressed.

One can say that Father Fessio's assessment of male and female roles is in accord with Vatican II's treatment of the laity[55] insofar as the Church is structured such that it allows for the diversity of roles:

> For just as in one body we have many members, yet all the members have not the same function, so we, the many, are one body in Christ, but severally members of one another [Romans 12.4-5].

In terms of responsibility, each individual is given a particular gift, necessary for the building up of Christ's Church. Father Fessio seems to associate this diversity with two distinct roles as in the reproductive act, which is in turn associated with male and female imagery in that Mary represents the Church and Christ represents God. In doing so, one can say that Father Fessio is limiting the diversity of gifts to conform to a sexual role. I argue that although male and females imagery is a necessary factor in God's revelation regarding the nature of the Church, to limit the diversity of roles in a sexual sense is to limit the nature of the gift itself. In other words, men and women each have viable gifts to contribute to the Church regardless of their gender.

In consequence, Christ has been equated with men, and the Church with women.[56] The Roman Catholic Church links women not only with the symbol of servant,[57] but also with that which is impure and incompatible with sacredness, while men are readily associated with priestly service and that which is holy. The result is a stereotype that is based upon the sex of an individual which ignores gifts and potentialities. It limits one to performing duties and roles that are acceptable only within the parameters of one's sex and, in doing so, fails to recognize the Spirit's challenge of making the gospel relevant for today. According to Lise Baroni, "The Church can and must renew its symbolism of the feminine if it is to challenge society in a prophetic way."[58]

From a practical stance, Fessio argues that permitting women to be acolytes

> ... would not lead to the invalidity of the sacrament [but would be] in serious disharmony with the very nature and character of the whole order of grace and redemption, the mediation of the priest and the symbolic character of men and women,[59]

since the acolyte, by reason of his assistance to the priest, becomes "...the hands of the priest"—one who represents Christ. Father Fessio's contention that women serving as acolytes would not cause the sacrament to become invalid seems to contradict his thought. He states that the acolyte becomes the "hands of the priest" and yet he contends that a woman's hands would not nullify the sacrament. Father Fessio seems to maintain that the Eucharist would lose its salvific effect if it was consecrated by a woman. Again, Father Fessio is limiting the salvific nature of the Church to a male flesh, when tradition reminds us that Jesus was made incarnate in a "human" flesh. Following my argument in Chapter 1, I observe that men and women are equally capable of representing Christ and the Church by virtue of their baptism. To deny that they are equally capable is to deny the effects of the sacrament itself.

Still on a practical note, Father Fessio argues that there will be a serious decline in candidates for the priesthood if the Church permitted girls to serve because altar serving is a direct source for priests, and no boy would want to serve alongside a girl. I think this argument appears quite childish. Girls and boys learn at a very young age to cooperate and to get along. In the public school system, boys and girls learn together and play together. They may be segregated when it comes to participating in activities that require physical contact, as in some sports, but mainly they learn while quite young to respect each other as individuals first—and as members of the opposite sex second. Further, in an age where men and women equally exercise positions of leadership on a social scale (though not yet in equal numbers), it should not seem irregular that in Church life, boys and girls serve alongside each other.

Further, statistics have shown a decline in priestly vocations in Canada since approximately 1970, due specifically to the greater number of renouncements as well as the greater number of deaths, particularly in Quebec.[60] It may be seriously doubted that allowing girls to serve at the altar alongside boys would reduce the number of candidates for priestly orders any more than the current statistics indicate. If anything, it might increase the amount of active participation in the Church. If girls were permitted to serve, it is only logical that this would help increase women's realization that they too are called to partake in the building up of Christ's Church. In this sense, girls who serve and feel comfortable at the altar could progress from serving Mass, to reading, ushering, being ministers of the Eucharist and lay presiders. In short, they would progress into active ministering roles—what better way to keep young women as well as young men interested in the Church? In my opinion, when the clergy (as well as the laity) feel comfortable with having girls and women serve near the altar, it would help calm their inhibitions about having women become priests.

From a pastoral stance, Father Fessio argues that there is a logical progression from altar boy to other forms of service, such as acolyte, lector and the priesthood. In this sense, the acceptance of altar girls would seem unfair as it would give them false hope of becoming priests. If this were so, why is there no restriction to women when it comes to being eucharistic ministers or lay presiders? Clearly these ministries involve just as much exposure to service at the altar as altar serving does. Does this mean that women should also be restricted from performing these roles? If this were the case, the Church would lose the benefits of many gifts and talents that were designed to be used in service. As Jean Forest notes:

> In the present shortage of sisters and priests, the work of these women is critical to the mission of the Church and if they find that they can no longer function within that framework, it will be the Church itself, and all its suffering others which will be the real loser.[61]

Another pastoral consideration Father Fessio notes is that altar girls present an identity problem because they are vested as priests. He argues that only boys can be authentic symbols for priests. I observe that symbols can be modified easily, depending on one's intention. When the understanding of a symbol shifts, so can its meaning. For example, if eucharistic ministers started to wear particular vestments, it would take on a specific meaning. When altar servers vest, they differ from priests in that they have a specific function that is different from that of the priests. In most cases, altar servers' garments differ from those of priests such that one can make the distinction. I would therefore maintain that altar girls do not create an identity problem by reason of their vestment based on the idea that they are actively engaged in serving at the altar, and not as priests.

Father Fessio's fourth consideration has to do with Church discipline. He maintains that if one chooses directly to violate Church discipline regarding the use of female altar servers, this practice will give way to other violations and eventually lead to the promotion of women priests and further division in the Roman Catholic Church. I do not think that promoting female altar servers violates Church discipline — much less tradition or even revelation. Since the Vatican has not said anything further in light of the "Bernier" case, it cannot be argued that the Vatican prohibits the use of altar girls. "Roman law operates on the principle that if it's not prohibited it's allowed."[62] Further, if the Pope himself has altar girls serving in his own parish, it is very difficult to argue that the Vatican is opposed to such a practice. The Rev. John Hibbard has maintained that

> There are just too many varying practices throughout the Church for the Vatican to make a statement that might possibly offend cultures where this would not be acceptable.[63]

Certainly the cultures who would take offense at such a practice would be those which continue to support the subordination of women to men. If the Vatican is truly "Christian" it should promote justice and equality among its churches. Certainly Christ broke with his culture in according women proper dignity and ministerial roles. If the Church wants to remain credible to its members and faithful to Christ's example, it should make a statement regarding altar servers that would promote justice and equality for women, regardless of the "culture" to which they belong.

It is difficult to know where to draw the line. The *Revised Code of Canon Law* has, however, clearly categorized the ministries of lector and acolyte as lay ministries that do not require ordination and further, as ones which "...are not intended as steps towards sacred orders."[64] Therefore, I observe that this aspect of Father Fessio's argument cannot be supported by the *Code*.

From a practical stance, one could imagine the eventual conflicts that would occur in a parish that officially recognized male lectors and acolytes and yet refused to do so with equally qualified female servers. Would this promote the fundamental equality described in canon 208? Further, although the female population that actively participates in the Mass largely outnumbers the men,[65] being of service is rooted in humility and should not promote or incite competition. If it does, this in itself would be a violation of Christ's Church—let alone Church discipline.

Lastly, Father Fessio argues that feminists who are concerned with the Roman Catholic Church are seeking to abolish the sexual distinction between men and women and ultimately want a gender-neutral society whereby the idea of God the Father will be eliminated. In this sense, he states that the Pope has no choice but to say "no" to altar girls, for otherwise the unique dignity that women already possess in the Church would be destroyed. I argue that although feminism is directly concerned with abolishing discrimination and discriminatory practices, it does not necessarily entail the promotion of a gender-neutral society. In Canada, many women who have been labeled as feminists are quite happy with the image of God the Father and are not seeking to change that concept.[66] The Catholic Network for Women's Equality is one example.[67] Formed in 1981, the group is an organization that promotes women's equality in the Church concerning various issues such as violence against women, equal pay for paid positions held by women who are employed by the Church, and the like. This group also promotes inclusive language in liturgies not to the point where every reference to God is changed to a female name, but in the sense that the gospel speaks to all people—not just to men.[68]

In short, the fact that Father Fessio was appointed to the synod by Pope John Paul II may lead one to speculate that his paper is indicative of the official Church's attitude when it comes to the promotion of more active roles for lay women in the Church. It is the fear that their male space will somehow be invaded and that their male power will be undermined. Priests must come to realize that women are capable of undertaking responsible leadership roles and that ministry in the Church is not meant to be reserved for men. As Lise Baroni notes,

> The competence of these women in filling a function where many expected them to fail has been a greater contribution to the advancement of the Church than certain liturgical reforms that followed Vatican II for it is the mental structure upon which our religious consciousness was built that has been changed.[69]

Perhaps signs like these will facilitate the ordination of women and abolish this systemic discrimination that the Roman Catholic Church continues to manifest.

Arguments for the Promotion of Women. In contrast, Bishop Hamelin's intervention to the Bishops' Synod in 1987 strongly promoted the participation of women in Church positions. On a practical note, he asserts that since women are not restricted from carrying out positions of authority and responsibility on a social level, the status of women in the Church should be comparable. For example, he notes that

> We must move aside the canonical obstacles which block the access of lay Catholics—and therefore of all Catholic women—to positions of responsibility which do not or should not require ordination.[70]

In this sense Bishop Hamelin seems to be moving away from official Church discipline, as outlined in the *Code of Canon Law*, to a more practical application and reading of the signs of the times:

> We must recognize that our mind-sets, our language and our practice do not always match the ringing affirmations of equality which are found in our declarations.[71]

He also stresses the duty that one shares as a member of Christ's Church to journey with Christ and seek to rediscover Jesus' attitude towards women and preserve the example He most strikingly set. He praises the women's movement that has been formed in Canada and acknowledges their struggle to promote "justice," "dignity" and "partnership" for women.[72] In this sense, he attributes their work to the baptismal calling felt by many men and women who seek to abolish many forms of discrimination in the Church and in society in general.

He also calls for the promotion of dialogue with Catholic women, in hopes of building stronger relationships in the face of stressful conflicts that arise when these types of issues surface. In Hamelin's words

> These tensions are impossible to avoid. We must live with them without breaking the bond of communion. They can be a stimulus to deepen the search for truth.[73]

He also points out the fact that although women form the majority in terms of active lay participation in the Church, they are absent when it comes to making decisions, because of their exclusion from ordained ministries. This is not only an injustice to women, it also has dire consequences. Hamelin explains:

> The very credibility of the Church is affected if we do not actively seek out the means to assure an equitable representation of women and men on all the levels of ecclesial life.[74]

In this sense, Hamelin's intervention calls for change—a change in perspective as well as action. He proposes a reexamination of the impact women's efforts have had in the life of the early Church as well as their contributions towards issues such as human rights, justice, peace and the like:

> That means that the faith voice of women is essential to the sign value of the Church as sacrament and to the witness which the Church is commanded to bear.[75]

He calls for the inclusion of women in positions that demand "real pastoral responsibilities, with the authority that such responsibilities entail"[76]—equality in terms of permanent installation of women acolytes and lectors.

Regarding the question of ordination for women, Hamelin asserts that those who support both sides have expressed valid concerns that need to be examined, possibly through the reflections of study groups, including lay men and women, theologians and clergy. His intervention closes with a reminder that Genesis teaches that God originally intended for the complete participation of women in Church life and in society:

> According to the heart of God, humanity is not humanity without the mutual presence of man and woman to each other, without the original covenant between them.[77]

From an American perspective, Archbishop Rembert Weakland, archbishop of the Milwaukee diocese, has also verbalized a "radical" inclusion for women in Church positions. The talk he gave at the Roman

Synod in October of 1987, for example, calls for an urgent response to women's concerns which directly relates to the Church's credibility as a whole.[78]

On a social scale, Archbishop Weakland claims that the Church must take specific actions against sexism which contributes to unjust ways and inequalities vis-à-vis women in the workplace. Such an undertaking would demand that the Church restructure its own organization. As I have noted with the altar serving issue, the Church cannot proclaim equality for women on a social scale, unless certain measures are taken to assure the equality of women within the Church.

Thus, Archbishop Weakland itemizes seven practical steps toward rectifying the inequalities that exist towards women in the Church, which would in turn permit the Church to remain credible to itself in its teaching and practice. Archbishop Weakland calls for inclusion of women in liturgical roles that do not require ordination. He also calls for the inclusion of women in administrative roles, such as positions in diocesan offices and the like. Inclusive language in liturgical and Church documents is also called for, as well as the promotion of nonpatriarchal aspects of historical and scriptural texts.

Further, Archbishop Weakland calls for "co-discipleship," which he defines as composed of "...a priestly people who share together the mission given us in baptism and who, thus, work together in mutual collaboration."[79] Although Archbishop Weakland's steps call for the inclusion of women in pastoral and liturgical functions, I maintain that the equality of women will not be completely achieved until they are admitted to the ministerial priesthood. Codiscipleship can only be achieved if the "mutual collaboration" exists on an egalitarian plane. The exclusion of women to the ministerial priesthood perpetuates the patriarchal structures that governed the social patterns of the early Church.

A Comparison. At this point, a brief comparison of the two perspectives may help to summarize the ongoing tensions that exist when the role of women in the Church is discussed.

On the one hand, we have the view that women should accept the current legislation regarding their roles. After all, their roles have been clearly defined. Although they are fully equal to men and share the same dignity, they differ in the way that they are called to serve Christ's Church. It is time for the Roman Catholic Church officials to stifle the issue by saying "no" to women lectors and acolytes, in order to dissuade women from seeking other roles that would assume a greater sense of responsibility and authority. If not, the Church is opening itself up to a lengthy battle against women who are seeking priestly ordination.

5. Women in the Catholic Church

On the other hand, we have the view that the Church should attempt to move away from Church discipline that restricts women's roles. The tension that this issue creates is unavoidable and should be addressed by following certain practical steps (already outlined). Then and only then can the Church truly remain credible for all of its members.

After having examined Father Fessio's paper in juxtaposition with Bishop Hamelin's, along with Archbishop Weakland's comments, I think that Father Fessio's solution appears short-term and lacks careful consideration for the consequences involved. If the Church seeks to stifle women at a time when vocations to the priesthood are declining considerably, it risks losing the majority of its active lay members. Father Fessio's argument closes with the assumption that the altar serving issue could create as much controversy as *Humanae Vitae* did.[80] I agree that the issue will create as much controversy as *Humanae Vitae* did. Not only did women and theologians support women's participation in liturgies, but at the 1987 Synod, Catholic bishops agreed that they would recommend that the current legislation regarding the restriction of female altar servers be revised.[81]

In short, in an age where women have demonstrated their abilities to perform responsible leadership roles in society, one can say that if the Roman Catholic Church maintains that women are to be excluded from authoritative positions of leadership, it will challenge the very credibility on which it was built. As Archbishop Vachon (of Quebec) states:

> The appeals of the Church to the world made in such documents as *Pacem in Terris* and *Gaudium et Spes* for the advancement of the status of women, are on the point of losing all impact unless the recognition of women as full members becomes simultaneously a reality within the Church itself.[82]

Although the Roman Catholic Church maintains in theory that men and women are coresponsible for the building up of God's kingdom on earth by virtue of their baptism, it must attempt to break down the barriers that have impeded women from doing so in practice. This attempt must be accompanied by the admission of lay women to liturgical roles including that of altar server, lector, acolyte, preaching as well as authoritative roles on all levels of Church life.[83] Consulting women and permitting them to actively participate in the preparation of Church documents that directly concern them are another area that needs to be addressed. Women must be permitted to share their common responsibility in the building up of Christ's Church by actualizing the potentialities of their gifts to the fullest. This would entail working alongside other members of the Church on an equal basis and participating actively at every level of Church life: ministry, Church documents, decision making, administrative tasks, and the like.

Women's Inequalities

By limiting ministries such as that of lector and acolyte positions that bear authoritative responsibilities to men, has the Roman Catholic Church restricted the effects of baptism in that "...the power to share in the priestly function of Christ"[84] is communicated only by the male gender of God's creation?

Lise Baroni has stated that one difficulty lies in the conflict between theory and practice when it comes to the equality of women. Although various Church documents have promoted the full equality of women in theory, she notes that in practice, women who are employed as pastoral workers are often secretaries at meetings, have little or no authority when it comes to making decisions that directly affect their work, and find their positions being threatened by seminarians or religious women who assume their responsibilities for lesser pay.[85] One will find that this type of treatment of women occurs at every level of the hierarchy. For example, in 1984, Pope John Paul II commissioned a group of two clerics and two lay members to interpret the *Code of Canon Law*. Both lay members were men. As Elisabeth Lacelle notes, considering the fact that there are women canonists and that the *Code of Canon Law* expresses a fundamental equality among all of God's people, women can no longer remain indifferent to this type of treatment.[86]

In this chapter, I have tried to outline the major tensions experienced by Canadian women seeking leadership roles in the Roman Catholic Church. In doing so, I observed that despite the shortage of priests, women have gifts and are capable of using their talents to serve Christ's Church in an official manner. Although the hierarchy documents the equality of women in theory, I maintain that the full equality of women cannot possibly be realized unless women are accorded responsible leadership roles. This would include women's full participation at every level of the hierarchy—including the ministerial priesthood. Although various clerical voices have called for women's inclusion to Church positions, the conflict between what the official Church professes and what it practices remains. Chapter 6 will treat the question of the ordination of women from a theological perspective and attempt to provide a contemporary setting which would allow for the liberation of women from clericalism, given women's legitimate call to vocations.

CHAPTER 6

A Contemporary Understanding of the Ordination of Women

In 1988, Pope John Paul II issued an apostolic letter entitled *On the Dignity and Vocation of Women on the Occasion of the Marian Year*. Although the letter does not focus on the ordination of women, I observe that several aspects treated parallel those set forth in the *Declaration on the Question of the Admission of Women to the Ministerial Priesthood*. The purpose of this chapter is to examine the Pope's recent letter in order to gain some insight as to the developments that have occurred since the *Declaration*. From there, attention will focus on the theological impediments that emerge when addressing the question of the ordination of women. To do this, I will readdress the service model of Jesus' ministry and reclaim women's legitimate call to vocations. In this manner, I will seek to outline a theology of liberation for women and present a brief synopsis of the argument put forth in this book.

"On the Dignity and Vocation of Women on the Occasion of the Marian Year"

Given the recent pressure for the ordination of women,[1] a contemporary understanding of where the official Church stands on the issue would seem appropriate. Like the *Declaration*, the apostolic letter begins by affirming women's value in the history of the early Christian Church. In defining what type of vocation seems appropriate for women, Pope John Paul II reflects on the manner in which scripture presents Mary as a model for women, whose virginal conception and birth of Jesus are characterized as "...the turning point of man's history on earth, understood as salvation history."[2] Mary is seen as a principal figure in terms of the Church's salvific mission, and is said to represent men and women.³ Yet, although Christ represents men and women, only men can represent Jesus. Should not the same hold true for women?

Men and Women in the Created Order. The encyclical stresses that men and women were created in the image and likeness of God,⁴ and maintains that they are equal. Scripture often speaks of God in masculine and feminine terms, even though God is divine and devoid of any masculine or feminine "bodily characteristics."⁵ I observe a contradiction here, with the *Declaration*'s emphasis on Jesus' maleness. If God is said to have no physical bodily characteristics, and if Jesus took on a "human" form, the physical bodily characteristics that he undertook would be of secondary importance. The form under which Jesus was revealed to man occurred in the form of a human flesh. In this sense, Jesus could represent men and women. The *Declaration*'s contention that women cannot represent Christ therefore remains problematic because it ignores the revelatory role of the Incarnation.

Jesus' Attitude Towards Women. The encyclical characterizes Jesus' behavior towards women as quite radical for his time.⁶ He revised the Mosaic laws regarding the status of women in Judea, and freely accepted women who accompanied him on his missionary journeys and spoke of them in his teachings. Indeed, various women remained faithful when the apostles were confused and full of doubt. Mary Magdalene is characterized as "the apostle of the Apostles."⁷ Although the encyclical attests to the significance of her role, the *Declaration* maintains that "...Jesus did not entrust the apostolic charge to women."⁸ If "apostolic mission" as described in the *Declaration* has to do with "official" and "public" proclamation of the risen Lord,⁹ in what way does Mary Magdalene's situation (cf. John 20.16-18) conflict with these criteria? Certainly, she witnessed the risen Lord, and was told to relate the good news to Jesus' "brethren" (RSV). Does this not constitute an "official" and "public" role?

Despite Jesus' "maleness," he permitted women various roles which are now restricted to the work of priests:

> It was women who anointed him, and women who proclaimed him, and women who prepared him for burial, and women who pronounced his return.¹⁰

In Chapter 2 of this work, I raised a legitimate concern regarding the historicity of Jesus' appointment of twelve "male" apostles. Coupled with the lack of scriptural evidence regarding the Twelve's activities, along with the aid of contemporary scholarship on the issue, I reached the conclusion that it was doubtful whether Jesus himself appointed twelve "male" apostles. The role of women in Jesus' ministry, however, has not been disputed. The fact that their involvement in Jesus' ministry as well as their functions in the early communities has been recorded throughout scripture is evidence that the historicity of their inclusion cannot be refuted.

Jesus' salvific mission had nothing to do with his physical bodily characteristics. The fact that the official Church continues to deny the access of women to the ministerial priesthood remains problematic because it assumes that women should be defined in terms of their biological functions. Let us now turn to the encyclical's argument regarding this issue.

Equality versus Diversity. Although the encyclical affirms the inherent equality of women and men, it maintains that men and women differ in the diversity of roles they are called to perform. Here, the encyclical calls attention to the special role that a mother undertakes. Although both the man and the woman share parenthood, the mother has a special role, given her "physical constitution."[11] For example, the woman carries and gives birth to a child, while apart from conception, the father's biological function remains inactive. In this sense, the joy a woman experiences immediately following her labor has been related to the Paschal Mystery, where the joy which accompanies the Good News immediately follows Jesus' bodily death.

It is interesting to note here that the encyclical cites the Lukan text when referring to Mary's motherhood. The text reads:

> As he said this, a woman in the crowd raised her voice and said to him, "Blessed is the womb that bore you, and the breasts that you sucked!" But he said, "Blessed *rather* are those who hear the word of God and keep it!" [Luke 11.27-28, RSV; emphasis added].

In this sense, the encyclical emphasizes that

> Jesus confirms the meaning of motherhood in reference to the body, but at the same time he indicates an even deeper meaning, which is connected with the order of the spirit.[12]

In what sense does Jesus "... confirm the meaning of motherhood in reference to the body"? Without being disrespectful to Mary, I observe that the message of Jesus is clear: "Blessed *rather* are those...." I interpret this to mean that Jesus disregards Mary's biological function here, and stresses the significance of one's fidelity to God's word, regardless of one's gender or physical functions. In this sense, Jesus indicates that keeping God's word is more important than one's bodily functions.

To use Elisabeth Schüssler-Fiorenza's words: "Faithful discipleship, not biological motherhood, is the eschatological calling of women."[13]

Therefore, Mary's discipleship was more significant than the biological role that she undertook as Jesus' mother. It is interesting to note here that the official Church has not accorded such an equation of biological roles for men. If the standard for women is rooted in their biological function as mothers, why is there no equivalent standard in a man's biological function as a father? Certainly such a contention would distort the dignity accorded celibacy within the priesthood.

Further, Glen Argan has observed that restricting women's roles because of their biology is sexist, just as the treatment of blacks in the United States has been racist, institutionally so prior to the Civil War. In this latter setting, blacks were said to have "good hands for picking cotton." Argan's observation has to do with a biological function, just as the role of women has been defined in terms of the "Marian nature of the Church as virgin, bride and mother." In Argan's words,

> To say that some people are naturally equipped—because of race or gender—for certain forms of service and not for others usually testifies to a deep-seated prejudice by those who perform those other forms of service.[14]

The encyclical also describes virginity as an appropriate vocation for single women, and fidelity within marriage.[15] Although virginity and marriage are two distinct states through which men and women may choose to respond to God's call, they are no doubt the means through which that call is answered. I observe that the call to discipleship touches every individual regardless of her or his gender. If all are called without genderal distinction, it seems untenable to insist that one's response is conditioned by the sex of that particular individual.

There is evidence that indicates that the early Christian Church functioned in such a manner that made no genderal distinction when regarding ministries.[16] When the second and third century churches deviated from this pattern and began to exclude women from performing certain roles, on account of certain cultural restrictions' being placed upon them, a cultural consideration was adapted and later deemed revelatory. In doing so, the second and third century churches preserved a cultural aspect and neglected to conform to the practices of the first century Church. It should also be noted here that the tradition of patriarchal-sexist theologizing of women emerged at this time.

The revelation of God occurred in the form of a human flesh. The fact that Jesus undertook a male form is secondary. If one regards Jesus' maleness as primary, one is ultimately saying that Jesus was made incarnate in the form of a man to redeem men, and not humankind. Such a contention remains unacceptable to Christian tradition.

Bridal Imagery. The encyclical maintains that when using spousal imagery to describe the relationship between Christ and his Church, one must note that, although the Church remains in a state of subjection to Christ, in the spousal relationship, husband and wife are mutually subjected to one another.[17] As a collective entity, men and women are called to become the "Bride" of Christ—his Church. Because Christ is the Bridegroom and Christ was made incarnate in the form of a man, Christ's love represents the Bridegroom's love and "men's" in particular.[18] What of mutuality? What of God's people? How is it that men and women both represent the Bride and yet only men represent the Bridegroom? If men and women are called to become Christ's Church, his Bride, then truly the only Bridegroom is Christ.

This argument appears almost identical to the one put forth in the *Declaration*. That is, only men can represent Christ, i.e., the Bridegroom, because Christ was a man. Here various contradictions come to mind. Other than those previously mentioned, I observe that if women are incapable of representing Christ, how is it that Christ can represent women? If women cannot represent Christ, there are dire implications surrounding the idea of salvation. If women cannot represent Christ, that is equivalent to saying that Christ came only for men. This I doubt. In Ruether's words

> Such a Christology makes it questionable whether women are actually represented or redeemed by Christ at all. Christ is presented to women as the reenforcer of their oppression, not as their redeemer.[19]

In my treatment of Jesus' "message" in Chapter 2, I observed that He proclaimed a "nonpatriarchal" image of God the Father. In this sense, Bernard Cooke has argued that Jesus' salvific mission should be appropriated as an "invitation" rather than God's "action" towards humankind. "Such a dependence involves no subordination; rather, it is one half of the most radical kind of personal equality."[20] This contention calls into question the very nature of the priesthood. If the priest represents Christ's salvific "invitation" I observe that the pyramidal structure of the current Church hierarchy denies the egalitarian nature with which Christ's mission was intended. Further, Christ transformed the understanding of Kingship in that His ministry was one of service. In the patriarchal order, the servants, many of whom were women, were the lowliest creatures on the social scale. If the discipleship of equals was patterned from Jesus' service model, women would definitely be included in this group. The current priesthood is somewhat modeled from the Old Testament notion of "cultic" priesthood. In such a setting,

> ... the bishop possesses a kind of regal—priestly eminence that lifts him to a distinct level above his people; they are more his charges and subjects than his fellow Christians.[21]

I observe that the latter model is hierarchic and self-serving. Such a structure could not possibly be modeled from Jesus' ministry of service. His whole message was based on the notion that He had come to "serve" and not to "be served." The notion that "cultic" overtones from the Old Testament concept of priesthood invaded the Church's tradition near the third or fourth century cannot be disputed. The fact that the Church has traditionally upheld such a practice, however, remains problematic. According to Rosemary Radford Ruether,

> ... one must ask whether the mere longevity of a practice counts absolutely as norm, especially when its dominical foundations are in doubt.[22]

If the Church intends to remain credible to itself as well as faithful to Christ's example, it cannot overlook these facts. The role of contemporary scholarship must seek to legitimize the historicity of Jesus' message. If it happens to uncover unjust practices that do not conform to Jesus' message, certainly Church officials cannot ignore these findings. Let us now turn to the concluding arguments used in the encyclical.

What Does the Official Church Offer for Women? In conclusion, the encyclical stresses that we must go back to Christ's teachings in order to overcome the tensions of our contemporary world. Here, I totally agree. It is not enough to look at the history of the tradition in the Church. When discussing the question of the ordination of women, it is essential to go back to Christ's example. What did he say? What did he do? How did he treat women? Did he outline criteria for the ministry of either men or women?

In this section, I have tried to outline the official Church's contemporary understanding of the vocation of women in light of the question of the ordination of women. When examined in conjunction with the *Declaration* issued in 1976, I find that the encyclical *On the Dignity and Vocation of Women on the Occasion of the Marian Year* offers no basis for an extension of roles for women in the Roman Catholic Church. Its

6. A Contemporary Understanding of the Ordination of Women

primary focus accords women a biological function. As I have noted, Jesus emphasized the discipleship of women, rather than their physical constitution. Yet, the encyclical simply reverberates with what was previously expressed in the *Declaration*: Since Christ was a man, and called only twelve men to become his apostles, only men can represent Christ and become priests. What, then, of women? In previous chapters, I have described a hierarchical, patriarchal and clerical Church which appears self-serving and which discriminates against women. Certainly the Roman Catholic Church has more to offer for women and men who attend Mass and function in their Church communities. What, then, is so attractive about the Church that, despite all of its flaws, has a membership of about 630 million people around the world?[23]

Despite its flaws, the Roman Catholic Church originated with Jesus Christ. This in itself is significant. Christ's message was radical; He proclaimed justice for all. The Christian experience is a faith experience — Believing in Christ means seeking Christ in one another and finding forgiveness despite the worst of evils. Christ died for humankind so that any individual could be redeemed. That in itself is reason enough to affiliate oneself with the Roman Catholic Church. Christ is the center of Roman Catholicism. The Church therefore is a framework for the expression of faith, hope and love. One can strive to be Christlike despite the injustices that have prevailed throughout the history of the Roman Catholic Church. In short, faith in Christ allows one to move beyond the institutionalized structure of the Roman Catholic Church — which remains in the care of human hands, restricted to human limitations. My point here is that even though Christ initiated the Church, the organizational character of the Church remains earthly and is not flawless. The recent reinstatement of Galileo is a good example of this. In 1633 he was condemned by the Church for theorizing that the earth was not at the center of the universe. The Church has since reinstated Galileo and admitted its error in judgment. It is to be hoped that women will not have to wait another three hundred years before the official Church comes to terms with its denial of women priests.[24]

Although the issue of women's empowerment and call to vocation readily comes to mind, let us turn our attention to the theology of women's ordination, as it will serve as the basis for the understanding of a theology of liberation for women within the Roman Catholic Church.

The Theology of the Ordination of Women

Up to this point, I have considered many facets of the question of the ordination of women. However, I have not discussed the theology of the ordination of women at length. Although there is a very practical problem with the shortage of priests, we must also examine the question from a theological perspective. Perhaps it would be appropriate to begin with the discussion of revelation.

Understanding How God Was Revealed. Coming to terms with the theological impediments against the ordination of women necessitates coming to terms with the dynamics involved in revelation. During Jesus' public life, He revealed His Father in various ways. The Catholic Church maintains that

> God the Father ... reveals himself by event and word to His people, and it is accomplished by the incarnate and personal intervention of Jesus Christ, Son of God.[25]

From a scriptural perspective, I observe that although Jesus was made incarnate in a male form, of significance here is the fact that he took on a "human" form, therefore representing men and women. Although this notion has been previously discussed,[26] I reiterate the importance of stressing Jesus' humanity rather than His maleness. I have previously stated that Jesus' maleness was central to His message. It would be inaccurate to suggest, however, that His maleness and the maleness of the Twelve was the content of His message. To do so would imply that Jesus revealed His Father so that only men could experience salvation.

God was also revealed "...in the Person and work of Jesus."[27] After having examined in Chapter 2 the role of women in the ministry of Jesus, I suggest that if Jesus included women in His ministry without making any distinction of roles in comparison to their male counterparts (with the exception of the twelve apostles), it follows that He willed that women be included as full members in His Church. This implies that as full members, women should not be excluded from performing duties which are exercised by men. In short, "Women should have their own share of responsibility and participation in the community life of society and likewise of the Church."[28]

Jesus also revealed His Father by what he said.[29] Here, I am sure anyone could select isolated incidents in which Jesus either "spoke" in favor of or against the participation of women in the building up of His

Church. For example, in the gospel of Luke, Jesus downplays Mary's biological function as a mother.[30] On the other hand, the gospel of Luke has Jesus in the company of the twelve apostles when He says: "Do this in remembrance of me" (Luke 22.19, RSV).

For every text that attaches significance to the maleness of the Twelve one can find a contrasting text that emphasizes one's spiritual being rather than one's bodily characteristics. In coming to terms with what Christ said and did, I observe that one must look to the heart of Jesus' message. In Chapter 3, I addressed the roles of women in the early Church in order to demonstrate that the early Church upheld no distinction of roles between men and women. In fact, women seemed to be among the leaders of house churches, and journeyed with other women and men who were dedicated to sharing Jesus' message and founding new churches. If the early Church found it suitable to include women among the missionaries and house church leaders and the like, one must seriously consider the cultural restrictions that later impeded women from performing similar leadership roles.

In 1976, when the Pontifical Biblical Commission was assigned to study the question of women's ordination from a scriptural perspective, the Commission concluded that although the New Testament does not conclusively settle the issue of women's ordination and that scripture alone does not justify women's exclusion from the ministerial priesthood, Christ's will would not be disobeyed if the Roman Catholic Church decided to ordain women.[31] Therefore, I maintain that the exclusion of women from the ministerial priesthood has no scriptural warrant, nor does it seem to be in accordance with what Christ willed.

Understanding Tradition in the Early Church. When discussing revelation and how God was revealed, one must consider the question of the ordination of women from a traditional perspective. In short, the Roman Catholic Church has maintained that the revelation of Jesus is contained in scripture only in part. It is also communicated by the "living" Church.[32] Therefore, the exclusion of women from the ministerial priesthood needs to be addressed from a traditional perspective. From a theological perspective the two-thousand-year practice of not ordaining women has been traditionally regarded by the hierarchy as a revelatory tradition.[33] Sandra M. Schneiders has recently documented that "ideology criticism," a new genre of biblical interpretation, seeks to discover the ideological bases under which scripture was written. This type of criticism has concerned feminist biblical scholars in terms of exposing androcentric texts. The latter have sought to

> ... identify the biased material in the text and to expose it against the claim that it is part of gospel revelation and therefore normative for Christian faith.[34]

Such a feminist critique was treated earlier in Chapter 3. I am reiterating the value of such an undertaking when regarding texts that are deemed revelatory in character.

Ideology criticism has demonstrated that sacred scripture cannot be relied upon for accurate historical accounts, nor does it contain cultural practices which are regarded as normative for a long period of time. One such example of how a cultural practice was adapted as revelatory is slavery. Slavery was universally accepted,[35] was sustained for a long period of time, and was somewhat based on a faith belief that slaves were inherently inferior to other people. In his first letter to the Corinthians, Paul urges slaves to accept their status, as long as they remain in Christ:

> Everyone should remain in the state in which he was called ... for he who was called in the Lord as a slave is a freed man of the Lord.... So, brethren, in whatever state each was called, there let him remain with God [I Corinthians 7.20, 22, 24, RSV].

Yet, it would be difficult today to argue that slavery belongs to a revelatory tradition.

Similarly, the subordination of women to men was universally accepted over a long period of time, and based on a belief that Eve was subordinate to Adam in the created order. Can we say without further debate, however, that the subordination of women belongs to a revelatory tradition? First, the exclusion of women from the roles of presider and leader of house church occurred at a time when the Church conformed to the social customs of the Greco-Roman culture. In this setting, women were not permitted to exercise a public authoritative role. Therefore, for the time that the church assemblies remained in homes, women were assigned duties and functions that were appropriate for women to carry out in their own homes. As soon as the church worship became public, women were excluded from having any official function. Therefore, I contend that women's exclusion from performing leadership roles that they had become familiar with had a direct relation to the social customs of the Roman world. As I have outlined in Chapter 3, how can this practice be deemed a revelatory tradition?

I observe also that the argument that stems from the two-thousand-year practice of not ordaining women can be challenged. The Roman Catholic Church maintains that this practice remains universal. The

Declaration argues that Christ commissioned his twelve male apostles and at no time did he "...entrust the apostolic charge to women."[36] Given Raymond Brown's insights regarding the development of Christian priesthood,[37] along with Hans Günther's contribution to our understanding of the numerological significance associated with the number 12,[38] I argue that if the Twelve were regarded as priests and women performed duties that were later exercised by priests, the contention that the Roman Catholic Church has never ordained women is questionable. Further, Mary Ann Rossi's work attests to the existence of female priests in the first ten centuries A.D. The exclusion of women can hardly be described as an "unbroken practice." If the exclusion of women from priestly orders was based on a revelatory tradition, how is it that the first century Church was comfortable with having women perform duties that were later performed by priests? In short if the service of the Twelve can be regarded as "priestly service" and if women performed duties that were similar and were not considered priests, I hold that when the Church became structured and institutionalized and conformed to the social restrictions that impeded women from performing leadership roles, the women became the objects of a discrimination which has continued to plague Christ's Church throughout the centuries. I observe that this practice has sustained itself for a long period of time because the hierarchy remains exclusively male.

Third, I argue that what has been sustained throughout the Roman Catholic Church's two-thousand-year history of not ordaining women is its patriarchal structure. In this setting, the exclusion of women from the ministerial priesthood became universal because the subordination of women to men was a common belief, and, while founding new churches in which all authority was undertaken by men, the organizational structure of the Church left no place for women. I therefore maintain that the exclusion of women from the ministerial priesthood was based on a human cultural tradition that has survived a two-thousand-year history because of the patriarchalism which has overcome Christ's Church. Hence, the contemporary Catholic Church must move beyond the theological impediments that restrict women's roles in order to survive.[39]

The Church's Ministry of Service

I have observed that Christ transformed the religious concepts of kingship in that his ministry was one of service. Although the concept of ministry in the early Church was treated in Chapter 4, perhaps it would be appropriate at this point to focus on the Church's portrayal of Christ's service, as its treatment bears significance to my discussion of the vocation issue.

To assist in my attempt to describe the Church's ministry of service, let us turn to the scholarship of Avery Dulles. His *Models of the Church* calls attention to five models which the Church portrays. Among them, he spends an entire chapter on the Church as servant. Let us briefly summarize Dulles' discussion as it may shed some light on the Church's mission given Christ's ministry of service.

Since Vatican II, the Church made a remarkable metanoïa regarding the relationship between the Church and the world. Prior to Vatican II, Dulles observes that the Church condemned certain modern developments which functioned autonomously and without the Church's authority.

Vatican II confirmed the secular world's accomplishments and acknowledged that the Church must strive to learn from them in order to effectively proclaim the gospel in an ever changing world. Since Christ came to serve, the Church must strive to serve all people — embracing modern developments and progressive technological improvements.[40]

At this point, certain observations may prove helpful. I think that Vatican II in many ways produced a healthy change of attitudes concerning various aspects of ecclesiology. Certainly the perspective of the Church on its relationship to the secular world is an indication that the Church had to keep up with modern times. Also, the service aspect of the Church was definitely revised at the occasion of Vatican II. In this setting, the Church commissioned itself to be more Christlike in its ministry of service to others and strove towards becoming a "community for others."[41]

Dulles develops this theme as it filters down to individual Christians in that each individual is called to serve others in Christ's name. In this setting, secular power can be transformed into power for service. Dulles seems to argue that the Church's structure impedes its mission of service. He quotes Bonhoeffer's call for a more "humble" Church:

> The Church is the Church only when it exists for others. To make a start, it should give away all its property to those in need. The clergy must live solely on the free-will offerings of their congregations, or possibly engage in some secular calling. The Church must share in the secular problems of ordinary human life, not dominating, but helping and serving.[42]

Perhaps readers of this book could take a moment and reflect on the ways in which the Church portrays its service model. A good exercise would be to enumerate the needs of one's own Church community which could be addressed more fully. This could be done in a community setting. Many people list the same areas that seem to be neglected in a specific community. Getting together and sharing thoughts on which areas need work in a community is a great exercise. It not only involves positive reflections, but permits an opportunity to identify community members' gifts and then outline the manner in which these gifts could be used in the community. Such mutual empowerment can be traced back to the type of ministries exercised in the early Church communities. I think the whole problem with the lack of vocations can be improved by involving more lay people to function within their communities given the talents they normally exercise in a secular setting. The Spirit is moving among Christians everywhere and is empowering individuals to serve as Christ did. Such a fostering of roles is evident from the *Vatican II* text *gaudium et spes*, which reads:

> Let the layman not imagine that his pastors are always such experts, that to every problem which arises, however complicated, they can readily give him a concrete solution, or even that such is their mission. Rather, enlightened by Christian wisdom and giving close attention to the teaching authority of the Church, let the layman take on his own distinctive role.[43]

Readers can decide for themselves if their Church community promotes this type of involvement. Prior to undertaking the question of vocations in the Roman Catholic Church, let us examine certain ministerial criteria outlined by contemporary scholarship.

A "Christian" Ministry of Service

At this point, let us briefly examine the ministerial models outlined by Bernard Cooke, Denise Lardner-Carmody and Edward Schillebeeckx, as their work in this field has greatly contributed to our modern understanding of the role of women in light of Christ's ministry of service. Let us commence with Bernard Cooke's discussion of the ministry of service.

Bernard Cooke. In his work *Ministry to Word and Sacraments*, Cooke maintains that any discussion of the ministry of service must begin by examining Jesus' mission. He therefore turns to scripture's characterization of Jesus as the "suffering servant." Although the latter is an Old Testament concept, Cooke observes that Jesus fulfilled all the criteria mentioned, and therefore realized all of the expectations in the Israelite tradition.

In the New Testament texts, the servant role is applied to his disciples as well, and is characteristic of the community leaders in Matthew 20.26-28. The text reads:

> It shall not be so among you; but whoever would be great among you must be your servant, and whoever would be first among you must be your slave; even as the son of man came not to be served but to serve, and to give his life as a ransom for many [RSV].

Cooke interprets this text to mean caring for the community in terms of a social responsibility which is rooted in the Old Testament understanding of the shepherding theme. In this setting, Jesus is the "good shepherd" himself who cares for His flock. This leadership characteristic is later handed down to his disciples, who exercised a leadership function in relation to Jesus' flock.

In terms of specific functions exercised, Cooke maintains that the shepherd's duties are in direct accordance with whatever the "flock" requires. Further, Cooke observes that the disciples are the flock and the shepherd simultaneously in that although Jesus remains the "great" shepherd, the disciples are to share His ministry in caring for the community. This model is certainly in keeping with Dulles' treatment of the Church as service. What is remarkable about both Cooke's and Dulles' comments is that they seem to be leaning towards an egalitarian Church structure which has no hierarchic power. The "power" as such is initiated within each Church community and parallels that of the early Church community's organizational character.

Another point which Cooke addresses has to do with forming church communities and keeping them together. As such, Cooke emphasizes the preservation of communities and the employing of gifts to unify the communities. In this setting, special charisms come from community members and are used to nurture that specific community.

At this point, Cooke calls our attention to the direct relationship between the ministry of service and the ministry of the word. Salvation comes from the word of God—Jesus. Faith in the word of God impacts healing and reconciliation. The ministry of service therefore provides a therapeutic action in Christ's name. Mental, spiritual and physical healing is derived from Christian service. The "service" of Christ's death reconciles man with God, himself and others. The disciples' service, therefore, is a reconciling task. To reconcile a community is to unify its character.[44]

6. A Contemporary Understanding of the Ordination of Women   131

A brief look at Cooke's treatment of the ministry of service can be summarized as follows: The ministry of service is rooted in Jesus' mission. The "servant" model is exemplified in the disciples' function as flock and shepherd. They become flock in that they represent Jesus' followers, and simultaneously shepherd as they are called to care for their respective communities. This includes a sharing of gifts for the unification and strengthening of the community. Further, the leaders are called to proclaim God's word, which is Jesus, from which healing and reconciliation occur. Jesus' ultimate "service" is manifested through his death and resurrection.

As Christians each individual is called forth to proclaim God's word and serve others. This implies a definite appropriation of gifts and a mutual empowerment. Cooke's treatment seems to be moving away from a Church whose organizational structure is hierarchic in character. Perhaps we should turn to Denise Lardner-Carmody's treatment of ministry as well as Schillebeeckx's before undertaking any further synopsis of Cooke's thought.

Denise Lardner-Carmody. In her work entitled *The Double-Cross: Ordination, Abortion and Catholic Feminism*, Lardner-Carmody begins her discussion of the ordination of women with a breakdown of the "service" aspect of ministry. Like Cooke, Lardner-Carmody professes that the leaders in the Church today should be the lowliest of servants. Since the past tradition in the Old Testament concept of priesthood was one of pomp and glory, the historicity of the priests' role became problematic. On the one hand, Lardner-Carmody states, their ministry was based on service. On the other, however, today's priesthood is often seen as an elite caste whose members are of a royal race. To reconcile the two images is quite impossible as the one negates the other. Perhaps we should continue with Lardner-Carmody's discussion prior to resolving these tensions.

She turns to a treatment of Christian ministry as service. Here, the names of three people readily come to her mind whose service to humanity exemplifies a Christian ministry. First, she mentions Pope John XXIII, who, according to Lardner-Carmody was a complete expression of God's love in his concern for "alienated" Catholics. Further, she stresses that he earned much respect for the humility which accompanied his pontifical authority. Second, she mentions the contribution of Martin Luther King, Jr., to the black communities as well as all oppressed peoples, in that he proclaimed himself as one of God's messengers and faithfully committed himself unto a sacrificial death. Third, she mentions Mother Teresa of Calcutta for her ministering service to the hopelessly sick and dying people of Calcutta, and her respect for all human life, no matter how meager. She identifies these three people because of their selflessness and their complete commitment to Christian service. We can all think of others who fit these criteria. She calls them "credible mediators of the power of Jesus' love" and presumes that women can qualify for such a priesthood.

Like Cooke, Lardner-Carmody defines three criteria suitable for Christian ministry. The first is preaching, in terms of proclaiming the Good News of Jesus Christ. This, she states, does not necessarily involve formal preaching or pulpit preaching. It has to do with seeking to abolish injustices that usually exhibit themselves among the poor and the oppressed. Few sermons touch on these subjects, she notes, primarily because the clergy do not experience these injustices firsthand. Viable preaching comes about when a group or individual seeks liberation from an oppressed state in light of the gospel. This type of preaching goes to the heart of the gospel.

The second criterion Lardner-Carmody mentions is celebrating. A Christian ministry should seek to celebrate the joy of the Good News and should celebrate the Eucharist as a liberating effect on our sinfulness. In Jesus, women can find liberation from oppressive hierarchic Church structures which perpetuate patriarchy and the sin of sexism.

Lardner-Carmody focuses, finally, on Christian ministry as healing. Although the sacrament of reconciliation has been limited to the priestly caste, she notes that women can be the agents of holistic healings—both of body and mind. The Spirit is moving women to reconcile the barriers that currently exclude them from the ministerial priesthood. This task can be expressed in various ways. Like Cooke, Lardner-Carmody calls for a reconciliation of community which would unify Christ's Church. This would probably involve a revision of the structural obstacles[45] that impede women's ordination.

In short, Lardner-Carmody's argument gives us an inkling of how the service model could enter the realms of Catholic priesthood. On the one hand, the image of servant and royalty must be reconciled. Perhaps Pope John XXIII exemplified an attempt to resolve this ambiguity when he called forth the Second Vatican Council. Certainly the Vatican texts bear witness to this fact.[46] The apparent lack of articulation of theories into practice however continues to burden Christ's Church. Lardner-Carmody's three criteria for Christian ministries—preaching, celebrating and reconciling, or healing—can all be manifested by women. Perhaps what needs to be most reconciled is the current hierarchic Church with that of Christ.

6. A Contemporary Understanding of the Ordination of Women 133

Edward Schillebeeckx. Let us now look at Schillebeeckx's treatment of the ministry of service in his work *The Church with a Human Face.* His observations are of a more practical nature. His discussion reiterates various concerns I noted earlier in this work. Notably, the idea that the ministry of word becomes completely schismatized from the sacraments, especially when the Church is currently experiencing a shortage of priests. In this setting, some parishes only celebrate the Eucharist a few times a year, more churches are being shut down and people are required to travel to neighboring towns to celebrate the Mass. Schillebeeckx also draws our attention to the phenomenon which occurs when various people journey with the sick and the dying, only to be replaced by a "stranger" who comes to administer last rites.[47]

I observe that Catholics are not only deprived of the sacraments because of the apparent shortage of priests. I think one should also consider the "ministering" functions of priests. I am referring to the ministering that usually arises vis-à-vis the sick, the bereaved, the separated and divorced, teens in turmoil, and others who are troubled. Granted, many parishes have various support groups which function very well. My point is that this is another area where the ministry of word and sacrament is separated because many pastoral assistants are not permitted to administer the sacraments.

Schillebeeckx articulates this very point quite well. His discussion turns to the notion of ordaining pastoral workers as deacons. The drawbacks involved in such an undertaking, he states, are that most deacons are already involved in secular careers and could not devote the time that the ministerial diaconate demands. Further, he notes, most deacons lack theological training perhaps because of their secular professions.

Therefore, Schillebecckx offers two alternatives. Either the whole ministerial aspect of the diaconate could be revised to include more theological training or a fourth ministry could arise which would supplement the episcopate, presbyterate and diaconate.[48] I observe that these alternatives would require some type of official designation. Unless the Vatican is prepared to completely revise the diaconate, such a practice would obviously exclude women. Since the diaconate program is currently carte blanche for married men, another injustice would prevail.

In short, Schillebeeckx finds it would greatly benefit the Church if more people were involved with the ministerial functions. All Christians are called through baptism to develop their gifts for the building up of Christ's Church. Certainly, Schillebeeckx's description would assist the conflicts which emerge in light of the current shortage of priests. This could not possibly be realized, however, unless the Vatican decided to officially recognize the ministry of women to its fullest. Vatican II called for a revival of the People of God, rooted in each individual's baptismal calling. If every individual has a specific vocation to fulfill, I observe that to limit the potentialities of that gift is sexist and discriminatory.

After having briefly examined the ministry of service according to Avery Dulles, Bernard Cooke, Denise Lardner-Carmody and Edward Schillebeeckx, the common theme that emerged throughout was the ministerial "calling" of each individual in any given community. Cooke especially touched upon the structure of the current Catholic Church, in comparison to the early Christian communities which functioned on an egalitarian plane. Cooke is not denying that a Church should have formal leaders. His argument leans, however, towards a mutual empowerment and leadership within certain communities based on an identification of gifts. Perhaps this would be a good time to introduce the area of vocations as perceived by the Roman Catholic Church, while keeping in mind the characteristics which my study of the ministry of service entailed.

The Official Teaching on Vocations

Perhaps the official teaching on vocations would be a good place to start. There are two expressions under which a vocation can be manifest: religious and clerical. The latter refers to a churchly office, whereas the former refers to the state of life which an individual can pursue. Basically, the nature of a vocation has two distinct qualities: divine and ecclesiastical. The divine has to do with a special calling whereas the ecclesiastical value has to do with a validation from Church authorities who then discern if the calling is authentic and provide certain direction to the individual in question. Marriage is also deemed an authentic vocation in that one's body is given to Christ as well as virginity, where the gift of one's body is reserved for Christ.

There are two obligations which arise when a vocation is to be followed. First, one must have received a call from within. Second, the denial or rejection of a divine calling is deemed sinful.[49]

Further, Vatican II has documented certain criteria for vocations in its *Decree on the Missionary Activity of the Church*.[50] The section on "missionaries" reads as follows:

6. A Contemporary Understanding of the Ordination of Women

> Every disciple of Christ has the obligation to do his part in spreading the faith. Yet Christ the Lord always calls whomever He chooses from among the number of His disciples, to be with Him and to be sent by Him to preach to the nations (cf. Mark 3.13f.). Therefore, through the Holy Spirit who distributes His charismatic gifts as He wills for the common good (cf. 1 Corinthians 12.11), Christ inspires the missionary vocation in the hearts of individuals.[51]

Such criteria seem inclusive of men and women. Given my discussion of the roles of women in Jesus' ministry in Chapter 2 of this work, contemporary scholarship has maintained that women were at the forefront of Jesus' ministry. Certainly women fulfilled the necessary criteria to be considered Jesus' disciples. Further, if the Spirit truly moves freely among Christians and bestows certain gifts for the benefit of Christian communities, certainly this freedom is devoid of any sexual distinction. Legitimate vocations, however, seem to be bound by this very distinction.

> For there are certain priests, religious and lay*men* who are prepared to undertake mission work ... who are endowed with the appropriate *natural* dispositions, character, and talent.[52]

Apparently, vocations undertake a hierarchic structure: priests, religious, then lay*men*. What of women? Does "appropriate natural disposition" have to do with the physical, bodily characteristics that a woman does not possess? Truly, women were among the group of Jesus' disciples in the Upper Room when the Holy Spirit came among them (cf. Acts 2.1-4). Male and female Catholics receive the Holy Spirit when they are baptized and united within Christ's mystical body. If the Holy Spirit bestows gifts upon men and women alike, the Roman Catholic Church must come to terms with the Spirit's action within women. To deny these gifts, denies the effects of the sacrament of baptism itself.

The "Vocations" Prayer. The same inconsistencies between what the church maintains in theory and what it maintains in practice are manifested in the "vocations" prayer. Written in 1983, this prayer is required to be used by every parish in the Winnipeg diocese. It reads as follows:

> O God, who have chosen the apostles to make disciples of all nations and who by Baptism and confirmation have called all of us to build up your Holy Church, we earnestly implore you to choose from among us, your children, many Priests, Deacons and Religious Brothers and Sisters who will love you with their whole heart and will gladly spend their entire lives to make you known and loved by all.[53]

Although the prayer seems very inclusive at the outset ("all of us"), the pyramidal structure maintains ("Priests, Deacons and Religious Brothers and Sisters"). Such a structure remains a barrier for women who truly feel the Spirit calling. It makes me wonder why the hierarchy continues to allow women's baptism, when it clearly denies the special graces that accompany the sacrament.

The Problem with the Lack of Vocations in the Roman Catholic Church. When regarding the apparent lack of vocations in the Roman Catholic Church, a common misconception is that Catholics have an attitude problem with the official Church. Who would want to associate with all the problems and scandals that the modern Church is experiencing? I observe that in order for people to change their attitude about the Roman Catholic Church, the Church must also change.

Significantly, the Church has prided itself in personifying strength, power and discipline. The Church that our contemporary world experiences is weak and vulnerable. Yet throughout all the scandals and all the conflicts, the Church appears strong and unscathed to many of the faithful. In order for people to change their attitudes about the Church, I observe that the Church must be true to itself and honest with the rest of the world. It is no longer acceptable to simply cover up the tragedies that have occurred. The Church must come to terms with its imperfections and deal with them before it has only a hierarchy and no faithful to support it.

What I am supporting is a process of self-examination that would consider several aspects of the Church's past and present. Although various conflicts need to be examined, for the purposes of this study, I will focus at this time on the place of women in the Church.

Towards a Renewal of the Hierarchy. On the whole, a look at the hierarchic order in the Church needs careful consideration. Without a doubt, any structure needs leadership and people in authority. But even a democracy has shown the importance of equal representation among leaders. For example, the Church claims to have the authority to pronounce official statements regarding family life and marriage. Yet, the clergy who are involved in the preparation of these documents have no notion of family life (excluding their own up-bringing) and no notion of what dynamics are involved in maintaining a healthy marriage. I admit that priests are being sought for counseling and through the sacrament of penance get an idea of the kinds of strains a marriage and family life can experience. However, I observe that since encyclicals like *Humanae Vitae* were published, the Church's faithful have been reluctant to confront clergy, much less to experience the sacrament of penance because fewer people agree with the Church's teaching on areas affecting their moral lives of which Church authorities have little knowledge.

A renewal of the hierarchy would also call for equal representation. That involves men and women priests. It is not enough to simply "consult" the lay faithful (i.e., women) at times of discussion, because the ultimate authority in the Church today lies with celibate, unwed men—the encyclical published in 1987 on the lay faithful is proof of this. One will recall that although lay people were consulted, including married women, not only were the propositions concerning women absent from the final draft, the report did not contain the information given by the Canadian bishops, and therefore gave Archbishop Chiasson the impression that the final report had been compiled prior to the Synod.[54] Women also have viable experiences and concerns that can contribute to the Church's perspective on modern life. In short, in order for the Church to remain truly relevant for its people, it has to look beyond the theological impediments that, in terms of the hierarchy's understanding, must be maintained.

The Legitimate Call to Vocation. The area of vocations also needs to be reconsidered:

> Spirit renewing the earth, renewing the hearts of all people; Burn in the weary soul, blow through the silent lips, come now awake us![55]

I observe that in coming to terms with the Spirit, the Church must remain open to what the Spirit is telling it. In short, Catholics must look at the conflicts that their modern-day Church is experiencing and seek to resolve them, not by covering up faults, but by looking at the root causes of failures. If the Church truly desires to remain credible to itself, it has to remain open to the people who are being called. Women have viable gifts and are being called to service. The Church has to acknowledge that call and permit women to undertake serious leadership and authoritative positions. By saying "no" to women priests, the Church is stifling the Spirit.

How can people become more accepting of the Church if the Church itself fails to acknowledge the gifts that women have? The Church emphasizes a "fundamental equality" among the People of God. Can the Church really remain credible for its people if it continues to exclude women from the ministerial priesthood on the basis of their sex?

Equal But Different. We have previously discussed the notion that although men and women are considered equal, they are nevertheless called to perform different duties in the building up of Christ's Church. I reiterate at this time that in terms of roles, women in the early Church did not seem to have been excluded from performing roles that were later exercised by priests. Despite their apparent biological function, women led house church assemblies and still today lead prayer services, lay liturgies and the like. The argument which stems from a woman's biological function seems to indicate that a woman is incapable of accomplishing any tasks outside her role as wife and mother. The position in which women find themselves today demonstrates that women are capable of maintaining successful authoritative careers while continuing to care for their husbands and families.

In terms of pastoral care, the role of the priest is becoming more and more marginal. In my discussion of the ministry of service, I observed that fewer parishes enjoy the ongoing availability of a pastor. By and large, people are being ministered to by women who make themselves readily available. They care for people who have pastoral concerns, yet they are incapable of administering the sacraments which ultimately convey God's love and healing. This is exercised by a "stranger" who visits only to administer the sacraments. As is the case with last rites, the person who administers the sacrament is a stranger—unlike the person who journeyed faithfully with the sick, the lonely and the dying.[56]

The Spiritual Effects of Women's Exclusion from the Ministerial Priesthood

Sandra M. Schneiders, in an article entitled "The Effects of Women's Experience on Their Spirituality,"[57] has documented certain effects that women's exclusion exhibits among certain aspects of women's spirituality. Although it is not my intent here to commence a lengthy discussion regarding Schneiders' perspective, I see some value in outlining her thought as my discussion of women's vocation and ministry to the priesthood directly concerns her agenda.

Schneiders' main focus is to discuss the effects of "male dominance" on women's spirituality. She does so by examining four dimensions of women's experience and then provides certain advantages that women have gained despite the effects of male dominating forces. From a ministerial perspective, she claims the denial of women to priestly roles has led to a spiritual "trauma" regarding the nurturing and development of young girls. In such a setting, they were socialized to envision a future of "nonpublic" roles in which women appeared as "male-dependent."[58] Schneiders indicates that the effects of women's exclusion from ministerial roles contribute to women's loss of self-worth and reinforces

6. A Contemporary Understanding of the Ordination of Women 139

their subordinate roles. The advantage in all of this, Schneiders contends, is that women are displaying and articulating the "servant" qualities of Jesus' ministry, and as a result respond to the needs of the oppressed in a more volatile and compassionate manner. To use her words:

> ... those who have been persecuted, humiliated, undervalued, and denied their rightful place in the society of the Church are singularly well equipped for identification with the great Minister, Jesus, who was himself a simple layman persecuted and disowned by the religious authorities of his day and who found in his solidarity with the poor and the unrecognized—the basis for a nonritualized ministry of personal service characterized by a gentleness and a powerlessness that were singularly revelatory of the true God.[59]

Schneiders' second element has to do with the effects of socialization. On a social scale, she notes that women are excluded from contributing to matters that directly affect them. For example, women are not consulted when Church policies are being formed, writers of Church documents relating to social problems do not invite women to share their thoughts, and even canon law is written and enforced by male voices. This leads to a lack of creativity for women and they begin to accept the monopoly of male authority figures for whom they work on a social level—to the point where they become more comfortable with male leaders. The benefit in all of this is that women have less difficulty including men and accepting them as partners and that women's adjustment to public secular roles is much easier than men's.

Third, Schneiders treats the effects of a masculine religious experience on the spirituality of women. In this setting, women are conditioned by a male mindset. Confessors, counselors and for the most part, theologians, remain male, who impart masculine spiritual practices. For example, apart from Mary of Nazareth, most of the role models in the Church remain men. The psychological advantage here, Schneiders contends, is that women can readily "...integrate the contrasexual side of [their] personality."[60] In contrast, men are taught to repress their feminine sides and become ashamed when "feminine" characteristics emerge in their personalities. This dynamic also enters the spiritual realm in that women have less difficulty coming to terms with their male spirituality because they have been so conditioned to submit to male images. Men who come to terms with their feminine spirituality often suppress their feelings and negate what they experience.[61]

Lastly, Schneiders treats the effects of an exclusively male God on women's spirituality. Although scripture describes God in masculine and feminine terms, women have been socialized to associate men only with the divine. This notion is also reflected in family life, where the father is considered the more dominant of the two parents and is usually the family head. Such a setting has left women no direct access to God other than through men. For example, Schneiders contends that all sacraments are administered by men and marital conflicts within a religious sphere are usually settled by a man (i.e., a male perspective). The positive aspects, Schneiders maintains, are that women have a better perception of God's "otherness" and transcendence, and are less "condemning" of other people. For example, clergy usually take it upon themselves to decide who should or should not receive the sacraments. Schneiders contends this results from man's association with the divine. Women, on the other hand, are less judgmental and have become more prayerful because access to the divine when one prays does not require a clerical intervention.[62]

Given Schneiders' discussion of the effects of the four elements treated on women's spirituality, I observe that the male dominating forces from a spiritual perspective also affect a woman's nurturing as well as her socialization. Despite the various advantages or benefits that have emerged, Schneiders repeatedly points out that she in no way condones such a pattern. Although certain effects Schneiders treats have already been touched upon in Chapter 5 (e.g., the effects of women's socialization in the workplace), the insights she offers in terms of a spiritual as well as a psychological level are very remarkable. She leaves me with a sense that everything women experience is directly related to her spiritual experience of a male-dominating pattern. Certainly, Schneiders' treatment of the effects on women's spirituality goes beyond women's exclusion from the ministerial priesthood. Perhaps if this vision were realized, it would also help correct other areas where women appear as the weaker parent, the submissive coworker, the emotional girlfriend, the battered wife, and so on.

Throughout this book, I have addressed the impediments which women experience from being full participants in Christ's Church. I have labeled this patriarchy, sexism, clericalism, elitism and discrimination. Perhaps, it would be appropriate to complete this work with a discussion which would focus on a liberation theology for women which would seek to outline a positive option for women who have been oppressed and socialized into thinking that God "revealed" the hierarchalism which predominates Christ's current Church.

A Theology of Liberation from Clericalism

> The Gospel has a sacred reverence for the dignity of conscience and its freedom of choice, constantly advises that all human talents be employed in God's service and men's and finally, commends all to the charity of all.[63]

Despite the egalitarian tone of this Vatican II passage, women have clearly no chance at serving Christ's Church, as long as they remain excluded from the ministerial priesthood. In Chapter 5 of this book, I spoke about a mutual empowering of men and women which stemmed from the service model of the early Christian community.

From a theological perspective, I also stated that only men are associated with the divine, and women remain in a subordinate position. The mutual empowering of men and women has to do with liberating oneself from a patriarchal and clerical Church. Men and women become disempowered within the Church's sacramentality, its teaching and its administration. In such a setting, the Church becomes identified with an "ecclesiastical superstructure" which promotes discrimination against women and upholds domination, control and clericalism. Rosemary Radford Ruether maintains that

> Instead, ministry must be understood as the means by which the community itself symbolizes its common life to itself and articulates different aspects of its need to empower and express that common life.[64]

Certainly Ruether touches upon the same criteria for ministry which Cooke, Schillebeeckx and Lardner-Carmody have, but she and Schüssler-Fiorenza have taken this entire discussion one step further. Ruether suggests that a liberation from clericalism involves a reclaiming of sacramental life. She begins with a process of reappropriating the sacrament of baptism as a conversion to an authenticity that has its own foundation. This conversion finds its own ground and is articulated within communal life. Although some type of leadership is necessary in any given community, Ruether holds that the authentic leadership originates once a certain community can assess its own values and gifts. In this manner a variety of needs can be engaged in, given the specific resources among community members. This way, the "leader" of the community does not have to master or engage in a number of ministries extending beyond his or her capacities or gifts. This type of ministry-sharing would also ensure that anyone would have the opportunity to contribute to the life of the community. Ruether contends that the function of a minister is to "teach" and "equip" the community with the necessary direction to fulfill their gifts.⁶⁵ She seems to suggest that this process can take place within the Roman Catholic Church structure or at least in such a setting that the Church can be made aware of it, for it is within a Church community setting that Catholics are socialized, and such an undertaking would have little impact on the structural organization of the Church if ministry is exercised autonomously.

Ruether's declericalizing process calls for a restructuring of the hierarchy and rethinking of the whole concept of ministry. Her process begins with the community members and ministry is exercised "from below." Such a conversion would be more appropriate within the Church itself and has endless possibilities. It involves a claiming of ourselves as a baptized People of God and a conversion of mentality regarding the whole function of Christ's Church here on earth. Such ministry is highly possible given the current shortage of priests. Although Ruether asserts that leadership is important for the unifying character in any given community, the skills required to consecrate the Eucharist are very minimal compared to those necessary to exercise other ministerial functions.⁶⁶ The leadership role in Ruether's process is more of a facilitator than a power monger. Certainly the only skills that women lack according to the Roman Catholic Church have to do with their biology.

Elisabeth Schüssler-Fiorenza has also described this process of self-awareness for men and women within the Roman Catholic Church setting. The *ekklēsia* of women or the concept of women-church is based on an awareness that men and women are Christ's Church. The word *ekklēsia* from the Greek refers to "...the public gathering of free citizens who assemble in order to determine their own and their children's communal well-being."⁶⁷ The women-church paradigm has to do with a conversion to discipleship to an egalitarian community which Jesus established. Schüssler-Fiorenza calls for an "equality from below" much like Ruether described a ministry from below. The former contends this conversion is also one of liberation for men and women from a hierarchic Church which remains patriarchal, oppressive and clerical.

The word of God is liberating if we remain open to the power of Jesus' love. This love was and still is based on a giving of oneself. The power of salvation

> ... is challenging us to be what we are capable of becoming, making us aware of potentialities we never dreamt we had, and providing resources of personal growth that by ourselves alone we would not have.⁶⁸

6. A Contemporary Understanding of the Ordination of Women

A reclaiming of ourselves in the face of a power structure like the Roman Catholic Church is a challenging task. It involves a transformation of power to a ministering service of love. We've already begun to see the impact of the shortage of priests upon our Church communities. Perhaps this is a "sign of the times" that a restructuring of the Church and a reclaiming of the egalitarian structure Jesus initiated in the early Christian communities is in order. Once men and women come to this stage of awareness and begin to identify their gifts, perhaps the Spirit of Christ will enable us to give from within.[69]

Conclusion

In this work, I have tried to move beyond the traditional arguments for the exclusion of women from the ministerial priesthood in the Roman Catholic Church. To do so, I have challenged the arguments presented in the *Declaration on the Question of the Admission of Women to the Ministerial Priesthood* and attempted to demonstrate that the use of contemporary scholarship is essential when regarding biblical texts that deal with women.

Having examined the role of women in the ministry of Jesus in Chapter 2, I observed that apart from the Twelve whose historicity can be challenged, Jesus did not exclude women from performing leadership roles. In fact, he commissioned Mary Magdalene to relate the news of his resurrection to the Twelve. She was accorded an official and public role. The notion that Christ "willed" that only men be priests because he commissioned twelve men to become his apostles cannot be maintained. A reading of the gospels demonstrates the conflicts that arise when coming to terms with what Jesus said and willed and to what extent the gospel writers authentically reflect Jesus' message.

Likewise, a reading of the texts that have been used in the *Declaration* to support the argument which favors the exclusion of women from the ministerial priesthood are equally controversial. Problems of biblical authorship recur, and it is quite difficult to assess the writer's main intent. With the assistance of contemporary feminist scholarship in the scriptural field, I observed that the texts that the *Declaration* used to support the arguments presented appear quite selective. When taken in the context of the letter as a whole, for example, the restrictions imposed upon women tend to deal with a particular situation in which proper order should be maintained. In this sense, extracting a specific instruction for women and judging this to be the norm for a long period of time remain absurd.

Having examined several Pauline texts that treat the role of women in an early church setting, I observed that women seemed to exercise various authoritative functions which men seemed comfortable with. In this sense, women exercised roles that were later performed by priests. When the Church became structured and conformed with the organizational model of the Roman empire in which women were restricted from holding any authoritative or leadership positions, the Church excluded women from authoritative roles in the worship community. How can this practice be considered a revelatory tradition in which God conveyed that only men be priests, if it is obvious that the early Church accorded roles to women that were later performed by priests? Given Mary Ann Rossi's work in this field, the exclusion of women priests cannot be viewed as a "constant" tradition, much less the will of Christ.

In Chapter 4, I focused on the roles that have been accorded to the lay faithful and noted that there is an apparent distinction between the roles that have been accorded to lay men and lay women. Again, I observed a contradiction of the term "fundamental equality" in that, although all the faithful are coresponsible in the building up of Christ's Church, there exists an apparent hierarchy in which clergy maintain the authority, lay men are allowed only certain duties, and lay women are permitted even fewer. If the contemporary Catholic Church could overcome the barriers that restrict lay women from performing duties comparable to lay men's (as they did in the early Christian community), it would definitely facilitate the ordination of women. Therefore, in an attempt to move beyond the injustices that restrict women from becoming priests, the Church must begin by correcting every level of the pyramidal structure. In this sense, women who feel they have been called to serve Christ's Church in a particular manner can be liberated in accepting the call.

On a pastoral note, statistics indicate that the number of available candidates to the priesthood is declining from year to year; and a couple of decades into the 21st century, if this decline continues, many parishes will have no priests. Already, women are ministering in parishes where the priest appears almost in the form of a "magician" who celebrates the essential sacraments and then goes on his way. In this setting, the priest's actions are being detached from the word of God in the sense that the ministry of word and sacrament is broken.[1]

Despite this apparent shortage of priests, the exclusion of women from the priesthood remains a serious injustice in the Roman Catholic Church. If Jesus chose only twelve men to be among his apostles and if women are not part of the Last Supper, the Roman Catholic Church is communicating that women are to be excluded from the Eucharist and from salvation. For reasons already stated this perspective is unacceptable.

I have tried to outline various aspects of the Church that require reconsideration and renewal. In doing so, I have maintained that women also have viable gifts to offer and that by impeding these gifts, the Roman Catholic Church continues to stifle the role of the Spirit which guides Christ's Church. To quote Elisabeth Schüssler-Fiorenza:

> Christian spirituality means eating together, sharing together, drinking together, talking with each other, receiving each other, experiencing God's presence through each other, and, in doing so, proclaiming the gospel as God's alternate vision for everyone, especially for those who are poor, outcast, and battered. As long as women Christians are excluded from breaking the bread and deciding their own spiritual welfare and commitment, *ekklēsia* as the discipleship of equals is not realized and the power of the gospel is greatly diminished.[2]

At this point my attention shifted from a ministry from above to a ministry from below. If men and women are reclaiming the gifts bestowed upon them at baptism, the initiation must come from below. Although many priests, bishops[3] and Catholic theologians[4] have strongly encouraged the hierarchy to become more inclusive regarding ministries for women as well as positions for women in administrative functions within the Church, the hierarchy has refused to reconsider the teaching put forth in the *Declaration* of 1976. Perhaps when the shortage of priests becomes so extreme that only the faithful remain—along with a few "token" priests, Church communities will undergo a radical transformation which will enable a mutual empowerment among the faithful and a metanoïa towards building a community that Christ truly intended. It would be very unfortunate if the official Church refused to acknowledge women priests until this time as many communities today lack the fruits of the gifts that are already within their midst.

Chapter Notes

1. The Ordination of Women

1. Leonard Swidler and Arlene Swidler, eds., *Women Priests: A Catholic Commentary on the Vatican Declaration* (New York: Paulist Press, 1974), p. 38.

2. The Biblical Commission is an advisory committee, "established in order to oversee proper biblical interpretation and to foster biblical studies." Swidler and Swidler, p. 38. The Commission was asked to study the exclusion of women from the ministerial priesthood from a biblical perspective.

3. John R. Donahue, "A Tale of Two Documents," in Swidler and Swidler, p. 25.

4. Swidler and Swidler, pp. 341-342.

5. *Ibid.*, p. 344.

6. Donahue, "A Tale of Two Documents," p. 28.

7. Swidler and Swidler, p. 40.

8. Patrick J. Dunn, *Priesthood: A Re-examination of the Roman Catholic Theology of the Presbyterate* (New York: Alba House, 1990), p. 45.

9. *Ibid.*, p. 235.

10. *Ibid.*, p. 124.

11. Pope John Paul II, *On the Dignity and Vocation of Women on the Occasion of the Marian Year* (Rome: Vatican Polygot Press, 1988), pp. 96-98.

12. *Ibid.*, p. 97.

13. *Ibid.*, p. 98.

14. For the dynamic between the rise of various customs (which can be designated as traditions) and the emergence of an authoritative interpretation of the implicit intent of Jesus (called Tradition), see Elisabeth Schüssler-Fiorenza, *In Memory of Her: A Feminist Theological Reconstruction of Christian Origins* (New York: Crossroad, 1983), pp. 14-21.

15. Raymond E. Brown, *Priest and Bishop, Biblical Reflections* (New York: Paulist Press, 1970), p. 18.

16. Elizabeth Tetlow, *Women and Ministry in the New Testament* (New York: Paulist Press, 1980), p. 49.

17. Donahue, "A Tale of Two Documents," p. 30.

18. *Ibid.*, p. 38.

19. Francine Cardman, "Tradition, Hermeneutics and Ordination," in James A. Coriden, ed., *Sexism and Church Law* (New York: Paulist Press, 1977), p. 63.

20. Joseph Komonchak, "Theological Questions on the Ordination of Women," *Catholic Mind* 75 (Jan. 1977), p. 25.
21. Rosemary Radford Ruether, "Women Priests and Church Tradition," in Swidler and Swidler, p. 236.
22. Karen Torjesen has argued that "the *Statutes of the Apostles* show that women also shared in the eucharistic ministry," in "The Early Controversies Over Female Leadership," *Christian History* 8, no. 1 (Issue 17), p. 24.
23. Elizabeth Carroll, "Women and Ministry," *Theological Studies* 36 (Dec. 1975), p. 673.
24. Rosemary Radford Ruether, "The Roman Catholic Story," in Rosemary Radford Ruether and Eleanor McLaughlin, eds., *Women of Spirit: Female Leadership in the Jewish & Christian Traditions* (New York: Simon & Schuster, 1979), p. 380.
25. Cardman, p. 68.
26. That is, with the exception of calling twelve male disciples to be a part of the official apostles. This notion will be given further consideration at a later time.
27. Edward J. Kilmartin, "Full Participation of Women in the Life of the Catholic Church," in James A. Coriden, ed., *Sexism and Church Law*, p. 127.
28. Rosemary Radford Ruether, *Sexism and God-Talk: Toward a Feminist Theology* (Boston: Beacon Press, 1983), p. 207.
29. It should be stressed that the use of the term "patriarchy" here does not intend a specific link with Judaism.
30. Swidler and Swidler, p. 39.
31. *Ibid.*, p. 40.
32. Sandra M. Schneiders has also noted this ambiguity in the sense that the *Declaration* fails to indicate "on what grounds it has decided that the behavior of Jesus in the matter of choosing the Twelve is binding insofar as it touches on the sex of the Twelve but not insofar as it touches on their race, ethnic identity, age, or other characteristics," in "Did Jesus Exclude Women from Priesthood?" in Swidler and Swidler, p. 227.
33. Bernard Cooke, *Ministry to Word and Sacraments* (Philadelphia: Fortress Press, 1976), p. 531.
34. Swidler and Swidler, p. 41.
35. Schneiders, "Did Jesus Exclude Women from Priesthood?" p. 231.
36. For further treatment, see Brown, *Priest and Bishop*, pp. 54–55.
37. Swidler and Swidler, p. 40.
38. *Ibid.*
39. Madeleine I. Boucher, "Women in the Apostolic Community," in Swidler and Swidler, p. 153.
40. Rosemary Radford Ruether, *New Woman/New Earth: Sexist Ideologies and Human Liberation* (New York: Seabury Press, 1975), pp. 74–75.
41. Pope John Paul II, *On the Dignity and Vocation of Women on the Occasion of the Marian Year*, p. 43.
42. Swidler and Swidler, p. 43.
43. *Ibid.*, p. 36.
44. Sonya A. Quitslund, "In the Image of Christ," in Swidler and Swidler, p. 263.
45. Swidler and Swidler, p. 43.

46. Quitslund, p. 263.
47. Sr. Joan Chittister, *Women, Ministry and the Church* (New York: Paulist Press, 1983), p. 100.
48. William J. Mc Donald et al., eds., *New Catholic Encyclopedia* (Washington, D.C.: Catholic University of America), vol. 7, p. 413.
49. Margaret Farley, "Moral Imperatives for the Ordination of Women," in Anne Marie Gardiner, ed., *Women and Catholic Priesthood: An Expanded Vision* (New York: Paulist Press, 1978), p. 40.
50. Rosemary Radford Ruether, "Ordination, What Is the Problem?" in Gardiner, pp. 31–32.
51. Swidler and Swidler, p. 44.
52. John R. Donahue, "Women, Priesthood and the Vatican," in *America* (April 2, 1977), p. 287.
53. Boucher, p. 155.
54. Ida Raming, *The Exclusion of Women from the Priesthood: Divine Law or Sex Discrimination,* transl. Norman R. Adams (Metuchen, N.J.: Scarecrow Press, 1976), see p. ix.
55. *Ibid.,* p. xiii.
56. Farley, p. 41.
57. Elizabeth Schüssler-Fiorenza, "Women Apostles: The Testament of Scripture," in Gardiner, p. 97.
58. Thomas Hopko, "On the Male Character of the Christian Priesthood," in Thomas Hopko, ed., *Women and the Priesthood* (New York: St. Vladimir's Seminary Press, 1983), pp. 97, 124.
59. *Ibid.,* pp. 111–112.
60. Swidler and Swidler, p. 44.
61. *Ibid.*
62. Boucher, pp. 154–155.
63. Walter M. Abbott, S.J., ed., *The Documents of Vatican II* (New York: Guild Press, 1966), p. 534.
64. For a good discussion of the theological problem with an exclusively male hierarchy, see Rosemary Radford Ruether, "The Female Nature of God: A Problem in Contemporary Religious Life," in "God as Father?" *Concilium,* vol. 143 (1981), pp. 61–66.
65. Monsignor Desmond Connell, "Women Priests: Why Not?" in Helmut Moll, ed., *The Church and Women: A Compendium* (San Francisco: Ignatius Press, 1988), p. 223.
66. For a good discussion of the "imageo dei" title, see Farley, pp. 35–51.
67. R.A. Norris, Jr., "The Ordination of Women and the Maleness of Christ," in Monica Furlong, ed., *Feminine in the Church* (London: SPCK, 1984), p. 81.
68. *Ibid.*
69. Cooke, *Ministry to Word and Sacraments,* p. 656.
70. Komonchak, p. 20.
71. *Ibid.*
72. *Ibid.*
73. Radford Ruether, *New Woman/New Earth,* p. 66.
74. Sidney Callahan, "Misunderstanding of Sexuality and Resistance to Women Priests," in Swidler and Swidler, p. 292.

75. Arthur A. Vogel, "Christ, Revelation and the Ordination of Women," in Marianne H. Micks and Charles P. Price, eds., *Toward a New Theology of Ordination: Essays on the Ordination of Women* (Somerville, Mass.: Greeno, Hadden, 1976), pp. 43–44.
76. Komonchak, p. 22.
77. Radford Ruether, "The Female Nature of God," pp. 65–66.
78. Swidler and Swidler, p. 43.
79. Komonchak, p. 22.
80. Chittister, *Women, Ministry and the Church*, p. 101.
81. Mc Donald et al., vol. 9, p. 415.
82. Chittister, *Women, Ministry and the Church*, p. 100.
83. John A. Hardon, *The Catholic Catechism* (Garden City, N.Y.: Doubleday, 1975), p. 521.
84. *Ibid.*
85. Mc Donald et al., vol. 11, p. 773.
86. Chittister, *Women, Ministry and the Church*, p. 100.
87. Connell, p. 221.
88. Cooke, *Ministry to Word and Sacraments*, p. 655.
89. Swidler and Swidler, p. 38.
90. *Ibid.*, p. 46.
91. *Ibid.*, p. 44.
92. *Ibid.*
93. *Ibid.*
94. Komonchak, p. 21.
95. Norris, p. 44.
96. Mc Donald et al., vol. 7, p. 413.
97. Vogel, p. 44.
98. Swidler and Swidler, p. 39.
99. Brown, *Priest and Bishop*, pp. 13–20.
100. Swidler and Swidler, p. 39.
101. *Ibid.*, p. 37.
102. Radford Ruether claims that Karl Rahner condemned the Declaration as "heretical" in *To Change the World: Christology and Cultural Criticism* (New York: Crossroad, 1981), p. 47. She also states that members of a Jesuit School of Theology in Berkeley "sent a statement directly to the Pope pointing out the historical, scriptural and theological untenability of the statement"; see Radford Reuther, ed., *Women of Spirit*, pp. 380–381.

2. Women in the Ministry of Jesus

1. Leonard Swidler has affirmed that "the status of women in Palestine during the time of Jesus was very decidedly that of inferiors." "Jesus Was a Feminist," in *Catholic World* (Jan. 1971), p. 178.
2. Schüssler-Fiorenza, "Women in the Early Christian Movement," in Carol P. Christ and Judith Plaskow, eds., *Womanspirit Rising: A Feminist Reader in Religion* (San Francisco: Harper and Row, 1979), p. 88.
3. These presuppositions stem from the Catholic understanding of Jesus of Nazareth. I am using these criteria as a basis for my interpretation of the role of women in the ministry of Jesus. Their significance will be explained as my

discussion of women unfolds. For a good discussion of the "historical" Jesus from a Christian perspective, see Edward Schillebeeckx, *The Church with a Human Face* (New York: Crossroad, 1985), Part One.

4. The *Declaration* stresses that although women were quite inferior in Jesus' culture, "his attitude towards women was quite different from that of his milieu, he deliberately and courageously broke with it"; Swidler and Swidler, pp. 38-39. From these observations, I maintain that the Roman Catholic Church has acknowledged that patriarchy was one of the cultural influences that affected the New Testament writers. The significance of this concept will be addressed when regarding the centrality of Jesus' maleness. For a good discussion of the implications which emerge and the pitfalls to avoid when patriarchal language is used to describe Jesus' cultural milieu, see Schüssler-Fiorenza, *In Memory of Her: A Feminist Theological Reconstruction of Christian Origins* (New York: Crossroad, 1983), pp. 106-110.

5. The significance of the Doctrine of the Incarnation has been discussed in Chapter One. I am reiterating this concept to emphasize that Jesus was nonetheless restricted to the limitations of his cultural milieu. In this sense, the delivery of his message would have been subject to the limitations of the conditions surrounding that very culture. Therefore, when one seeks to interpret Jesus' treatment of women, one must bear these aspects in mind.

6. This notion should be kept in mind when discussing Jesus' calling of the Twelve. The significance of choosing twelve male apostles to carry on his work has historical implications.

7. Several feminists have completely rejected Christianity because of Christ's maleness. In my opinion, the very fact that Christ was a male is central to his ministry—especially when discussing the roles he prescribed for women.

8. Swidler and Swidler, p. 44.

9. See Letha Scanzoni and Nancy Hardesty, *All We're Meant to Be* (Waco, Texas: Word Books, 1974), Chapter Five. Although women were considered "unclean" during menstruation and after childbirth, in Mark 5.25-27, Jesus heals a woman who has been suffering from a hemorrhage for the last twelve years. Not only did she physically suffer but this woman had become a social outcast. Further, as noted by Judith Sanderson, "Jesus and Women," in *The Other Side* (July/Aug. 1973), p. 20, "she was not allowed to take part in any religious proceedings, could not come into the temple, could not touch other persons and had to be separated from her husband. She was a despised and solitary woman." Of significance here is Jesus' attitude toward her. After she simply touches his clothes, Jesus publicly insists on knowing who this woman is. In doing so, Jesus praises her for her faith and demonstrates that "her violation of that taboo i.e., the restriction concerning an unclean woman led to her healing."

10. Scanzoni and Hardesty, p. 6.

11. Leonard Swidler, "Jesus Was a Feminist," p. 177.

12. Further treatment will follow when examining Jesus' attitude toward women in the canonical accounts.

13. Bernard Cooke, "Non-Patriarchal Salvation," in Joann Wolski Conn, ed., *Women's Spirituality: Resources for Christian Development* (New York: Paulist Press, 1986), p. 277.

14. Schüssler-Fiorenza, "Women in the Early Christian Movement," p. 86.

15. John Drane, *Introducing the New Testament* (San Francisco: Harper

and Row, 1986), p. 181. I am using Schüssler-Fiorenza's terminology here as a caution to exclusively attributing the four canonical accounts to men.

16. Ben Witherington, *Women in the Earliest Churches* (New York: Cambridge University Press, 1984), p. 159.
17. *Ibid.*, p. 160.
18. Elisabeth Moltmann-Wendel, *The Women Around Jesus* (New York: Crossroad, 1982), p. 108.
19. Schüssler-Fiorenza, *In Memory of Her*, p. 316.
20. *Ibid.*, p. 318.
21. *Ibid.*, p. 319.
22. Schüssler-Fiorenza dates John's gospel approximately twenty to thirty years after Mark's in *In Memory of Her*, p. 323.
23. Evelyn Stagg and Frank Stagg, *Women in the World of Jesus* (Philadelphia: Westminster Press, 1978), p. 235.
24. Raymond E. Brown, "Roles of Women in the Fourth Gospel," *Theological Studies* 30 (April, 1975), pp. 690–691.
25. Stagg and Stagg, p. 233.
26. Schüssler-Fiorenza, *In Memory of Her*, p. 235.
27. Evelyn and Frank Stagg (p. 219) have identified an extensive list of women in Luke's gospel. Among them are "Elizabeth, Mary, Anna, the widow of Serepta, the widow of Nain, a sinful woman who anointed Jesus, the many women who accompanied Jesus on his preaching missions, the woman whom Jesus rebuked, a crippled woman, a widow before a judge, a widow who gave two mites, some women at the burial of Jesus, and women at the open tomb."
28. *Ibid.*
29. Constance F. Parvey, "The Theology and Leadership of Women in the New Testament," in Radford Ruether, ed., *Religion & Sexism: Images of Women in the Jewish & Christian Traditions* (New York: Simon & Schuster, 1974), p. 139.
30. Witherington, p. 129.
31. James Coriden et al., eds., *The Code of Canon Law: Text and Commentary* (New York: Paulist Press, 1985), pp. 122–123.
32. Witherington, pp. 173–174.
33. *Ibid.*, p. 174.
34. Tetlow, p. 98.
35. *Ibid.*, pp. 100–101.
36. Stagg and Stagg, p. 217.
37. Barbara J. MacHaffie, *Her Story: Women in Christian Tradition* (Philadelphia: Fortress Press, 1986), p. 15.
38. *Ibid.*
39. Schüssler-Fiorenza, *In Memory of Her*, p. 329.
40. Tetlow, p. 112.
41. Moltmann-Wendel, p. 25.
42. Schüssler-Fiorenza, *In Memory of Her*, p. 329.
43. Alicia Faxon, *Women and Jesus* (Philadelphia: United Church Press, 1973), p. 27.
44. Elizabeth E. Platt, "The Ministry of Mary of Bethany," *Theology Today* 34 (1977), p. 32.
45. Schüssler-Fiorenza, *In Memory of Her*, p. 331.

46. Platt, p. 37.
47. *Ibid.*
48. Tetow, p. 120.
49. Schüssler-Fiorenza, *In Memory of Her,* p. xiv.
50. Radford Ruether, *New Woman/New Earth: Sexist Ideologies & Human Liberation* (New York: Seabury Press, 1975), p. 65.
51. Faxon, p. 83.
52. For a good discussion of the "biblical" Mary Magdalene, see Moltmann-Wendel, pp. 75-90.
53. Stagg and Stagg, p. 123.
54. Tetlow, p. 103.
55. Leonard Swidler, *Biblical Affirmations of Women* (Philadelphia: Westminster Press, 1979), p. 195.
56. *Ibid.,* p. 305.
57. Tetlow, p. 118.
58. *Ibid.*
59. *Ibid.,* p. 119. See also Moltmann-Wendel, pp. 72-75.
60. As Schüssler-Fiorenza has observed, "The apostle Peter, who according to some traditions was the first witness to the resurrection, has been hailed through the centuries as the first among the apostles, whereas the apostle Mary of Magdala, who according to other traditions was the primary witness to the resurrection, has lived in Christian memory as a repentant whore and sinner." *But She Said: Feminist Practices of Biblical Interpretation* (Boston: Beacon Press, 1992), p. 80.
61. Schüssler-Fiorenza, *In Memory of Her,* p. 333.
62. According to Faxon, p. 89, "Jesus' encouragement of women disciples was not only an acceptance of their grateful response to him after their healings or conversions but was an even more positive statement of his attitude toward women as equals of men and equally valuable as disciples."
63. Schüssler-Fiorenza, *In Memory of Her,* p. 332.
64. Swidler and Swidler, p. 39.
65. For a good discussion of Mary's treatment in the New Testament, see Raymond E. Brown, "Mary in the New Testament and in Catholic Life," in *America* (May 15, 1982), pp. 374-379.
66. Pope John Paul II, *On the Dignity and Vocation of Women on the Occasion of the Marian Year,* p. 116. For a good discussion of Mary's theological significance within Roman Catholicism, see Cardinal Joseph Ratzinger, "On the Position of Mariology and Marian Spirituality Within the Totality of Faith and Theology," transl. Graham Harrison, in Moll, pp. 67-79.
67. For a good discussion of this parallel, see Faxon, pp. 21-29.
68. Anthony J. Tambasco, *What Are They Saying About Mary?* (New Jersey: Paulist Press, 1984), p. 77.
69. Radford Ruether, *Mary—The Feminine Face of the Church* (Philadelphia: Westminster Press, 1977), p. 37.
70. *Ibid.,* p. 38.
71. *Ibid.,* p. 39.
72. Rosemary Radford Ruether is a feminist scholar whose work has made a significant contribution to our understanding of the historical roles of women in the Christian tradition.

73. See John 2.3–5, 2.12.
74. Tetlow, pp. 102–103.
75. *Ibid.*, p. 110.
76. Schüssler-Fiorenza, *In Memory of Her*, p. 327.
77. Tetlow, p. 110.
78. Radford Ruether, *Mary—The Feminine Face of the Church*, p. 38.
79. *Ibid.*, p. 39.
80. Tambasco, p. 30.
81. Radford Ruether, *Mary—The Feminine Face of the Church*, p. 39.
82. *Ibid.*, p. 40.
83. For example, Mary seems to have persuaded Jesus to perform his first miracle. For a good discussion of the marriage at Cana text, see Faxon, pp. 21–29.
84. Tambasco, p. 81.
85. See discussion in Schüssler-Fiorenza, "The Sophia—God of Jesus and the Discipleship of Women," in *Women's Spirituality: Resources for Christian Development*, pp. 261–273.
86. Swidler and Swidler, p. 39. The *Didascalia* also hints that Jesus excluded women from the group of apostles: "For our master Jesus Christ sent us, the twelve, to teach all nations, but He did not command the women to teach, nor to speak in the church and address the people.... For there abode with us Mary Magdalene and the sisters of Lazarus, ... and since he did not command them to teach alongside us, neither is it right for other women to teach." Karen Torjesen (p. 21) notes that "these apostolic sayings offer a clear statement of the theological justification used for the exclusion of women, but they do not provide insight into the actual motives for the exclusion of women from church offices. Nor do they give a description of the circumstances under which this exclusion seemed necessary."
87. Heinz Günther, *The Footprints of Jesus' Twelve in Early Christian Traditions: A Study in the Meaning of Religious Symbolism* (New York: Peter Lang Press, 1985), p. 30.
88. Drane, p. 243. Similarly, Bernard Cooke maintains in *Ministry to Word and Sacraments*, p. 531, that: "Apart from their presence at the supper and at the post-Resurrection meals, there is practically nothing in the New Testament that might refer to a special role of the Twelve in early Christian worship."
89. Günther, p. 29.
90. Tetlow, p. 117.
91. As Günther (p. 31) notes, "the disparate function played by the twelve in these early materials, along with their mysterious disappearance even before the start of the earliest Christian mission, does not suggest their appointment by the earthly Jesus."
92. Schüssler-Fiorenza, *In Memory of Her*, p. 325.
93. Swidler and Swidler, p. 39.
94. Günther, p. 65.
95. *Ibid.*, p. 68.
96. *Ibid.*, p. 67.
97. *Ibid.* For complete discussion of the Qumran texts, see pp. 75–86.
98. Stagg and Stagg, pp. 123–124.
99. For complete discussion, see Tetlow, pp. 60–62. Various biblical scholars

have questioned whether the earthly Jesus did in fact appoint the twelve to continue his earthly ministry. Given several scholarly interpretations of the twelve in early Christian tradition, Heinz Günther has concluded (p. 55) that "the creation of the twelve concept ... falls into the earliest post-Easter period of the Christian community [and therefore], the claim that Jesus had appointed them during his earthly ministry is, in view of the absence of historical evidence, anything but self-evident."

100. Günther, p. 67.
101. Tetlow, p. 62.
102. Swidler and Swidler, p. 39.
103. Brown, *Priest and Bishop,* pp. 13–20.
104. Schneiders, "Did Jesus Exclude Women from Priesthood?" p. 230. Further, Günther (p. 96) has noted that "no specific leadership role is assigned to them [i.e., the unknown group of twelve witnesses mentioned in Paul's letter to the Corinthians]. The twelve stand side by side with other equally privileged individuals or groups of witnesses as 'the five hundred' and 'all the apostles.'"
105. Schneiders, "Did Jesus Exclude Women from Priesthood?" pp. 228–229.
106. Tetlow, p. 64.
107. Schneiders, "Did Jesus Exclude Women from Priesthood?" p. 230. See also Robert Jewett, "Paul, Phoebe, and the Spanish Mission," in Neusner et al., eds., *The Social World of Formative Christianity and Judaism* (Philadelphia: Fortress Press, 1988), pp. 142–161. Jewett claims (p. 149) that: "The host or hostess of house churches was usually a person of high social standing and means, with a house large enough for the church to gather, who presided over the eucharistic celebrations and was responsible for the ordering of the congregation."
108. Schneiders has characterized women's activity as "the precursors of present-day priests" in "Did Jesus Exclude Women from Priesthood?" p. 230.
109. Schüssler-Fiorenza, *In Memory of Her,* p. 324.
110. Günther, p. 28.
111. Tetlow, p. 131.

3. The Role of Women in the Early Church

1. Randy Peterson, "What About Paul?" in *Christian History* 8, no. 1 (Issue 17), p. 26. He, along with other contemporary scholars, has noted that Paul's writings in particular give a detailed account as to women's roles in the early Christian community. See also MacHaffie, pp. 18–21.
2. Abbott, p. 116.
3. Avery Dulles, S.J., "The Authority of Scripture: A Catholic Perspective," in F. Greenspahn, ed., *Scripture in the Jewish and Christian Traditions* (Nashville, Tenn.: Abingdon Press, 1982), p. 40. For a good discussion regarding the interpretation of biblical sources that deal with feminist issues, see Rosemary Radford Ruether, "Feminist Interpretation: A Method of Correlation," in Letty M. Russell, ed., *Feminist Interpretation of the Bible* (New York: Basil Blackwell, 1985), pp. 111–124.
4. Vatican II expressed that "sacred tradition and sacred scripture form one sacred deposit of the word of God, which is committed to the Church"

(Abbott, p. 117). I am using these terms in the sense that when dealing with scripture and tradition, one flows from the next, and it is impossible to separate one from the other, as scripture records tradition and vice versa.

5. Sandra M. Schneiders, *Beyond Patching: Faith and Feminism in the Catholic Church* (New York: Paulist Press, 1991), pp. 65–71.

6. Brendan Byrne, S.J., *Paul and the Christian Woman* (Homebush, NSW: St. Paul Publications, 1988), p. 99.

7. Many scholars have held this view. For further treatment, see Virginia Mollenkott, *Women, Men and the Bible* (Nashville, Tenn.: Abingdon Press, 1977); various articles written by Elisabeth Schüssler-Fiorenza including "Women in the Early Christian Movement," in Carol P. Christ and Judith Plaskow, eds., *Womanspirit Rising* (San Francisco: Harper and Row, 1979), "Women in the New Testament," in *New Catholic World* (Nov./Dec., 1976), pp. 256–260 and "Women in Pre-Pauline and Pauline Churches," in *Union Seminary Quarterly Review* 33 (Spring and Summer, 1978), pp. 153–166; Leonard Swidler, *Women in Judaism: The Status of Women in Formative Judaism* (New Jersey: Scarecrow Press, 1976), as well as other sources listed in the bibliography.

8. McDonald et al., vol. 11, p. 9.

9. Florence M. Gillman, *Women Who Knew Paul* (Collegeville, Minn.: The Liturgical Press, 1991), p. 14.

10. Mollenkott, p. 91.

11. Another example of this type appears in I Cor. 14.35–37.

12. Schüssler-Fiorenza, *In Memory of Her*, p. 29.

13. *Ibid.*, pp. 32–33.

14. *Ibid.*, p. 32.

15. *Ibid.*, p. 34.

16. *Ibid.*, p. 36.

17. *Ibid.*, p. 60.

18. For complete discussion, see William Oddie, *What Will Happen to God? Feminism and the Reconstruction of Christian Belief* (San Francisco: Ignatius Press, 1988), pp. 141–146.

19. *Ibid.*, p. 143.

20. *Ibid.*, p. 146.

21. Schüssler-Fiorenza, *In Memory of Her*, p. 61.

22. Oddie, p. 155.

23. *Ibid.*, p. 153.

24. Swidler and Swidler, pp. 44–45.

25. For an excellent discussion of the sources involved in Brooten's reconstruction, see her article, "Early Christian Women and Their Cultural Context: Issues of Method in Historical Reconstruction," in Adela Yarbro Collins, ed., *Feminist Perspectives on Biblical Scholarship* (Chico, Calif.: Scholars Press, 1985), pp. 65–91. Brooten quotes a series of articles that reflect the work that is being done by contemporary scholars in the field of historical reconstruction.

26. Witherington, p. 24.

27. Swidler and Swidler, p. 41.

28. Schüssler-Fiorenza stresses that women in the egalitarian movement, (i.e., in the Christian community) were not marginal figures. Rather, she insists

they exercised responsible leadership roles. For a good discussion of these roles, see "Word, Spirit, Power," in Rosemary Radford Ruether and Eleanor McLaughlin, eds., *Women of Spirit: Female Leadership in the Jewish and Christian Traditions* (New York: Simon and Schuster, 1979).

29. Schüssler-Fiorenza, "Women in Pre-Pauline and Pauline Churches," p. 154.

30. Louise Harris, *Women in the Christian Church* (Brighton, Michigan: Green Oaks Press, 1988), p. 5.

31. Gillman devotes an entire chapter to Paul's co-workers, pp. 43-58.

32. *Ibid.,* p. 52.

33. Swidler and Swidler, p. 41.

34. Walter L. Liefield, "Women, Submission and Ministry in I Corinthians," in Alvera Mickelson, ed., *Women, Authority, & the Bible* (Downers Grove, Illinois: Intervarsity Press, 1986), p. 149.

35. Arlene Swidler, *Woman in a Man's Church* (New York: Paulist Press, 1972), p. 35.

36. Joan Morris, *The Lady Was a Bishop* (New York: Macmillan, 1973). Other biblical scholars such as C.K. Barrett and H. Conzelmann have also argued in favor of this view.

37. Byrne, p. 62.

38. Barbara Hall, "Paul and Women," in *Theology Today* (April 1974), pp. 50-55. See also William O. Walker, Jr., "The Theology of Woman's Place and the Paulinist Tradition," in *The Bible and Feminist Hermeneutics,* p. 103. Walker cites numerous scholars who have regarded the text as a "post-Pauline interpolation."

39. For a good discussion of Galatians 3.28, see Schüssler-Fiorenza, *In Memory of Her,* pp. 205-218.

40. Witherington, p. 72.

41. Peterson, p. 28.

42. Schüssler-Fiorenza, *In Memory of Her,* pp. 231-232. Walter L. Liefield (p. 151) also maintains this view of propriety.

43. Swidler and Swidler, p. 41.

44. *Ibid.,* p. 206. Liefield contends this passage has to do with judging prophecies on p. 150.

45. Schüssler-Fiorenza, *In Memory of Her,* p. 176.

46. *Ibid.,* p. 229.

47. Swidler and Swidler, p. 41.

48. Barbara Hall (p. 50) holds this view, along with various biblical scholars. Walker has theorized that the passages in the New Testament that discuss the subordination of woman to man have a common source that originated in the post-apostolic period and not with Paul. For complete discussion, see Walker, pp. 101-112. See also MacHaffie, pp. 18-19. She contends that the New Testament texts that have often been quoted to support the subordination of women were written at a later time when the Church began to take on a more hierarchical structure that conformed with the Greco-Roman model of patriarchy.

It should be noted, however, that there is no "homogeneous" body of scholarly feminist opinion on the subject which this work explores.

49. David Scholer, "I Timothy 2:9-15 and the Place of Women in the Church's Ministry," in Mickelsen, p. 202.

It is interesting to note here that Catherine Kroeger, in her article "The Neglected History of Women in the Early Church" in *Christian History* 8, no. 1 (Issue 17), has theorized that the restriction for women from teaching has to do with the content of the message itself, rather than the act of teaching. Her contention is based on the verb used to restrict women. She has suggested that the word *didasko* is the restriction concerning "false teaching."

50. Schüssler-Fiorenza, *In Memory of Her,* p. 290.
51. *Ibid.*, p. 172. Also, Robert Jewett (p. 148) attests to Phoebe's solidarity with Paul in "Paul, Phoebe, and the Spanish Mission."
52. Byrne, p. 70.
53. Gillman contends (p. 61) that the Greek term *diakonissa,* the feminine form for "deacon," does not appear in Paul's time.
54. Roger Gryson, *The Ministry of Women in the Early Church,* transl. Jean LaPorte and Mary Louise Hall (Collegeville, Minn.: Liturgical Press, 1976), pp. 3-4.
55. Schüssler-Fiorenza, "Word, Spirit and Power," p. 36.
56. For the complete discussion see Scanzoni and Hardesty, p. 62.
57. Manfred Hauke has devoted an entire chapter to his observations regarding the ordination of women to a permanent diaconate. For a good discussion of the deacon/deaconess distinction according to the *Didaskalia* and the *Apostolic Constitutions,* see "Observations on the Ordination of Women to the Diaconate," transl. Graham Harrison, in Moll, pp. 117-139.
58. Schüssler-Fiorenza contends that the ministries performed in the early Church were not limited to "specific gender roles and functions," in "Word, Spirit and Power," p. 36.
59. Schüssler-Fiorenza, *In Memory of Her,* p. 172.
60. *Ibid.*, p. 170. Robert Jewett speculates that Phoebe was the congregation's leader based on the fact that wealthy women usually occupied a large enough house to permit communities to gather there. In such a setting the hostess, in this case Phoebe, would lead the congregation and preside at the Eucharist. For complete discussion, see Jewett, pp. 142-161.
61. Schüssler-Fiorenza, "Women in the New Testament," p. 260.
62. *Ibid.* See also Scanzoni and Hardesty, p. 62, and Byrne, p. 70.
63. Suzanne Heine, *Women and Early Christianity* (Minneapolis: Augsburg, 1987), p. 89. See also Leonard Swidler, *Biblical Affirmations of Women,* p. 309.
64. Catherine Kroeger, "The Neglected History of Women in the Early Church," in *Christian History* 8, no. 1 (Issue 17), p. 7.
65. For complete discussion, see Jewett, pp. 142-161.
66. *Ibid.*, pp. 151-155.
67. The *New Catholic Encyclopedia* (eds. William J. Mc Donald et al.) defines the term "Apostle" as "...one of the Twelve intimate followers of Jesus who were commissioned by Him to preach His gospel" (vol. 1, p. 679). It is interesting to note here that "the term is rightly considered one of the most significant New Testament terms that provides a basis and model for the Church's concept of priestly ministry." Mary Ann Getty, "God's Fellow Worker and Apostleship," in Swidler and Swidler, p. 179.
68. Christ and Plaskow, p. 89.
69. "...Women were the primary apostolic witnesses of Jesus' ministry, his

suffering and death, his burial and his resurrection. They were moreover sent to proclaim the message of the Twelve." *Ibid.*, p. 90.
  70. Bernard Cooke, *Ministry to Word and Sacraments*, p. 531.
  71. Swidler and Swidler, p. 41.
  72. *Ibid.*, p. 40.
  73. *Ibid.*, p. 38.
  74. Bernadette Brooten, "Junia ... Outstanding Among the Apostles" (Romans 16:7), in Swidler and Swidler, p. 141. See also Byrne, pp. 72–73.
  75. Kroeger, p. 7.
  76. Brooten, "Junia ... Outstanding Among the Apostles," p. 141.
  77. *Ibid.* For the complete discussion, see pp. 141–143.
  78. Cooke, *Ministry to Word and Sacraments*, p. 531.
  79. Schüssler-Fiorenza, *In Memory of Her*, p. 172.
  80. *Ibid.*
  81. Gillman, p. 69.
  82. Cooke, *Ministry to Word and Sacraments*, p. 532.
  83. Schüssler-Fiorenza, *In Memory of Her*, p. 172.
  84. *Ibid.*, p. 299.
  85. Lesly F. Massey, *Women and the New Testament: An Analysis of Scripture in Light of New Testament Era Culture* (Jefferson, N.C.: McFarland, 1989), p. 76.
  86. *Ibid.*, p. 78.
  87. *Ibid.*, pp. 76–79.
  88. Cooke, *Ministry to Word and Sacraments*, p. 532.
  89. McDonald et al., vol. 11, p. 867.
  90. Schüssler-Fiorenza, *In Memory of Her*, p. 175.
  91. *Ibid.*, p. 175.
  92. *Ibid.*, p. 177. Harris has also argued that Lydia established and presided over a church in her house in *Women in the Christian Church*, p. 4. For a good discussion of Lydia, see Gillman, pp. 30–38. She contends that Lydia's baptism was by immersion, and indicates that Paul would already have had female "coworkers" as it would not have been proper for a man to conduct such an act.
  93. Kroeger, p. 24. See also Schüssler-Fiorenza, "Word, Spirit and Power," p. 32. She contends that wealthy women founded house churches and that they functioned independently from Paul.
  94. Kroeger, p. 24.
  95. *Ibid.* Adolf Harnack contends that the two women mentioned in Phil. 4.2, 3 were presiders in their house churches. For complete discussion, see Harris, pp. 4ff.
  96. Schüssler-Fiorenza notes that among the thirty-six people listed in Romans 16 who perform active ministries within the early Church, sixteen of them are women, and eighteen of them are men. This leads her to conclude that the structure of the early Church gatherings was egalitarian vis-à-vis ministerial duties in "Word, Spirit and Power," p. 36.
  97. Sister Mary McKenna, *Women of the Church* (New York: P.J. Kennedy & Sons, 1967), pp. 37–38.
  98. Massey, p. 65.
  99. G.A. Buttrick et al., eds., *The Interpreter's Bible* (Abingdon, New York: Cokesbury Press, 1957), vol. 9, p. 130.

100. Massey, p. 65.
101. Lesly F. Massey (pp. 66–67) has offered that the term "enroll," meaning to place on a list, suggests a special function on the basis that the qualifications given for widows are comparable to those of elders and deacons in the same letter.
102. *Ibid.*, p. 68.
103. *Ibid.*, p. 69.
104. Gryson, p. 56.
105. According to McDonald et al., the "Testament of our Lord Jesus Christ" is a reworking of Hippolytus' *Apostolic Tradition* from the fifth century, which has been characterized as "the fullest and most important source extant for the Roman liturgy and for the constitution of the Church and the administration of the sacraments in the 2d and 3d centuries" (vol. 6, p. 1141).
106. Kroeger, p. 11.
107. Bonnie Bowman Thurston, *The Widows: A Women's Ministry in the Early Church* (Minneapolis: Fortress Press, 1989), p. 44.
108. Lucretia Marmon, "Why Can't Women Be Priests Again?" in *Glamour* (Sept. 1991), p. 112.
109. Mary Ann Rossi, "Priesthood, Precedent or Prejudice: On Recovering the Women Priests of Early Christianity," in Judith Plaskow et al., eds., *Journal of Feminist Studies in Religion* 7, no. 1 (Spring 1991), p. 81.
110. Swidler and Swidler, p. 42.
111. *Ibid.*, p. 39.
112. Christ and Plaskow, pp. 86–87.
113. *Ibid.*, p. 91.

4. Overcoming the Lay-Clergy Dualism

1. MacHaffie, p. 29.
2. For complete discussion, see Edward Schillebeeckx, *Ministry: Leadership in the Community of Jesus Christ* (New York: Crossroad, 1981), pp. 38–65. Rosemary Radford Ruether also affirms this viewpoint in *New Woman/New Earth*, pp. 74–78.
3. McDonald et al., vol. 8, p. 331.
4. Isidore Gorski, "Commentary on the Decree on the Apostolate of the Laity," in Timothy E. O'Connell, ed., *Vatican II and Its Documents* (Wilmington, Del.: Michael Glazier Press, 1986), p. 74.
5. Edward Schillebeeckx, *The Definition of a Christian Layman* (Staten Island, New York: Alba House, 1963), p. 10.
6. *Ibid.*, p. 20.
7. Bishop James L. Doyle, "We Are the Church," in *National Bulletin on Liturgy*, vol. 20, no. 109 (May-June, 1987), p. 182.
8. This is an extract from a lecture entitled, "Developments in the Lay-Church since Vatican II—Focus on Canada" (unpublished), presented by Mary Matthews during a 1987 Regis College lecture series entitled *In Celebration of the Lay-Church.*
9. *Ibid.*
10. Roger Haight, "The Ministry of the Laity: History, Principles, Challenges" (unpublished). Regis College lecture series, 1987.

11. For the sake of brevity, I will refer to this conference as the "Bishops' Synod" in future citings.
12. Abbott, p. 57.
13. O'Connell, p. 75.
14. Abbott states (p. 56) that the people of God all share in Christ's office as King, prophet and priest.
15. *Ibid.*, p. 491.
16. "Selection from Homily of Pope Paul VI to the Third World Congress of Lay Apostolate on the Layman's Sphere of Action, Oct. 15, 1967," in Odile Liebard, ed., *Clergy and Laity* (Wilmington, N.C.: McGrath, 1978), pp. 291-292.
17. The *Lineamenta* is the name used for the working paper that was published in preparation for the 1987 Bishops' Synod (Ottawa, Canada: C.C.C.B., 1985), p. 9.
18. O'Connell, p. 145.
19. Abbott, pp. 543-544.
20. Most Rev. Henri Légaré O.M.I., "Task of the Whole Church," in *National Bulletin on Liturgy* no. 8 (March-April, 1975), p. 95.
21. Alan F. Blakley, "Decree on the Apostolate of Lay People," in O'Connell, p. 146.
22. Mary Matthews, "Developments in the Lay-Liturgy since Vatican II— Focus on Canada" (unpublished). 1987 Regis College lecture series.
23. *Ibid.*
24. Rosemary Haughton, "Lay Community, a Prophetic Movement," in *Compass* 4 (Oct. 1987), p. 14.
25. *Ibid.*, p. 17.
26. *Ibid.*, p. 14.
27. Matthews, "Where We Are Today," in *National Bulletin on Liturgy* 8, p. 19.
28. Haight, p. 5.
29. Coriden et al., p. 139.
30. Gorski, p. 79.
31. John Martin, "Canon Law Discovers the Laity," in *Compass* 4 (Oct. 1987), p. 24.
32. *Ibid.*, p. 25.
33. Coriden et al., pp. 122-123.
34. Canon 208 states, "In virtue of their re-birth in Christ there exists among all the Christian faithful a true equality with regard to dignity and the activity whereby all co-operate in the building up of the body of Christ in accordance with each one's own condition and function." *Ibid.*, p. 139.
35. *Ibid.*, p. 131.
36. *Ibid.*, p. 141.
37. *Ibid.*
38. *Ibid.*, p. 67.
39. John Huels, *The Pastoral Companion* (Quincy, Ill.: The Franciscan Herald Press, 1986), p. 87.
40. Coriden et al., p. 437.
41. It is interesting to note here that the term "pastoral" is defined as "pertaining to the duties of a minister" in *Winston's Dictionary* (Holt, Rinehart and

Winston of Canada, 1965), p. 452, and therefore indicates a rather inclusive role for women.

42. Coriden et al., p. 168.
43. Martin, p. 25.
44. Avery Dulles S.J., *The Reshaping of Catholicism: Current Challenges in the Theology of Church* (San Francisco: Harper and Row, 1988), p. 188.
45. *Ibid.*
46. *Lineamenta*, p. 11.
47. *Ibid.*, pp. 16–17.
48. *Ibid.*, p. 16.
49. *Synod of Bishops: Rome, 1987* (Ottawa, Canada: C.C.C.B., 1987), p. 1.
50. *Ibid.*
51. *Ibid.*, p. 3.
52. *Ibid.*, p. 6.
53. *Ibid.*
54. *Ibid.*, pp. 9–10.
55. *Ibid.*, p. 10.
56. Michael McAteer, "Catholics Learn New Buzzword," in *The Toronto Star* (Oct. 1986).
57. *Ibid.*
58. Murray Lewis, "Synod: We Missed a Wonderful Chance," in *The Prairie Messenger* (March 21, 1988), p. 1.
59. *Ibid.*
60. For further treatment, see Richard McBrien, *Ministry* (San Francisco: Harper and Row, 1987), pp. 71ff.
61. *Ibid.*, p. 13.
62. Swidler and Swidler, p. 41.
63. In likeness to Elizabeth Tetlow, Edward Schillebeeckx has argued that the choosing of twelve male apostles "is a symbol of Israel's twelve patriarchs and tribes, and of the whole of Israel as a sign of the eschatological community of mankind," in *The Church with a Human Face*, p. 75.
64. *Ibid.*, p. 76.
65. *Ibid.*, p. 77.
66. Roger Haight (p. 9) explains: "In the fifth century at the Council of Chalcedon it was prescribed that ordination was only valid if the candidate were ordained for a specific community.... There was to be no absolute or universal ordination of a priest as such apart from a community. A priest was bound to his community because ministry was precisely for the building up of a specific community."
67. As he states: "Though they may neglect it in the course of their practical Christian activity, all Christian Churches in all periods of history admit in some form the principle that Christ alone is the ultimate possessor of priesthood and ministry and authority in the Church. This means that the understanding of Christ's own ministry is determinative of any insight into Christian ministry, whether it be the ministry of the community as a whole or that of the ordained minister." Cooke, *Ministry to Word and Sacraments,* p. 36.
68. *Ibid.*, p. 38.
69. *Ibid.*, p. 39.
70. Cooke notes that although no hierarchical order was established, it

appears that specific functions were outlined on an egalitarian level. For example, he describes Peter's role as "one of fostering the communal life of the believing followers of Jesus. In this sense, those who were commissioned to special responsibility within the apostolic community are meant to carry on essentially the same task as Jesus: to shepherd the flock" (*Ministry to Word and Sacraments,* pp. 40–41). Therefore, Cooke is leaning toward the concept of a mutual support among the early Christian community members.

71. *Ibid.,* p. 37.
72. Tetlow, p. 96.
73. Cooke, *Ministry to Word and Sacraments,* pp. 42–43.
74. *Ibid.,* p. 43.
75. *Ibid.*
76. *Ibid.* For further discussion, see pp. 43–44.
77. *Ibid.,* p. 64.
78. McBrien, p. 31.
79. Edward Schillebeeckx, *Ministry,* p. 11.
80. *Ibid.,* p. 13.
81. Van A. Harvey, *A Handbook of Theological Terms* (New York: Macmillan, 1964), p. 26.
82. Swidler and Swidler, p. 40.
83. Schillebeeckx, *Ministry,* p. 37.
84. McDonald et al., vol. 3, p. 423.
85. Schillebeeckx, *Ministry,* Chapter II.

5. Women in the Catholic Church

1. For example *On the Dignity and Vocation of Women on the Occasion of the Marian Year* (Rome: Vatican Polygot Press), issued by Pope John Paul II in 1988, confirms the teaching outlined in the *Declaration.*

2. Sr. Thérèse-André, *Projet vocationnel* (unpublished). This report was a brief presented by the diocesan commission for vocations in St. Boniface, 1990.

3. *Human Resources in the Catholic Church of Canada, 1987–88 (Remunerated Personnel)* (Ottawa, Canada: C.C.C.B., 1988), p. 47. Although this report shows that the decline among priests in the last few years has been notably less than others, in 1988, 34 percent of Canadian priests were at least 65 years of age. Since the percentage of priests between the ages of 50 and 64 in 1988 was 39 percent, I observe that the 65 and older category is increasing. Since the number of priests over the age of 50 in 1988 represents 73 percent of the total number of priests, it is plausible to suggest that the next few decades will witness an even greater decline in the number of active priests in Canada.

4. For a good breakdown of the statistics which deal with the lack of available priests on an international plane, see Patrick J. Dunn, pp. 7–9.

5. "The Role of the Laity ... An Interview with Mary Matthews," in *Canadian Catholic Review* (June 1987), p. 220.

6. Lise Baroni, "The Creative Emergence of Women Working in the Church," in *Women, for What World, in What Church?* Donum Dei Series #30, Canadian Religious Conference (Ottawa, 1985), p. 49.

7. Marty Gervais, "Women Keeping the Faith for a Chance at Ordination," in *The Saturday Windsor Star* (June 11, 1988), p. 6.

8. Abbott, p. 30.
9. Coriden et al., p. 139.
10. Dunn, p. 119.
11. Mary Ellen Sheehan, "When Sleeping Women Awake...," *Women for What World, in What Church?* p. 79.
12. Arlene Swidler, p. 65.
13. *Ibid.*, pp. 68-69.
14. Elisabeth J. Lacelle, "Should the Church Come Forward as a Project for a New Humanity?" in *Women, for What World, in What Church?* p. 99.
15. Sheehan, pp. 75-83.
16. Mary Beth Murphy, "Fourth Pastoral Draft Called the Worst," in *The Milwaukee Sentinel* (Sept. 11, 1992).
17. Murphy, "Final Draft of Pastoral on Women Called Inferior," in *The Milwaukee Sentinel* (Sept. 12, 1992).
18. Mark Lisheron, "Weakland Calls for Women in Vatican," in *The Milwaukee Journal* (Dec. 6, 1992).
19. Abbott, p. 30.
20. Ramon Gonzalez, "Women Not Yet Welcome in Heart of Church," in *The Prairie Messenger* (May 17, 1993), p. 2.
21. Jean Forest, "Women in the Canadian Context," in *Women and the Church,* eds. Michael W. Higgins and Douglas R. Letson (Toronto, Canada: Griffin House, 1986), p. 166.
22. *Ibid.*, p. 166.
23. Carolyn Osiek, in her work *Beyond Anger: On Being a Feminist in the Church* (New York: Paulist Press, 1986), has documented a series of situations in which women have come to be excluded from their church, and the manner in which they have chosen to cope with their situation. Her work bears relevance to my discussion of women as it demonstrates the manner in which the official Church continues to alienate women in various ways, including ministerial service.
24. *Ibid.*, p. 173.
25. *Ibid.*
26. For complete discussion, see Grace M. Anderson and Juanne Nancarrow-Clarke, *God Calls: Man Chooses—A Study of Women in Ministry* (Burlington, Ontario: Trinity Press, 1990), Chapter Two. Although their survey includes women from various denominations, I argue that their findings are equally applicable to Catholic women because Catholic women experience comparable tensions due to their specifically female nature. For a good discussion of the "silencing" of women in the Roman Catholic Church, see Elisabeth Schüssler-Fiorenza, "Breaking the Silence—Becoming Visible," in Elisabeth Schüssler-Fiorenza and Mary Collins, eds., *Women, Invisible in Church and Theology* (Edinburgh: T. & T. Clark, Ltd., 1985), *Concilium* vol. 182, pp. 3-16.
27. Baroni, p. 64.
28. *Ibid.*, pp. 66-67.
29. Elisabeth J. Lacelle, "From Today to Tomorrow: Women in the Canadian Catholic Church," in Higgins and Letson, eds., *Women and the Church,* p. 156.
30. For complete discussion, see Schüssler-Fiorenza, "Breaking the Silence—Becoming Visible," in Schüssler-Fiorenza and Collins, pp. 3-16.

31. Jerry Filteau, "Religious Want Full Place at Roman Synod," in *The Prairie Messenger* (April 19, 1993), p. 4.

32. Cindy Wooden, "Pope, Québec Bishops Differ on Role of Women," in *The Prairie Messenger* (May 17, 1993), p. 6.

33. *Ibid.*, p. 180.

34. *Ibid.*, p. 179.

35. *Ibid.*, p. 180.

36. Abbott, p. 60.

37. For example, Radford Ruether notes that in the United States, there is a membership of 2,000 priests that belong to a "Priests for Equality" group who support the ordination of women. "The Roman Catholic Story" in Radford Ruether and McLaughlin, p. 379.

38. Baroni, p. 52.

39. Sidney Callahan, "Then and Now, Women Won't Take No for an Answer," in *The Prairie Messenger* (June 21, 1993), p. 15.

40. Dolores Leckey, "Power-sharing Essential to Equality of Sexes," in *The Prairie Messenger* (June 14, 1993), p. 12.

41. *Ibid.*

42. Coriden et al., p. 167.

43. Baroni, p. 54.

44. Bishop Robert Lebel, "The Role of Women in Family Ministry and the Life of the Church," in Michael W. Higgins and Douglas R. Letson, p. 177.

45. Kaye Ashe, *Today's Woman, Tomorrow's Church* (Chicago: Thomas More Press, 1983), p. 178.

46. *Ibid.*, p. 184.

47. Coriden et al., p. 139.

48. *Ibid.*, p. 167.

49. The paper was reprinted in *Origins* 17 #22 (Nov. 12, 1987), pp. 398–399.

50. Thomas C. Fox, "Altar-Girl Issue Seen as Symbol in Rome," *National Catholic Reporter* (Nov. 6, 1987), p. 20.

51. This information is documented in a letter written by Fr. Francis Morrisey to me and remains among my personal notes for this book. Permission was granted to reveal the contents of his letter.

52. Fox, p. 20.

53. Father Joseph Fessio, "Reasons Given Against Women Acolytes and Lectors," in *Origins* 17 #22, (Nov. 12, 1987), p. 398.

54. *Ibid.*

55. Abbott, p. 58.

56. Baroni, p. 57.

57. *Ibid.*

58. *Ibid.*

59. Fessio, p. 399.

60. *Human Resources in the Catholic Church of Canada, 1987-88,* eds. C.C.C.B., p. 38.

61. Forest, p. 169.

62. Art Babych, "Altar Girls Not a Vatican but Diocesan Issue," in *The Prairie Messenger* (June 21, 1993), p. 6.

63. *Ibid.*

64. Coriden et al., p. 168.

65. Bishop Hamelin, "Access of Women to Church Positions," in *Synod of Bishops* (Ottawa, Canada: C.C.C.B., 1987), p. 8.
66. Forest, p. 164.
67. "Women's Ordination Conference Broadens Horizons," *Catholic New Times* (June 12, 1988), p. 1.
68. Marty Gervais, *The Saturday Windsor Star* (June 11, 1988), p. 6.
69. Baroni, p. 51.
70. Hamelin, p. 7.
71. *Ibid.*
72. *Ibid.*, p. 8.
73. *Ibid.*
74. *Ibid.*
75. *Ibid.*
76. *Ibid.*
77. *Ibid.*
78. For complete discussion of this talk, see the appendix.
79. Weakland, p. 5.
80. Gervais, p. 6.
81. Mary McIver, "Barred from the Church Altar," in *Maclean's* (July 6, 1987), p. 45.
82. Paule Cantin, "Opening Address," in *Women, for What World, in What Church?* Donum Dei Series #30, Canadian Religious Conference (Ottawa, 1985), p. 14.
83. These recommendations were made by Fr. Weakland O.S.B., Archbishop of Milwaukee, Wisconsin, in his talk presented to the Synod of Bishops in 1987. I have included his talk in this work; see appendix.
84. McDonald et al., vol. 2, p. 65.
85. Baroni, pp. 55–56.
86. Lacelle, "Should the Church Come Forward as a Project for a New Humanity," p. 92.

6. A Contemporary Understanding of the Ordination of Women

1. Radford Ruether, "Ordination: What Is the Problem?" p. 32.
2. Pope John Paul II, *On the Dignity and Vocation of Women on the Occasion of the Marian Year* (Ottawa, Canada: C.C.C.B., 1988), p. 9.
3. *Ibid.*, p. 13.
4. *Ibid.*, p. 19.
5. *Ibid.*, p. 29.
6. *Ibid.*, p. 48.
7. *Ibid.*, p. 62.
8. Swidler and Swidler, p. 40.
9. *Ibid.*, p. 41.
10. Sister Joan Chittister O.S.B., *Woman Strength: Modern Church, Modern Women* (Kansas City, MO: Sheed & Ward, 1990), p. 44.
11. Pope John Paul II, *On the Dignity and Vocation of Women on the Occasion of the Marian Year*, p. 68.

12. *Ibid.*, p. 72.
13. Elisabeth Schüssler-Fiorenza, *In Memory of Her*, p. 146.
14. Glen Argan, "Excluding Women from Priestly Ministry Based on Narrow View," in *The Prairie Messenger* (April 12, 1993), p. 18.
15. Pope John Paul II, *On the Dignity and Vocation of Women on the Occasion of the Marian Year*, p. 64.
16. See Chapter Three of this work.
17. Pope John Paul II, *On the Dignity and Vocation of Women on the Occasion of the Marian Year*, p. 91.
18. *Ibid.*, p. 96.
19. Radford Ruether, "John Paul II and the Growing Alienation of Women from the Church," in Hans Kung and Leonard Swidler, eds., *The Church in Anguish* (San Francisco: Harper and Row, 1987), p. 281.
20. Cooke, "Non-Patriarchal Salvation," p. 281.
21. This notion of eminence is associated with priesthood in the *Didascalia* which Bernard Cooke claims was strongly influenced by "Jewish thinking" and "Old Testament religion," in *Ministry to Word and Sacraments*, p. 542.
22. Radford Ruether, "Women Priests and Church Tradition," in Swidler and Swidler, p. 237.
23. This figure was taken from Rosemary Radford Ruether, *Contemporary Roman Catholicism: Crises and Challenges* (Kansas City, MO: Sheed & Ward, 1987), p. 65.
24. This information is documented in Lisheron, "Weakland Calls for Women in Vatican," in *The Milwaukee Journal* (December 6, 1992).
25. This teaching is documented in McDonald et al., vol. 14, p. 225.
26. See Chapter One of this work.
27. McDonald et al., vol. 14, p. 225.
28. Edward J. Kilmartin, S.J., "Full Participation of Women in the Life of the Catholic Church," in Coriden, ed., *Sexism and Church Law* (New York: Paulist Press, 1977), p. 110.
29. The *New Catholic Encyclopedia* documents that "The Apostles preached to us the gospel received from Jesus Christ." McDonald et al., vol. 14, p. 225.
30. See Luke 11.27-28. This passage has been previously discussed in Chapter Two of this work.
31. For the complete discussion, see Appendix II in Swidler and Swidler, pp. 338-346.
32. McDonald et al., vol. 14, p. 225.
33. For the complete discussion, see Swidler and Swidler, p. 38.
34. Sandra M. Schneiders, *The Revelatory Text: Interpreting the New Testament as Sacred Scripture* (San Francisco: Harper Collins, 1991), p. 120.
35. McDonald et al., vol. 13, p. 281.
36. Swidler and Swidler, pp. 40-41.
37. Raymond Brown contends that the development of Christian priesthood per se did not occur until the year A.D. 70. For complete discussion, see *Priest and Bishop*, pp. 13-21.
38. See Chapter Two of this work.
39. For a good discussion of the dynamics which revelation and the prophetic tradition imply, see Radford Ruether, "Feminist Interpretation: A Method of Correlation," pp. 111-124.

40. Avery Dulles S.J., *Models of the Church* (New York: Image Books, 1974), pp. 95–98.
41. *Ibid.,* p. 99.
42. *Ibid.,* p. 100.
43. Abbott, p. 242.
44. For complete discussion, see Cooke, *Ministry to Word and Sacraments,* pp. 343–349.
45. For complete discussion, see Denise Lardner-Carmody, *The Double Cross: Ordination, Abortion and Catholic Feminism* (New York: Crossroad, 1986), Part I.
46. I am thinking here of the "Pastoral Constitution on the Church in the Modern World," as well as the "Decree on the Apostolate of the Laity," in Abbott, ed., *The Documents of Vatican II.*
47. Edward Schillebeeckx, *The Church with a Human Face,* p. 265.
48. *Ibid.,* p. 266.
49. This information is documented in McDonald et al., vol. 14, p. 735.
50. See Abbott, pp. 584–633.
51. *Ibid.,* pp. 613–614.
52. *Ibid.,* p. 614.
53. This prayer is a matter of public knowledge. No permission was required to reprint it.
54. For the complete discussion, see Chapter Four of this work.
55. These are lyrics taken from a song entitled "Spirit Blowing Through Creation," in *Gather* #191 (Chicago: GIA Publications, Inc., 1988). In a recent interview, the Pope reiterated that the shortage of priests was not a sign of the times because the Church maintains Jesus' promise in Matthew 28.20. Roles for women in the Church, he said, are "deeply rooted in Christian anthropology and sacramentology." For complete discussion, see "Pope Speaks Out on the Role of Laity and of Women in the Church," in *The Prairie Messenger* (July 19, 1993), pp. 18–19.
56. This point is reiterated by Edward J. Kilmartin S.J., in Coriden, *Sexism and Church Law,* p. 127.
57. Sandra M. Schneiders, "The Effects of Women's Experience on Their Spirituality," in Wolski Conn, pp. 31–48.
58. *Ibid.,* p. 32.
59. *Ibid.,* p. 35.
60. *Ibid.,* p. 40.
61. *Ibid.,* p. 41.
62. *Ibid.,* p. 44.
63. Abbott, p. 240.
64. Radford Ruether, *Women-Church: Theology and Practice of Feminist Liturgical Communities* (San Francisco: Harper and Row, 1985), p. 87.
65. *Ibid.,* p. 90.
66. *Ibid.*
67. Elisabeth Schüssler-Fiorenza, "The Will to Choose or to Reject: Continuing Our Critical Work," in Russell, p. 126.
68. Cooke, "Non-Patriarchal Salvation," p. 281.
69. Elisabeth Schüssler-Fiorenza in Chapter Six of her book *But She Said: Feminist Practices of Biblical Interpretation* (Boston, Mass.: Beacon Press, 1992)

has discussed the educational practices within the theological discipline for women. Although the theological education of women is to some degree a secular matter, it bears a certain amount of significance to my discussion of the ordination of women as it also calls for a conversion of sorts. Further, theological institutes are more and more responsible for the training of ministers and teachers. This in turn contributes to the socialization of parishioners and the philosophies of Church structure. In short, if theological institutes in their teaching and administering functions promote patriarchy and sexism, certainly a conversion is also required at this level. Schüssler-Fiorenza articulates this position rather well and enumerates various ways in which this process can be accomplished.

Conclusion

1. Kilmartin, p. 127.
2. Schüssler-Fiorenza, *In Memory of Her,* pp. 345-346.
3. Archbishop Rembert G. Weakland's support for women priests continues, despite the Pope's fear of "radical feminism" in John Thavis' article "Pope Wary—Fearful—of 'Radical Feminism'," in *The Prairie Messenger* (July 19, 1993), pp. 1-2.
4. In a recent interview, Edward Schillebeeckx observed that the exclusion of women from the ministerial priesthood is a discriminatory practice based on a cultural restriction. The Church, he noted, should prepare for women's ordination or it could meet a horrible schism. He also observed that the Anglican Church's decision to confer ordination upon its female members was an important step toward ecumenism because Catholics are leaning in this direction. This interview was recently conducted by Rev. Francesco Strazzari and published in Italian. The English title has been translated as *I Am a Happy Theologian* by Agostino Bono in his article "Church Should Prepare for Women Priests," in *The Prairie Messenger* (July 5, 1993), p. 20.

Appendix

An Address by the Most Rev. Rembert G. Weakland, O.S.B. Archbishop of Milwaukee, to the Roman Synod, October 1987

Pope John XXIII, in his encyclical, Pacem in Terris (1963), stated: "Since women are becoming ever more conscious of their human dignity, they will not tolerate being treated as mere material instruments, but demand rights befitting a human person both in domestic and public life" (#41). The Synod of Bishops in 1971 added to this concept the importance of the role of women in the Church. Implementing that agenda on the role of women in Church and society is perhaps the most significant challenge we face today as disciples of Christ.

Many women, it is true, are satisfied with the present situation. The hearing sessions conducted by the bishops of the United States in preparation for this Synod and for a pastoral letter they are preparing as a response to women's concerns for Church and Society in the United States attest to the love but also the frustration so many women feel at this point with regard to their Church.

The intensity of that feeling places an urgency upon all of us. This is not just an issue affecting some regions of the world but one which definitely touches the credibility of the Church's teaching on human dignity everywhere on this planet.

In the past, women contributed much to the life of the Church, especially in the areas of education and health services. In being grateful for their contributions of the past, we must look forward to the full expression of their codiscipleship in the Church today and in the future.

Women, as members of the Church, are not expecting all the answers from those holding authority in the Church, but only that women be partners in finding the solutions. Most of all, they want Church leaders to treat them as Jesus treated women. His approach to women was open, trusting, and respectful.

Women in the Gospels ministered to, with, and for Jesus. He, in turn, was sensitive to their needs. Women ask for the same kinds of mutual relationships in the Church they serve today, relationships that are not paternalistic nor condescending, that do not create passivity and dependency.

The bishops of the United States have been faithful in upholding the teaching of the Church as stated in the Declaration of the Sacred Congregation for the Doctrine of the Faith (*Inter Insigniores* 1976), namely, that "the Church, in fidelity to the example of the Lord, does not consider herself authorized to admit women to priestly ordination." That same document affirms that nonordination to priesthood must not be seen as a manifestation of baptismal inferiority. Honesty forces us to admit, however, that the issue was raised by men and women in almost every hearing around the nation.

Many questioned, too, why so many aspects of jurisdiction in the Church are tied into the power of Orders and felt that leadership roles for women in the Church would be excluded without some change in this regard.

In their desire to be codisciples in the Kingdom, women rightly cite Mary as the first disciple, the first who heard God's word and said her *fiat*. Many see her as a feminine image of partnership with God. Her courage and her fidelity make her an admirable model for all. She exemplified that unique blend of gentleness and firmness, of personal sacrifice and God's grace, that permitted her to be God's partner in the birth of Jesus. Mary is also a model of how God favors the lowly and humble; Mary identified with those who were poor and suffering and showed God's liberating energies working in and with her. Thus, she brings hope to those in need.

Because so often today Society tends to treat women as inferior or as objects, it is important that the Church struggle to root out all vestiges of such sexism. In society this implies, for example, that the Church must respond to women's concerns about such issues as just wages and equality with men in the work force, about the value of parenting and family life. Women in Society tend to be economically disadvantaged because of such discrimination (this is especially true among women of color); this must not also be true in Church life. Sexism, denoting an expression of inferiority because of being a woman, must be guarded against in Church teaching and action. For example, in Society and Church one must guard against reducing the human person—man or woman—to a selective collection of psychological characteristics.

This Synod could recommend that some practical steps be taken at once to remedy the situation—at least in part:

- by permitting all laity (thus, also women) to function in all liturgical roles that do not demand priestly ordination (e.g., altar server, lector, acolyte, preaching);

- by opening to all laity (thus, also women) decision-making and administrative roles on all levels of Church life (e.g., in the diocesan offices—as chancellor, in every aspect of the tribunal system; on the level of the universal Church—major positions in the *curia* and diplomatic corps);
- by a sensitivity to language in liturgical and other official texts so that it will always include women;
- by avoidance of perpetuating the negative and condescending cultural aspects of patriarchy inherent in some of the historical and biblical narratives;
- by fostering collaborative models of working with clergy that are mutually supportive in pastoral ministry and are not based on any manifestations of inferiority or dependency;
- by continuing to support family values and the specific role of women in the home without denying women major roles in public and societal life;
- by fighting against all forces that degrade women and view them as objects, such as pornography, prostitution, and the like.

Codiscipleship means we are not isolated individuals in the Church but, rather, a priestly people who share together the mission given us in baptism and who, thus, work together in mutual collaboration. Codiscipleship will lead to a new realization and appreciation for the gifts of women in particular in the Church today. In gratitude for their specific contributions of the past we must then seek new ways with them of assuring their full participation in Church and in Society, now and in the future.

Bibliography

Abbott, Walter, S.J., ed. *The Documents of Vatican II* (New York: Guild Press, 1966). This work compiles the documents which resulted from Vatican II, along with several appendices which contain supplementary talks that were omitted from the documents themselves. This lengthy work is an excellent source for all Catholics, as it represents a turning point in the history of the Roman Catholic Church.

Anderson, Grace M., and Juanne Nancarrow-Clarke. *God Calls: Man Chooses—A Study of Women in Ministry* (Burlington, Ontario: Trinity Press, 1990). This research paper probes the lives of Canadian women in four seminaries of different denominations. This study addresses the conflicts and dynamics which surround women in ministry. The work includes a well-documented bibliography as well as three appendices which contain valuable research notes for anyone attempting to engage in a similar study.

Argan, Glen. "Excluding Women from Priestly Ministry Based on Narrow View," in *The Prairie Messenger* (April 12, 1993), p. 18. This article relates the biological exclusion of women to the ministerial priesthood with comparable prejudices which were used to characterize certain people because of their ethnicity or gender.

Ashe, Kaye. *Today's Woman, Tomorrow's Church* (Chicago, Illinois: Thomas More Press, 1983). This work represents the findings of a questionnaire which was circulated among Catholic women. It documents women's experiences, tensions, hopes and visions. Chapter Five concludes with four addresses from groups and organizations that are committed to the fostering of equality for women within the Church. The work concludes with a very detailed bibliography, along with helpful suggestions for future readings.

Babych, Art. "Altar Girls Not a Vatican but Diocesan Issue," in *The Prairie Messenger* (June 21, 1993), p. 6. This article reiterates the conflicts which have contributed to the official Church's silence regarding the question of altar girls.

Baroni, Lise. "The Creative Emergence of Women Working in the Church," in *Women, for What World, in What Church?* Donum Dei Series #30, Canadian Religious Conference (Ottawa, 1985), pp. 45–68. This talk builds upon the mandate which the gospel initiates for men and women to work (co-responsibly) for the Church's credibility regarding issues such as justice and equality in today's world.

Bono, Agostino. "Church Should Prepare for Women Priests," in *The Prairie Messenger* (July 5, 1993), p. 20. This article documents comments made by Edward Schillebeeckx which regard women's exclusion from juridical and authoritative positions in the Church today as a discriminatory practice.

Boucher, Madeleine I. "Women and the Apostolic Community," in Swidler and Swidler, eds., *Women Priests* (New York: Paulist Press, 1974), pp. 152-155. In this brief article, Boucher challenges the *Declaration*'s exclusion of women from the ministerial priesthood based upon the practice of the apostolic community, and in doing so, raises various points which seem to discredit the *Declaration*'s claim.

Brooten, Bernadette. "Early Christian Women and Their Cultural Context," in *Feminist Perspectives on Biblical Scholarship* (Chico, California: Scholars Press, 1985), pp. 65-91. In this article, Brooten offers a biblical methodology in terms of a feminist reconstruction of women's historicity derived from a feminist perspective, instead of a male-oriented framework. This is a well-documented paper which offers a refreshing perspective in terms of the manner in which research is done and of the methodology itself.

_____. "Junia ... Outstanding Among the Apostles," (Romans 16:7) in Swidler and Swidler, eds., *Women Priests* (New York: Paulist Press, 1974), pp. 141-144. In this article, Brooten challenges Junia's gender and examines the implications which result from the context in Romans 16:7.

Brown, Raymond E. "Mary in the New Testament and in Catholic Life," in *America* (May 15, 1982), pp. 374-379. This brief article discusses Mary's treatment in the New Testament. Brown's main thesis is that Mary was an exemplary disciple whose spirit of service remains a role model for all Catholics to strive to imitate. Brown demonstrates his ability to treat numerous biblical texts accurately given the limited space available.

_____. *Priest and Bishop: Biblical Reflections* (New York: Paulist Press, 1970). A brief but significant work which begins with the biblical foundations for Catholic priesthood. From there, Brown's attention shifts to the role of the bishops, and concludes with a short discussion of the hierarchy and its function. In doing so, Brown calls attention to the historicity of Catholic priesthood and demonstrates his scholarly expertise regarding scriptural tradition.

_____. "Roles of Women in the Fourth Gospel," *Theological Studies* 30 (April, 1975), pp. 688-699. In this article, Raymond Brown's attention focuses primarily on the manner in which women are portrayed in the Fourth Gospel. His sources are very well documented, and Brown touches upon other related themes which bear significance to any study of women's roles in scripture and in the early Church.

Buttrick, G.A., et al., eds. *The Interpreter's Bible* (Abingdon, New York: Cokesbury Press, 1957). This is a twelve-volume alphabetical work which provides prefaces, introductions, maps and articles for the interpretive study of Old Testament and New Testament texts. Although dated, it provides a sound body of information regarding any biblical text.

Byrne, Brendan, S.J. *Paul and the Christian Woman* (Homebush, NSW: St. Paul Publications, 1988). This study examines certain Pauline texts which describe women or assign women certain functions, and seeks to establish the writings' context and meaning. It is well documented in terms of scripture and recent biblical scholarship.

Callahan, Sidney. "Misunderstanding of Sexuality and Resistance to Women Priests," in Swidler and Swidler, eds., *Women Priests* (New York: Paulist Press, 1974), pp. 291-294. In this article, Callahan defends her support of women's ordination from a gender-related perspective.

———. "Then and Now, Women Won't Take No for an Answer," in *The Prairie Messenger* (June 21, 1993), p. 15. This article documents the action of 100 women who recently gathered in New York to publicly demand justice for women in the Church.

Cantin, Paule. "Opening Address," in Donum Dei Series #30, Canadian Religious Conference (Ottawa, 1985), pp. 13-17. As the title suggests, this talk was the "opening address" for the Canadian Religious Conference in 1985. As such, it states the purpose of the conference as the recognition that men and women are the Church, and that each have gifts which should be employed to their fullest, regardless of one's gender, race or color.

Cardman, Francine. "Tradition, Hermeneutics, and Ordination," in James A. Coriden, ed., *Sexism and Church Law* (New York: Paulist Press, 1977), pp. 58-81. In this well-documented article, Cardman examines what tradition is, how it is defined, and how it is significant to the historical and theological aspects involved when considering the exclusion of women from the ministerial priesthood.

Carroll, Elizabeth. "Women and Ministry," in *Theological Studies* 36 (December, 1975), pp. 660-687. In her article, Elizabeth Carroll examines the *Declaration*'s restriction of women to the ministerial priesthood. In doing so, she calls for a restructuring of the ministerial parameters which exclude women from serving Christ's church. Carroll's argument is clear and to the point and demonstrates the feminist pursuit of a more egalitarian Church structure.

Chittister, Sr. Joan. *Woman Strength: Modern Church, Modern Women* (Kansas City, MO: Sheed & Ward, 1990). This is a collection of sixteen essays which discuss contemporary issues facing women and Catholicism. Chittister also touches upon issues such as spirituality, politics and ministry which relate to men and women alike. It is a good source book for feminists as well.

———. *Women, Ministry and the Church* (New York: Paulist Press, 1983). In this work, Sister Joan treats the role of women in Roman Catholicism from a pastoral perspective. She also touches upon women in religious life and calls for a renewal of traditional teachings in the Church. This work demonstrates Sr. Joan's dedication toward women's ministerial functions in the Church whether lay or religious. It outlines basic guidelines for authentic challenges which men and women experience in a contemporary setting.

Connell, Monsignor Desmond. "Women Priests: Why Not?" in Helmut Moll, ed., *The Church and Women: A Compendium* (San Francisco: Ignatius Press, 1988), pp. 207-227. In this article, Monsignor Connell reflects upon the question of women's ordination from various perspectives, including the common priesthood of all believers, symbolic and sacramental representation and Christ's salvific mission. In doing so, Connell articulates the arguments stated in the *Declaration* and concludes that a woman's "proper" role accorded through creation prevents her from representing Christ, "because the *Head* of the race is a man." For reasons already stated throughout this book, this remains unacceptable to Christian tradition.

Cooke, Bernard. *Ministry to Word and Sacraments* (Philadelphia: Fortress Press, 1976). This lengthy work provides an accurate description of Christian ministry in the early Christian communities, along with the historical emergence of Christian ministry as we experience in a contemporary Roman Catholic setting. Cooke discusses specific questions regarding the exercise of Christian ministry. This is an excellent resource which touches upon various facets of ministry including historical and theological elements.

_____. "Non-Patriarchal Salvation," in *Women's Spirituality: Resources for Christian Development,* ed. Joann Wolski Conn (New York: Paulist Press, 1986), pp. 274-286. This brief yet significant study examines the "maleness" of God from a theological perspective. In doing so, Cooke very aptly observes the "non-patriarchal" character of Jesus' salvific action toward humankind.

Coriden, James A., ed. *Sexism and Church Law* (New York: Paulist Press, 1977). This is a compilation of articles which discuss the origin of ecclesiastical laws that remain unjust toward women in the Roman Catholic Church. In doing so, they provide a wealth of information and incite dialogue regarding a revision of laws which continue to perpetuate a systemic discrimination against women. Appendices contain the *Biblical Commission Report: Can Women Be Priests?* and the *Declaration on the Question of the Admission of Women to the Ministerial Priesthood.*

_____, et al., eds. *The Code of Canon Law: A Text and Commentary* (New York: Paulist Press, 1985). This is an excellent guide which includes background information and discusses dynamics which surround the issues at hand. It is a good source for the laws and juridical codes which govern the current Roman Catholic Church.

Donahue, John R. "A Tale of Two Documents," in Swidler and Swidler, eds., *Women Priests* (New York: Paulist Press, 1974), pp. 25-34. This article lays the groundwork and background for the Biblical Commission's Report regarding women's ordination and the *Declaration* of 1976 which forbids women access to ministerial orders. Although the essay is brief, Donahue manages to uncover the main conflicts involved and his sources are very well documented.

_____. "Women, Priesthood and the Vatican," in *America* (April 2, 1977), pp. 285-289. In this brief article, John R. Donahue calls into question the *Declaration*'s use of scripture, tradition and theology to defend the exclusion of women from the ministerial priesthood. He describes the *Declaration*'s argument as a "negative agenda" and concludes with a vision of a more egalitarian practice of ministry in the Church. This article comes to terms with the issues at hand, and demonstrates the extent to which the *Declaration*'s restriction against women remains unsettling to modern-day priests.

Doyle, James L. "We Are the Church," in *National Bulletin on Liturgy,* vol. 20, no. 109 (May-June, 1987), pp. 182-183. This talk was presented in homily style, and attempts to portray the Church as the people of God. As such, this concept remains impractical because it is limited to the confines of a hierarchic and pyramidal structure. This talk reiterates a traditionalist perspective, and offers no practical signs of the need to declericalize the current Church structure.

Drane, John. *Introducing the New Testament* (San Francisco: Harper and Row, 1986). This illuminating work gives a detailed introduction to the New Testament. Drane draws attention to the religious and social customs under which it was written and gives a detailed background of its significance to the formation of the early Church. This work serves as a basic guide for an elementary study of scripture.

Dulles, Avery, S.J. "The Authority of Scripture: A Catholic Perspective," in Frederick E. Greenspahn, ed., *Scripture in the Jewish and Christian Traditions* (Nashville, Tenn.: Abingdon Press, 1982), pp. 13-40. In this study, Dulles examines the question of authority and its relationship to scripture and tradition in the Roman Catholic Church.

_____. *Models of the Church* (New York: Image Books, 1974). In this book, Avery Dulles develops a system of models which describes five dimensions of Catholic ecclesiology. In doing so, he offers new insights for ministry which are usually characterized by the most obvious, traditional model. This book could be used in various ways, including private reflection or as a starting point for Catholic discussion groups.

_____. *The Reshaping of Catholicism: Current Challenges in the Theology of Church* (San Francisco: Harper and Row, 1988). This book is a compilation of previously published articles which were revised for publication. As such, each chapter discusses certain issues which have plagued Roman Catholicism since Vatican II. In this manner, it can be read as an historical account of the Church's conflicts, as Dulles gives very accurate information surrounding the drafting of conciliar documents and the like.

Dunn, Patrick J. *Priesthood: A Re-examination of the Roman Catholic Theology of the Presbyterate* (New York: Alba House, 1990). This work focuses on the rediscovery of the ordained presbyter. Dunn touches upon the scriptural foundations which have governed the form under which the current presbyterate functions, and gives a detailed perspective on the history surrounding the modern Roman Catholic Church's understanding of the presbyterate in the light of contemporary questions.

Farley, Margaret. "Moral Imperatives for the Ordination of Women," in Anne Marie Gardiner, S.S.N.D., ed., *Women and Catholic Priesthood: An Expanded Vision* (New York: Paulist Press, 1976), pp. 35-51. In this well-documented article, Farley examines the moral implications surrounding the question of women in ministry, and challenges the arguments used to justify women's exclusion from Catholic priesthood.

Faxon, Alicia. *Women and Jesus* (Philadelphia: United Church Press, 1973). A work which attempts to recover women's significance within biblical texts, and apply Jesus' message to modern-day questions. Sources are well documented, and the book includes an annotated bib- liography.

Fessio, Father Joseph. "Reasons Given Against Women Acolytes and Lectors," in *Origins* 17, no. 22 (Nov. 12, 1987), pp. 397-399. This paper was circulated by Fr. Fessio himself at the occasion of the Synod of Bishops in 1987. It reiterates the traditional arguments used to justify the exclusion of female altar-servers from theological and practical perspectives.

Bibliography

Filteau, Jerry. "Religious Want Full Place at Roman Synod," in *The Prairie Messenger* (April 19, 1993), p. 4. This article documents a plea from women religious to be included among full members who will deliberate their fate at the Synod of Bishops in 1994. It bears significance to the study of women priests because women religious experience a systemic discrimination as well.

Forest, Jean. "Women in the Canadian Context," in Michael W. Higgins and Douglas R. Letson, eds., *Women and the Church* (Toronto, Canada: Griffin House, 1986), pp. 163-172. In this article, Forest examines women's strengths and giftedness within Roman Catholicism, outlining the need for reconsideration of women's ministerial roles in the Church.

Fox, Thomas C. "Altar-Girl Issue Seen as Symbol in Rome," in *National Catholic Reporter* (Nov. 6, 1987), p. 20. This article documents Rome's official refusal to discuss the issue of altar girls in the Church.

Furlong, Monica, ed. *Feminine in the Church* (London: SPCK, 1984). This collection of essays focuses on the ordination of women in the Anglican Church, and includes a detailed study about women's status on the ecclesiastical as well as social scale. In doing so, one will observe that certain questions treated from an Anglican perspective parallel those which emerge in the Catholic Church. This work contributes to the ongoing tensions which women experience in a Roman Catholic setting and perhaps provides a motif of solidarity for women in all Christian churches.

Gardiner, Anne Marie, ed. *Women and Catholic Priesthood: An Expanded Vision* (New York: Paulist Press, 1976). This work documents the presentations given at the Detroit Ordination Conference. It contains dialogue, prayer and various appendices including a roster of people who attended the conference.

Gervais, Marty. "Women Keeping the Faith for a Chance at Ordination," in *The Saturday Windsor Star* (June 11, 1988), p. 6. This article documents the actions taken by a group of Catholic women who belong to an organization called *Catholic Network for Women's Equality*. The illustration which accompanies the article really carries the group's point across.

Getty, Mary Ann. "God's Fellow Worker and Apostleship," in Swidler and Swidler, eds., *Women Priests* (New York: Paulist Press, 1974), pp. 176-182. In this article, Getty examines the language used in the *Declaration* to determine the context between official public ministry and the service rendered by women in Paul's gospel (i.e., the gospel attributed to Paul).

Gillman, Florence M. *Women Who Knew Paul* (Collegeville, Minn.: The Liturgical Press, 1991). This work gathers information about the women who surrounded Paul and explores their significance in detail. In doing so, Gillman probes scripture as well as nonliterary works in an attempt to gain historical accuracy as well as the traditional perspective regarding these women's roles. The work is well documented and gives a helpful list of works for further reading.

Gonzalez, Ramon. "Women Not Yet Welcome in Heart of Church," in *The Prairie Messenger* (May 17, 1993), p. 2. This article documents recent comments made by Mary Malone regarding the Church's official refusal to accept women as full members.

Greenspahn, Frederick E., ed. *Scripture in the Jewish and Christian Traditions*

(Nashville, Tenn.: Abingdon Press, 1982). This is a collection of works which examine scripture and its significance, authority and interpretation from various perspectives. It is a good starting point for the study of scripture in light of Jewish, Catholic and Protestant traditions.

Gryson, Roger. *The Ministry of Women in the Early Church,* transl. Jean LaPorte and Mary Louise Hall (Collegeville, Minn.: Liturgical Press, 1976). This study probes various texts and Church documents in search of the historicity and authenticity of the deaconess' role and function in the early Church tradition. This is an extensive research work and is very well documented.

Günther, Heinz. *The Footprints of Jesus' Twelve in Early Christian Traditions: A Study in the Meaning of Religious Symbolism* (New York: Peter Lang Press, 1985). In this work, Günther examines the historicity of the Twelve's biblical tradition. In doing so, Günther makes use of the Qumran texts as well as important findings regarding the numerological symbolism attached to the *Twelve.* The work includes a detailed bibliography, an index of quotations and a subject index.

Haight, Roger, S.J. "The Ministry of the Laity: History, Principles, Challenges" (unpublished, Regis College Lecture Series, 1987). In this talk, Roger Haight outlines a theology of ministry rooted in Jesus' community of believers. Much of his discussion finds similar parallels in Edward Schillebeeckx's *The Church with a Human Face.* He also addresses challenges for future synods including a declericalizing of the current hierarchy.

Hall, Barbara. "Paul and Women," in *Theology Today* 31 (April 1974), pp. 50-57. Here Hall treats various biblical passages attributed to Paul, and demonstrates that certain texts deemed exclusionary to women can be interpreted as specific instructions given to certain communities regarding proper conduct during worship services. Hall claims that Paul's texts can be interpreted in favor of women's active participation, conforming to Christ's example.

Hamelin, Bishop Jean Guy. "Access of Women to Church Positions," in *Synod of Bishops* (Rome: CCCB, 1987), pp. 7-8. In this intervention, Bishop Hamelin appeals for women's recognition and access to responsible leadership roles within the Roman Catholic Church.

Hardon, John A. *The Catholic Catechism* (Garden City, New York: Doubleday, 1975). This work gives an accurate account of the doctrines, morality, spirituality, rituals and worship that are contained in Catholic faith. It is an excellent resource for catechists, parents, and anyone wanting to research the most basic tenets on which the Catholic faith was built.

Harris, Louise. *Women in the Christian Church* (Brighton, Michigan: Green Oak Press, 1988). This illustrative book traces the historical, scriptural and traditional path of women's position and eventual exclusion from leadership roles. The appendix contains the names and epitaphs of distinguished women in Christian history.

Harvey, Van A. *A Handbook of Theological Terms* (New York: Macmillan, 1964). This is a handy alphabetical guide of the terminology used in systematic and philosophical theology.

Haughton, Rosemary. "Lay Community, a Prophetic Movement," in *Compass* 4 (Oct. 1987), pp. 13-17. In this brief article, Rosemary Haughton describes the manner in which laypersons are restructuring their concept of ministry into creative and concrete undertakings which are rooted in Christ's example. In doing so, Haughton centers upon a North American social perspective.

Hauke, Manfred. "Observations on the Ordination of Women to the Diaconate," transl. Graham Harrison, in Helmut Moll, ed., *The Church and Women: A Compendium* (San Francisco: Ignatius Press, 1988), pp. 117-139. This article examines the current debate over the official recognition of women deacons in the Roman Catholic Church. Hauke outlines the theological, pastoral and historical significance of ordaining women deacons, and concludes that it is theologically impossible to do so within the current Catholic mindset. What is required is an emphasis on a ministry of service exemplified by men and women alike.

Heine, Suzanne. *Women and Early Christianity* (Minneapolis: Augsburg Publishing House, 1987). A feminist interpretation of women's roles in the early tradition of the Roman Catholic Church. Scriptural and bibliographical sources are well documented.

Higgins, Michael W., and Douglas R. Letson, eds. *Women and the Church: A Sourcebook* (Toronto, Canada: Griffin House, 1986). An excellent resource for educators and students concerned with the critical issues which surround any study of women in the Church.

The Holy Bible, R.S.V. (New York: Collins, 1973).

Hopko, Thomas, ed. *Women and the Priesthood* (New York: St. Vladimir's Seminary Press, 1983). This work is a series of essays which discuss the priesthood of women in the Orthodox tradition. It touches upon various questions which emerge in the study of the exclusion of women from the ministerial priesthood in the Roman Catholic Church as many of the historical and scriptural materials recur in both traditions. It exemplifies the struggle which other Christian churches are currently encountering to redefine appropriate roles for women in light of Christian tradition.

Huels, John. *The Pastoral Companion* (Quincy, Ill.: The Franciscan Herald Press, 1986). This is an excellent reference for the code of canon law. It also serves as a guide for Catholic ministry.

Human Resources in the Catholic Church of Canada, 1987-88 (Remunerated Personnel) (Ottawa, Canada: C.C.C.B., 1988). This booklet accurately documents the statistical information on the number of available priests in the Canadian Catholic Church. It demonstrates the shortage of priests today, and projects a serious decline in the number of available priests for the years to come.

Jewett, Robert. "Paul, Phoebe and the Spanish Mission," in Jacob Neusner et al., eds., *The Social World of Formative Christianity and Judaism* (Philadelphia: Fortress Press, 1988), pp. 142-161. This work examines the social dynamics which surrounded Paul as a missionary figure. Jewett calls attention to Phoebe's missionary activity and postulates that she was a key figure in Paul's attempt to evangelize Spain. This article is very well documented with contemporary biblical scholarship, and demonstrates Jewett's ability to articulate converging ideas in such a limited setting.

John Paul II. *On the Dignity and Vocation of Women on the Occasion of the Marian Year* (Rome: Vatican Polygot Press, 1988). This is an

Apostolic letter which attempts to correlate the theological understanding for the dignity of women with the diversity of roles that men and women perform in the Roman Catholic Church. It gives a clear perception of the theological impediments which restrict the role of women in the Roman Catholic Church.

Kilmartin, Edward J., S.J. "Full Participation of Women in the Life of the Catholic Church," in James A. Coriden, ed., *Sexism and Church Law* (New York: Paulist Press, 1977), pp. 109-135. In this article, Kilmartin traces the development of the official Church's policies regarding the inclusion of women in Church positions between 1971 and 1976. He then proceeds to examine the official Church's arguments regarding the apparent exclusion of women from certain roles. This article is well documented and includes a postscript following the Vatican's official word on the subject contained in the *Declaration* in 1976.

Komonchak, Joseph. "Theological Questions on the Ordination of Women," *Catholic Mind* 75 (Jan. 1977), pp. 13-28. This brief article examines the theological basis for the restriction of women priests. In doing so, Komonchak wrestles with the main arguments presented in the *Declaration*. Despite the article's brevity, Komonchak clarifies the most basic reasons for which the *Declaration* considers it appropriate to restrict women from ministerial service.

Kroeger, Catherine. "The Neglected History of Women in the Early Church," in *Christian History* 8, no. 1 (Issue 17), pp. 6-11. In this brief article, Catherine Kroeger searches to uncover the prominence of women in early Christianity.

Küng, Hans, and Leonard Swidler, eds. *The Church in Anguish* (San Francisco: Harper and Row, 1987). This series of essays probes the thought of various Catholic theologians who discuss serious issues which Vatican II addressed that are still in need of renewal and re-examination within the Church today, and will continue to plague Catholicism if Roman officials neglect to address them. This work could serve as a sourcebook for contemporary catholicism as each chapter treats a different issue.

Lacelle, Elisabeth J. "From Today to Tomorrow: Women in the Canadian Catholic Church," in Michael W. Higgins and Douglas R. Letson, eds., *Women and the Church* (Toronto, Canada: Griffin House, 1986), pp. 151-158. This article traces the historical development of an ad hoc committee formed in 1984 to study the role of women in the Church along with the C.C.C.B. (Canadian Conference of Catholic Bishops). This paper is well documented and gives a brief but concise account of the committee's struggles and accomplishments.

_____. "Should the Church Come Forward as a Project for a New Humanity," in Donum Dei Series #30, Canadian Religious Conference (Ottawa, 1985), pp. 85-103. This talk focuses on the giftedness and potential of God's people and calls these gifts to action for the benefit of all.

Lardner-Carmody, Denise. *The Double-Cross: Ordination, Abortion and Catholic Feminism* (New York: Crossroad, 1986). In this work, Denise Lardner-Carmody reflects on two very significant issues for women: ordination and abortion in relation to a feminist spirituality. This is a feminist work which stems from Catholic tradition. Lardner-Carmody raises various issues which could easily stimulate private reflection or group discussions.

Lebel, Bishop Robert. "The Role of Women in Family Ministry and the Life of the Church," in Higgins and Letson, eds., *Women and the Church* (Toronto, Canada: Griffin House, 1986), pp. 176-178. In this brief statement, Bishop Lebel identifies the feminist movement within the Church as a "positive reality." In doing so, he states that the Church must move beyond women's roles as wives and mothers and seriously discuss active and responsible roles which women can undertake. This talk is definitely a positive step in according women their proper dignity in the Church. However, the article (dated 1980) is indicative of the inability of the hierarchy to actually listen to what its people are saying.

Leckey, Dolores. "Power-Sharing Essential to Equality of Sexes," in *The Prairie Messenger* (June 14, 1993), p. 12. This brief article discusses the dynamics involved in partnership within marriage and their extension into the social sphere.

Légaré, Rev. Henri, OMI. "Task of the Whole Church," in *National Bulletin on Liturgy* 8 (March-April, 1975), pp. 93-96. This talk's main message focuses on the lay-faithful's task of evangelizing rooted in baptism and confirmation. It is a gospel-centered message which draws upon the traditional understandings of laity and clergy.

Lewis, Murray. "Synod: We Missed a Wonderful Chance," in *The Prairie Messenger* (March 21, 1988), p. 1. This article documents the Canadian bishops' disappointment following the Synod of Bishops in Rome of 1987. It is indicative of the monopoly that the official Church exercises even among its clergy.

Liebard, Odile M. *Clergy and Laity* (Wilmington, N.C.: McGrath, 1978). This work documents the Catholic Church's teaching on clergy and laity. It provides the history, tradition and challenges for the future. This work has been well researched and would serve as an excellent teaching and pastoral guide.

Liefeld, Walter L. "Women, Submission and Ministry in I Corinthians," in Alvera Mickelsen, ed., *Women, Authority, & the Bible* (Downers Grove, Illinois: Intervarsity Press, 1986), pp. 134-160. Here, Liefeld gives an in-depth look at the tensions which scholars identify while searching to interpret I Corinthians 11.2-16 as well as I Corinthians 14.33b-40. The work includes an interesting response by Alan F. Johnson, professor of New Testament and theological ethics at Wheaton College in Illinois.

Lineamenta (Ottawa, Canada: CCCB, 1985). This was the official working paper in preparation for the 1987 Synod of Bishops. Each section ends with a series of questions designed to evaluate the current situation. It is a good indication of the tensions regarding the laity's role in the Church and in the secular sphere.

Lisheron, Mark. "Weakland Calls for Women in Vatican," in *The Milwaukee Journal* (December 6, 1992). This article documents Archbishop Rembert G. Weakland's comments regarding the installation of women within the bureaucratic departments of the Vatican, while maintaining that the exclusion of women to the ministerial priesthood reinforces the Church's attitude that women are inferior to men.

McAteer, Michael. "Catholics Learn New Buzzword," in *The Toronto Star* (Oct. 1986). This article focuses on the spirit of coresponsibility Canadian bishops sensed they would carry to the Roman Synod in 1987. The article also gives statistical information regarding the survey which was circulated in an attempt to identify the Canadian Catholic Church's strengths and weaknesses.

McBrien, Richard. *Ministry* (San Francisco: Harper and Row, 1987). In this work, Richard McBrien discusses a theology of ministry and outlines practical pastoral guidelines for clergy, religious educators, chaplains and anyone who engages in Church ministries exercised by clergy or laity. The work includes a list of materials for suggested readings, as well as an appendix of pastoral reflections from the United States bishops.

Mc Donald, William J., et al., eds. *New Catholic Encyclopedia* (Washington, D.C.: Catholic University of America, 1967). A seventeen-volume work which serves as an excellent resource for the history, theology, and social elements in Roman Catholicism. It even includes resources which touch upon other Christian subjects.

MacHaffie, Barbara J. *Her Story: Women in Christian Tradition* (Philadelphia: Fortress Press, 1986). This study probes the social and cultural tradition surrounding women in the early Church from a feminist perspective. Each chapter is well documented and includes an extensive list of materials for further reading.

McIver, Mary. "Barred from the Church Altar," in *Maclean's* (July 6, 1987), p. 45. This article documents the official Church's restriction imposed upon an eleven-year-old girl who wished to serve at a Mass that celebrated her parish's 100th anniversary. Comments were printed from Sarah, her mother Suzanne, and Church canonist Fr. Francis Morrisey.

McKenna, Sister Mary. *Women of the Church* (New York: P.J. Kennedy & Sons, 1967). This work probes the historicity of women's roles in the tradition of the Roman Catholic Church. Although somewhat dated, the historical information is accurate and well documented.

Marmon, Lucretia. "Why Can't Women Be Priests Again?" in *Glamour* (Sept. 1991), p. 112. This very brief article uncovers Dr. Mary Ann Rossi's research and eventual translation of Giorgio Otranto's work which documents the existence of female priests in the Roman Catholic Church's tradition.

Martin, John. "Canon Law Discovers the Laity," in *Compass* 4 (Oct. 1987), pp. 22-25. In this brief article, John Martin manages to critique the role of the laity in the former code of canon law in comparison to that in the revised 1983 edition of the code. He raises some significant questions and charts a course for the work that needs to be accomplished on a more practical level. Although quite limited in terms of space, the article very efficiently discusses the main issues at hand and explains the technicalities involved.

Massey, Lesly F. *Women and the New Testament: An Analysis of Scripture in Light of New Testament Era Culture* (Jefferson, N.C.: McFarland & Co., 1989). This work examines the position of women in the New Testament, and seeks to redefine their roles within their social and cultural parameters. In doing so, Massey calls attention to the liberating word when appropriated from a feminist perspective.

Matthews, Mary. "Developments in the Lay-Church Since Vatican II — Focus on

Canada" (unpublished, Regis College Lecture Series, 1987). As the title suggests, this talk discusses the Canadian Catholic Church's growth in its identification as a lay church. In doing so, Mary Matthews aptly handles various canonical and conciliar texts which give the "official" treatment of the laity. The talk concludes with an enumeration of priorities which were expressed to the bishops in October of 1986.

———. "Where We Are Today," in *National Bulletin on Liturgy* 8, pp. 19–28. Here, Mary Matthews discusses the main tensions lay people encounter in the Canadian Catholic Church with a strong emphasis on ministry.

Metz, Johannes-Baptist, and Edward Schillebeeckx, eds., "God as Father?" *Concilium* vol. 143 (New York: Seabury Press, 1981). In this *Concilium* issue, various scholars address the topic of the Fatherhood of God. Essays include historical approaches, theological issues, practical implications, and the like. The reader will come to appreciate the innovative concepts which these authors offer.

Mickelsen, Alvera, ed. *Women, Authority and the Bible* (Downers Grove, Illinois: Intervarsity Press, 1986). This work probes the scriptural teaching set forth regarding women, and challenges the authority from which this teaching has been defined.

Micks, Marianne H., and Charles P. Price, eds. *Towards a New Theology of Ordination: Essays on the Ordination of Women* (Mass.: Greeno, Hadden, 1976). This work is a collection of nine essays which discuss the ordination of women in the Episcopal Church. A careful reading of the text demonstrates the similarities with which the Episcopal churches wrestle and those which continue to plague the Roman Catholic Church. For example, this work treats such questions as authority in ministry, the role of women in the early church, and the significance of the "Abba" father model. A reading of the text enriches the Roman Catholic understanding because it calls into question similar issues, and offers new insight as to how these issues can be resolved.

Moll, Helmut, ed. *The Church and Women: A Compendium* (San Francisco: Ignatius Press, 1988). This is a compilation of sixteen dialogical essays which attempt to resolve an issue which emerges in North American and German churches alike: What is the specific identity of women in the Church and how can this identity shape roles for women in such a setting? These essays present moral and theological approaches from contemporary Catholic theologians concerned with this issue. As such, these essays are quite traditional and reiterate the *Declaration*'s teaching on the admission of women to priestly orders. The contributors remain quite resistant to contemporary feminist scholarship, and I would caution anyone reading this work to recognize the blinders these authors have obviously not shed.

Mollenkott, Virginia. *Women, Men and the Bible* (New York: Crossroad, 1989). This is a revised edition which includes bibliographical notes and a six-session study guide designed for private or group use.

Moltmann-Wendel, Elisabeth. *The Women Around Jesus,* transl. John Bowden (New York: Crossroad, 1982). In this work, Elisabeth Moltmann-Wendel seeks to rediscover the biblical images of certain women whose significance has been repressed through biblical translations, historical Church traditions and the like. In doing so, Moltmann-Wendel describes these women as actively engaged in ministerial roles which she very illustratively demonstrates through art work and paintings. The work heightens women's self-awareness and impels its readers toward justice and equality for all.

Morris, Joan. *The Lady Was a Bishop* (New York: MacMillan, 1973). In this work, Joan Morris explores the history of women leaders in early Christianity, with particular emphasis on the episcopate, the community overseers. Her work abounds in bibliographical sources and is well documented.

Murphy, Mary Beth. "Final Draft of Pastoral on Women Called Inferior," in *Milwaukee Sentinel* (Sept. 12, 1992). This article documents the American bishops' indecisiveness regarding the contents of the Pastoral on Women. It also mentions the Vatican's interference and outside influence on the writing committee which can be attributed to the division which exists between the bishops and the Vatican.

_____. "Fourth Pastoral Draft Called the Worst," in *The Milwaukee Sentinel* (Sept. 11, 1992). This article documents the extent to which the role of women in the Church is seriously being addressed among American bishops. The lengthy debates regarding the Pastoral on Women certainly attest to the complexities involved when considering the role of women in the Church today.

Norris, R.A., Jr. "The Ordination of Women and the Maleness of Christ," in Monica Furlong, ed., *Feminine in the Church* (London: SPCK, 1984), pp. 71-85. In this article, Norris maintains that the exclusion of women to the presbyterate based on Christ's maleness is contrary to Christian doctrine. His thought here is indicative of the struggles that various modern-day priests encounter.

O'Connell, Timothy E., ed. *Vatican II and Its Documents* (Wilmington, Delaware: Michael Glazier Press, 1986). This work is a compilation of essays which discuss specific facets of the Vatican II documents. As such, each essay unfolds the basic content of a certain document, the work that has occurred since, and the work that remains to be done. This is a good resource for classroom discussion or private reflection.

Oddie, William. *What Will Happen to God? Feminism and the Reconstruction of Christian Belief* (San Francisco: Ignatius Press, 1988). This work examines the methodology which contemporary feminist scholars are currently employing and their reconstructive techniques. Oddie supports the traditional perspective on women's "place" in society and in religious institutions.

Osiek, Carolyn. *Beyond Anger: On Being a Feminist in the Church* (New York: Paulist Press, 1986). This work is addressed to North American women who find themselves in a Catholic setting. As such, Osiek's main goal is to impel hope in situations which continue to plague women and to demonstrate a reconciliation that can liberate women from discrimination and oppression. This is a work about self-awareness and dignity for Catholic women.

Parvey, Constance F. "The Theology and Leadership of Women in the New Testament," in Rosemary Radford Ruether, ed., *Religion and Sexism: Images of Women in the Jewish and Christian Traditions* (New York: Simon & Schuster Press, 1974), pp. 117-149. This is a very detailed study which identifies certain roles for women in scripture as reflected through a first-century Jewish and cultural framework. Parvey's main contention is that the cultural guidelines exemplified for women in scripture were later adapted as a moral code for all women for all time. This work is a good source for those attempting to identify roles for women in the early Church.

Peterson, Randy. "What About Paul?" in *Christian History* 8, no. 1 (Issue 17), pp. 26-31. This article examines the basis for Paul's statements regarding the role of women in early church assemblies. There are no bibliographical notes, but scriptural sources are well documented.

Platt, Elizabeth E. "The Ministry of Mary of Bethany," in *Theology Today* 34 (1977), pp. 29-39. In this article, Elizabeth E. Platt examines the canonical accounts relating the story of the woman who anointed Jesus in search of criteria for women's ministries in a contemporary setting. Although this study is quite brief, Platt manages to treat the four accounts separately, and in doing so, seeks to identify the significance each writer conveys for a contemporary understanding of women's roles.

"Pope Speaks Out on the Role of Laity and of Women in the Church," in *The Prairie Messenger* (July 19, 1993), pp. 18-19. This article reiterates Pope John Paul II's refusal to confer ordination upon women, based on the traditional arguments which impede such a practice. The text cited in the article is an excerpt from his remarks of July 2, 1993, to United States bishops.

Quitslund, Sonya A. "In the Image of Christ," in Swidler and Swidler, eds., *Women Priests* (New York: Paulist Press, 1974), pp. 260-270. This article challenges the *Declaration*'s claim that women cannot sacramentally represent Christ. Although brief, it is well documented and offers innovative insights regarding the conflicts involved.

Radford Ruether, Rosemary. *Contemporary Roman Catholicism: Crises and Challenges* (Kansas City, Mo.: Sheed & Ward, 1987). This work examines the significance and future of the institutional Roman Catholic Church in light of contemporary challenges. Although Ruether's starting point is American Catholicism, the issues treated are applicable internationally.

_____. "The Female Nature of God: A Problem in Contemporary Religious Life," in "God as Father?" *Concilium* 143 (1981), pp. 61-66. In this article, Ruether raises several implications which result from according God an exclusively male presence. From there, she turns to acknowledging God as a spiritual being which is beyond male or female characteristics in an attempt to move away from the patriarchal overtones which personify the Roman Catholic portrayal of God as father.

_____. "Feminist Interpretation: A Method of Correlation," in Letty M. Russell, ed., *Feminist Interpretation of the Bible* (New York: Basil Blackwell, Inc., 1985), pp. 111-124. In this article, Ruether maintains that women's experience does indeed affect the manner in which scripture was shaped and the manner in which theological tradition was and still is handed on today.

_____. "John Paul II and the Growing Alienation of Women from the Church," in Küng and Swidler, eds., *The Church in Anguish* (San Francisco: Harper and Row, 1987), pp. 279-283. In this brief article, Ruether manages to identify some of the root causes for women's alienation from the Roman Catholic Church today. In doing so, she touches upon a feminist theology and challenges the Roman Catholic Church to revamp its patriarchal structure.

_____. *Mary—The Feminine Face of the Church* (Philadelphia: Westminster Press, 1977). This work studies the feminine aspects of the Roman Catholic Church tradition, with a strong emphasis on Mary. Each chapter concludes with a few discussion questions for the reader's own reflection. Included is a guide for a study of this work which can be structured in small groups.
_____. *New Woman/New Earth: Sexist Ideologies & Human Liberation* (New York: Seabury Press, 1975). This work discusses the religious aspects of women's sexual roles, in light of the teaching put forth within Roman Catholicism.
_____. "Ordination: What Is the Problem?" in Anne Marie Gardiner, S.S.N.D., ed., *Women and Catholic Priesthood: An Expanded Vision* (New York: Paulist Press, 1976), pp. 30–34. In this brief article Ruether challenges the patriarchal and hierarchic structure of the Roman Catholic Church and identifies its exclusion of women from the ministerial priesthood as an idolatrous sin of sexism.
_____. "The Roman Catholic Story," in Ruether and McLaughlin, eds., *Women of Spirit: Female Leadership in the Jewish & Christian Traditions* (New York: Simon & Schuster Press, 1979), pp. 373–383. In this brief article, Ruether documents the struggle for women's ordination within Roman Catholicism, and challenges the hierarchy to change its traditional mindset.
_____. *Sexism and God-Talk: Toward a Feminist Theology* (Mass.: Beacon Press, 1983). This work discusses a Christian theology from a feminist perspective and seeks to liberate men and especially women from the structural parameters of Roman Catholicism within this framework.
_____. *To Change the World: Christological and Cultural Criticism* (New York: Crossroad, 1981). This work is a collection of five essays which discuss a christological approach to contemporary questions. As such, it is a good starting point for discussion groups or private reflection.
_____. *Women-Church: Theology and Practice of Feminist Liturgical Communities* (San Francisco: Harper and Row, 1985). This book is designed to respond to Catholic women's needs which are continuously being thwarted by the official Church. In doing so, this work provides an outlet for women's liberation through faith as well as worship. It is an important resource which includes various liturgies and theological reflections.
_____. "Women Priests and Church Tradition," in Swidler and Swidler, eds., *Women Priests: A Catholic Commentary on the Vatican Declaration* (New York: Paulist Press, 1974), pp. 234–238. In this brief article, Ruether challenges the *Declaration*'s claim that the exclusion of women from priestly orders is an "unbroken" tradition, and manages to cast some doubt as to the validity of such a claim.
_____, and Eleanor McLaughlin, eds. *Women of Spirit: Female Leadership in the Jewish and Christian Traditions* (New York: Simon & Schuster Press, 1979). This work contains a series of essays which treat the leadership of women in the Jewish and Christian traditions. It seeks to reclaim women's history despite the patriarchal character which predominates historical as well as biblical sources. The contributors provide an excellent resource for recovering women's roles in the early Jewish and Christian traditions.

Raming, Ida. *The Exclusion of Women from the Priesthood: Divine Law or Sex Discrimination,* transl. Norman R. Adams (New Jersey: Scarecrow Press,

1976). This work examines the legal and historical impediments for women's exclusion from the ministerial priesthood in light of the traditional understanding of priesthood and ecclesiology. This is an excellent source for the history of the juridical tradition in the Roman Catholic Church.

Ratzinger, Joseph Cardinal. "On the Position of Mariology and Marian Spirituality Within the Totality of Faith and Theology," transl. Graham Harrison, in Helmut Moll, ed., *The Church and Women: A Compendium* (San Francisco: Ignatius Press, 1988), pp. 67-79. Here, Cardinal Ratzinger traces the development and significance of Mariology within Roman Catholic tradition. In doing so, Ratzinger relates Mary's "biological" function with women's "proper" role in the created order. As such, Ratzinger reiterates the traditional perspective on women's passivity and subordinate state.

"The Role of the Laity ... an Interview with Mary Matthews," in *Canadian Catholic Review* (June 1987), pp. 219-222. In this brief interview, Mary Matthews speaks about the Canadian aspects of Catholic laity. The introduction gives a good synopsis of her involvement within the Canadian Catholic Church in the last twenty years.

Rossi, Mary Ann. "Priesthood, Precedent, and Prejudice: On Recovering the Women Priests of Early Christianity," in Judith Plaskow et al., eds., *Journal of Feminist Studies in Religion* 7, no. 1 (Spring, 1991), pp. 73-93. In this article Mary Ann Rossi translates Giorgio Otranto's Italian text which uncovers historical and archaeological evidence which supports the existence of women priests as late as the fifth century A.D. This paper is very detailed and abounds in bibliographical information regarding the priesthood of women.

Russell, Letty M., ed. *Feminist Interpretation of the Bible* (New York: Basil Blackwell Ltd., 1985). This work is a compilation of essays which discuss various issues that relate to a feminist hermeneutical approach for a study of the liberating word of God. The work abounds in feminist biblical scholarships, and includes a postscript which describes the journey one encounters when searching for biblical truths and spiritual wholeness.

Sanderson, Judith. "Jesus and Women," in *The Other Side* (July-August, 1973), pp. 16-21, 35-36. In this brief article, Judith Sanderson demonstrates the manner in which Jesus' treatment of women was quite revolutionary, given women's cultural condition in first century Palestine. In doing so, Sanderson discusses various scriptural texts in which Jesus accords women freedom and dignity, despite religious and social customs of the day. This article has no secondary references, although scriptural sources abound and are well documented.

Scanzoni, Letha, and Nancy Hardesty. *All We're Meant to Be* (Waco, Texas: Word Books, 1974). In this work, authors Letha Scanzoni and Nancy Hardesty develop a biblical approach to men's and especially women's modern day issues. In doing so, they call their readers' attention to the sociological, biblical and psychological elements which contribute to our modern day identification of men and women. The work includes a helpful study guide which can assist an individual or group who is currently encountering similar conflicts.

Schillebeeckx, Edward. *The Church with a Human Face* (New York: Crossroad,

1985). This work is a continued reflection of the same author's book *Ministry,* published in 1981. It includes an extensive bibliography and an index of biblical references and names. This book probes modern day questions and conflicts in the light of the practice of the early Christian communities. The historicity of the Christian tradition is well documented. This book is a good resource for biblical studies as well.

_____. *The Definition of a Christian Layman* (Staten Island, New York: Alba House, 1963). This is a handy guide which traces the historical development and theological significance of the Christian laity.

_____. *Ministry: Leadership in the Community of Jesus Christ* (New York: Crossroad, 1981). This work reflects upon the theological understanding of ministry in the early Christian communities and its development and practice throughout the historical tradition of Roman Catholicism. The work closes with an interesting perspective on the Church of the future. The work is well documented with bibliographical information.

Schneiders, Sandra M. *Beyond Patching: Faith and Feminism in the Catholic Church* (New York: Paulist Press, 1991). A good introduction on feminist theology and spirituality which serves as a basic guide for the vocabulary, methodologies and framework which Catholic feminism explores.

_____. "Did Jesus Exclude Women from Priesthood?" in Swidler and Swidler, eds., *Women Priests: A Catholic Commentary on the Vatican Declaration* (New York: Paulist Press, 1974), pp. 227-233. In this brief but well documented article, Schneiders challenges the *Declaration*'s claim that Christ's will would be transgressed if the Church decided to ordain women. In doing so, Schneiders manages to shed some doubt as to the plausibility of such a claim.

_____. "The Effects of Women's Experience on Their Spirituality," in Joann Wolski Conn, ed., *Women's Spirituality: Resources for Christian Development* (New York: Paulist Press, 1986), pp. 31-48. As the title suggests, this article examines the effects of male dominance on women's spirituality. This article is well documented and describes psychological and sociological patterns which women display when experiencing a dominating male behavior.

_____. *The Revelatory Text: Interpreting the New Testament as Sacred Scripture* (San Francisco: HarperCollins, 1991). This work offers a methodology for the study and interpretation of the New Testament as a sacred text. This is a good resource for pastors, teachers and students. References are well documented, and the book includes a wide range of thought.

Scholer, David M. "I Timothy 2:9-15 & the Place of Women in the Church's Ministry," in Alvera Mickelsen, ed., *Women, Authority & the Bible* (Downers Grove, Illinois: Intervarsity Press, 1986), pp. 193-219. In this article, David M. Scholer maintains that proper interpretation is vital when regarding texts (attributed to Paul) which discuss women in ministry. Scholer offers his own exegesis of the texts involved and concludes that proper conduct is discussed when regarding a specific situation and that prescriptions given throughout these texts were not meant to be interpreted as a code for women's conduct in varying circumstances.

Schüssler-Fiorenza, Elisabeth. "Breaking the Silence — Becoming Visible," in E. Schüssler-Fiorenza and Mary Collins, eds., *Women, Invisible in Church and Theology* (Edinburgh: T. and T. Clark, Ltd., 1985), vol. 182, pp. 3-16. This article calls attention to the patriarchal castes and ideologies which continue to exclude women from positions of authority and decision-making in the Church. In doing so, Schüssler-Fiorenza demands the full participation of women in the shape of a discipleship of equals as a liberating motif for women's spirituality.

_____. *But She Said: Feminist Practices of Biblical Interpretation* (Boston: Beacon Press, 1992). In this work, Elisabeth Schüssler-Fiorenza continues her quest for a critical feminist biblical hermeneutic. Anyone endeavoring to read this book should perhaps begin with *Bread Not Stone* by the same author, as *But She Said* serves as a sequel to that work.

_____. *In Memory of Her: A Feminist Reconstruction of Christian Origins* (New York: Crossroad, 1983). A feminist scholarly work which heightens one's awareness of the androcentrism that predominates scripture and the Roman Catholic tradition. As a biblical scholar, Schüssler-Fiorenza builds upon a feminist hermeneutic of historical reconstruction. This work is dynamic, scholarly and very complex. I would suggest an in-depth knowledge of scripture prior to undertaking the reading of this work.

_____. "The Sophia—God of Jesus and the Discipleship of Women," in Joann Wolski Conn, ed., *Women's Spirituality: Resources for Christian Development* (New York: Paulist Press, 1986), pp. 261-273. In this article, Schüssler-Fiorenza maintains that the God that Jesus proclaimed was one of justice and equality for all. This in turn is used to justify the inclusion of various women disciples in scripture, regardless of the patriarchal character which dominated women in that particular social setting.

_____. "The Will to Choose or to Reject: Continuing Our Critical Work," in Letty M. Russell, ed., *Feminist Interpretation of the Bible* (New York: Basil Blackwell, Inc., 1985), pp. 125-136. In this article, Schüssler-Fiorenza proposes a feminist method for the interpretation of the Bible whose goal is to liberate women from certain dominating forces she identifies as patriarchy. In doing so, revelation is defined as women's struggle to overcome patriarchy, rather than the biblical texts themselves. This is an excellent method which can be applied to most biblical texts.

_____. "Women Apostles: The Testament of Scripture," in Anne Marie Gardiner, S.S.N.D., ed., *Women and Catholic Priesthood: An Expanded Vision* (New York: Paulist Press, 1976), pp. 94-102. In this well-documented though brief article, Schüssler-Fiorenza challenges the exclusion of women from the ministerial priesthood from a scriptural perspective.

_____. "Women in Pre-Pauline and Pauline Churches," in *Union Seminary Quarterly Review* 33 (Spring and Summer 1978), pp. 153-166. This article basically follows the same schema as "Women in the New Testament" but is more detailed and includes bibliographical notes.

_____. "Women in the Early Christian Movement," in Carol P. Christ and Judith Plaskow, eds., *Womanspirit Rising: A Feminist Reader in Religion* (San Francisco: Harper and Row, 1979), pp. 84-92. This article is published in a larger work which focuses on women's spirituality and the feminist challenge to Christian tradition. Schüssler-Fiorenza's article in particular calls attention to women's role in early Christian tradition.

_____. "Women in the New Testament," in *New Catholic World* (Nov./Dec.,

1976), pp. 256-260. This article gives a brief synopsis of the women who figured prominently in the early Christian communities. Scriptural sources are well documented.

———. "Word, Spirit and Power: Women in Early Christian Communities," in Ruether and McLaughlin, eds., *Women of Spirit*, pp. 29-70. In this well-documented article, Schüssler-Fiorenza challenges the notion that women were insignificant in scripture and in the early Church by introducing secondary source material. This is an excellent resource for any study regarding women in the Bible.

"Selection from Homily of Pope Paul VI to the Third World Congress of Lay Apostolate on the Layman's Sphere of Action," in Odile M. Liebard, ed., *Clergy and Laity* (Wilmington, N.C.: McGrath, 1978), pp. 289-295. This article documents the Catholic Church's teaching on clergy and laity.

Sheehan, Mary Ellen. "When Sleeping Women Awake ... A Reflection on Women's Experience in the Catholic Church Today," in *Women, for What World, in What Church?* Donum Dei Series #30, Canadian Religious Conference (Ottawa, 1985), pp. 69-83. This talk reflects upon reclaiming full membership for women in the Church as disciples and equals based upon the community which Jesus inspired and loved through a giving of himself. In baptism, all are invited to exemplify Jesus' life of service and commitment to community.

Stagg, Evelyn, and Frank Stagg. *Women in the World of Jesus* (Philadelphia: Westminster Press, 1978). This book explores the world into which Jesus came, as well as the one which Jesus came to liberate, by probing the religious and cultural settings which defined first-century Judaism. In doing so, Evelyn Stagg and Frank Stagg question women's identity, Jesus' treatment of women, and the early Church's perspective on women, bearing in mind that Jesus remains a fundamental and authoritative source for contemporary theology. This work has well documented sources and appeals to contemporary feminist scholarship.

Swidler, Arlene. *Woman in a Man's Church* (New York: Paulist Press, 1972). Although somewhat dated, this work calls attention to various questions which are still relevant for contemporary women. Each section examines women in a particular situation and concludes with a series of questions designed to incite further reflection either privately or in small groups.

Swidler, Leonard. *Biblical Affirmations of Women* (Philadelphia: Westminster Press, 1979). This work searches for the treatment of women in biblical tradition and seeks to identify the positive elements in women's lives despite the restrictions imposed upon women, in a culturally governed text. In doing so, Swidler calls attention to women's social and religious status and impels his readers to look beyond the language of the text and extract positive characteristics that appropriately define women. Swidler's work is richly documented and abounds in biblical as well as scholarly sources. It gives a wonderful introduction to the significance of women in biblical tradition.

———. "Jesus Was a Feminist," in *Catholic World* (Jan. 1971), pp. 177-183. In this brief article, Leonard Swidler accords Jesus the title of a feminist or one who promotes the dignity and equality of all people, regardless of their sex, color or race. To do this, Swidler undertakes the study of certain scriptural texts which demonstrate Jesus' special interest in and compassion for the poor and the disadvantaged, most of whom, Swidler attests, were women. Swidler's article depends solely on scriptural texts and is devoid of any secondary source material.

_____. *Women in Judaism: The Status of Women in Formative Judaism* (New Jersey: Scarecrow Press, 1976). This study examines the social and religious standing of women when Judaism emerged as an organized religion—notably between the second and fifth centuries A.D. Swidler employs an historical-critical methodology and offers a well-documented study.

_____, and Arlene Swidler, eds. *Women Priests: A Catholic Commentary on the Vatican Declaration* (New York: Paulist Press, 1974). This excellent source gives an overview of the main questions surrounding the *Declaration*'s argument. These questions are treated in various articles. Also included in this work is a commentary on the *Declaration* and *The Biblical Commission's Report: Can Women Be Priests?*

Synod of Bishops: Rome, 1987 (Ottawa, Canada: C.C.C.B., 1987). This series documents five interventions given by the Canadian bishops at the Synod of Bishops in Rome of 1987. It also includes two reports following the synod, as well as a message from the world synod of bishops.

"The Synod Propositions," in *Origins* (Dec. 31, 1987), vol. 17, no. 29. This is a series of 54 propositions which reflect the Synod of Bishops' (1987) deliberations.

Tambasco, Anthony J. *What Are They Saying About Mary?* (New Jersey: Paulist Press, 1984). This work discusses Mary's significance as virgin and saint. It documents the traditional understanding of Mary of Nazareth.

Tetlow, Elizabeth. *Women and Ministry in the New Testament* (New York: Paulist Press, 1980). This work presents a feminist interpretation of scripture in light of the *Declaration*'s exclusion of women priests based on Jesus' ministry and exclusion of women from the Twelve. Tetlow seeks to extract the cultural aspects which shaped scriptural texts in an attempt to redefine appropriate roles for women within Roman Catholicism. Her work includes an appendix which discusses the ministerial evidence found in biblical texts. This work is a good introduction for anyone who wishes to learn more about women's status and function in Jesus' ministry.

Thavis, John. "Pope Wary—Fearful—of 'Radical Feminism'," in *The Prairie Messenger* (July 19, 1993), pp. 1-2. In this article, Pope John Paul II labels feminists' work toward the ordination of women as "extreme" and "bitter," and strongly refutes the notion that Roman Catholicism is plagued by a power-oriented hierarchy.

Sr. Thérèse-André. *Projet vocationnel* (unpublished). This work documents the statistical information regarding the shortage of priests. Although this report was drafted on a diocesan level, it indicates that the number of available priests by the year 2000 will have seriously declined.

Thurston, Bonnie Bowman. *The Widows: A Women's Ministry in the Early Church* (Minneapolis, MN: Fortress Press, 1989). This work probes the early Christian centuries in an attempt to define the history of and scriptural foundation for widows. Bowman Thurston uncovers widows' role and function in early Christianity.

Tolbert, Mary Ann, ed. *The Bible and Feminist Hermeneutics* (Semeia 28, 1983). This work examines a feminist critical hermeneutic for biblical interpretation in the light of Jewish and Christian traditions.

Torjesen, Karen. "The Early Controversies Over Female Leadership," in *Christian History* vol. 8, no. 1 (Issue 17), pp. 20-24. In this brief article, Torjesen examines the evolution of Church documents which restrict women's leadership and calls into question the conflicts which made their exclusion a painful reality and a prescription in the Church for a long period of time. In doing so, Torjesen demonstrates her knowledge of early Church documents and her ability to focus on the issues at hand.

Vogel, Arthur A. "Christ, Revelation and the Ordination of Women," in Marianne H. Micks and Charles P. Price, eds., *Toward a New Theology of Ordination: Essays on the Ordination of Women* (Somerville, Mass.: Greeno, 1976), pp. 42-51. In this article, Vogel challenges the theological and traditional arguments which the ordination of women calls into question.

Walker, William O., Jr. "The Theology of Woman's Place and the Paulinist Tradition," in Mary Ann Tolbert, ed., *The Bible & Feminist Hermeneutics* (Semeia 28, 1983), pp. 101-112. In this article, Walker maintains that the New Testament texts (attributed to Paul) which support the subordination of women emerged from a specific source which was neither apostolic nor apparent throughout the early Church.

Weakland, Reverend Rembert G. *Talk/Roman Synod—October, 1987* (unpublished). This "talk" was presented at the occasion of the Synod of Bishops in 1987 and supports more authoritative roles for women and their full equality within the Church.

Witherington, Ben. *Women in the Earliest Churches* (New York: Cambridge University Press, 1984). This study probes the biblical texts which discuss women's significance in the early Christian communities. This is an academic work which makes use of various journals and commentaries.

Wolski Conn, Joann, ed. *Women's Spirituality: Resources for Christian Development* (New York: Paulist Press, 1986). This collection of essays discusses various issues in women's spirituality by probing women's psychological and religious developmental patterns within Christian tradition. It serves as an excellent resource book for Christian educators, psychologists, counselors and students.

Women, for What World, in What Church? Donum Dei Series #30, Canadian Religious Conference (Ottawa, 1985). This collection of essays reflects on the situation of women in the Church today, and identifies a contradiction with the gospel. From there, the attention shifts to the dynamics with which reconciliation can occur for women at every level of the hierarchy, including social and religious spheres. This is a significant study which accurately describes the historical, traditional and social contexts for the discrimination against women in the Church today.

"Women's Ordination Conference Broadens Horizons," in *Catholic New Times* (June 12, 1988), p. 1. This article defines the *Catholic Network for Women's Equality*'s raison d'être, and names the newly elected five-member group which was chosen to represent the organization.

Wooden, Cindy. "Pope, Québec Bishops Differ on Role of Women," in *The*

Prairie Messenger (May 17, 1993), p. 6. This article documents the Pope's refusal to include women as full members of the Church, despite a plea from the Québec bishops to reconsider the role of women in a society which encourages the equality of men and women alike.

Index

Aaron 23
"Abba" 31
Abraham 96
Access of Women to Church Positions 106
Acts 33, 40, 45, 64, 67, 86, 135
Adam 23, 25, 126
altar servers 79, 80, 103, 104, 105, 108-111, 113-115
Anderson, Grace M. 99
androcentrism 37, 53, 54
Andronicus 65, 66
Apollos 57
apostle 4, 8, 12-14, 18-20, 22, 25, 37, 41, 42, 45, 46, 48, 49, 51, 63-65, 68, 82, 85, 88-90, 118, 119, 123, 125, 127, 135, 145, 146
Apostolic Constitutions 62, 68
Aquila 57, 60, 65-67
Aquinas, Thomas 16, 18
Argan, Glen 120
Ashe, Kaye 105

baptism 2, 19, 20, 26, 35, 62, 65, 66, 74, 77, 78, 81-83, 94, 98, 109, 112, 115, 116, 134, 135, 147
Baroni, Lise 99, 100, 103, 104, 108, 112, 116
Bernier, Sandra 106, 110
Bible 3, 4, 12, 21, 29, 37, 38, 51-54, 56, 99, 103, 125, 145
bishops 13, 18, 68, 73, 75, 88, 89, 95-97, 122, 147
Bishops' Synod 76, 80-82, 84, 90, 101, 102, 106, 112

Blakley, Alan F. 75
"Body of Christ" 106
Bonhoeffer 128
Boucher, Madeleine I. 16, 18
Bride-Bridegroom analogy 9, 22, 24, 55, 107, 121
Brooten, Bernadette 56, 65
Brown, Raymond E. 9, 13, 26, 33, 127
Byrne, Brendan, S.J. 52, 58

C.C.C.B. (Canadian Conference of Catholic Bishops) 96
C.T.S.C. (Canadian Theological Students' Conference) 96
Calcutta 132
Callahan, Sidney 21, 103
Cardman, Francine 10, 11
caro 15, 25
Carroll, Elizabeth 10, 11
Carter, Cardinal 75
Catholic Network for Women's Equality 111
Cenchreae 4, 63
Chiasson, Archbishop 83, 84, 137
Chittister, Sister Joan 15, 22, 23
Chrysostom, John 65
The Church with a Human Face 133
Civil War 120
Clarke, Juanne Nancarrow 99
clericalism 95, 96, 100, 116, 140-142
Colossians 67
confirmation 82
Connell, Monsignor Desmond 23, 24

Cooke, Bernard 13, 20, 24, 30, 31, 64–66, 86–88, 121, 129, 130–132, 134, 141
Coriden, James A. 79
Corinthians 8, 53, 57–60, 62, 64–66, 126, 135
Council of Chalcedon 89
Council of Trent 22
culture 11, 16, 23, 29–33, 47, 52, 53, 56, 57, 61, 72, 82, 87, 102, 110, 111, 120, 125, 126

David 23, 30
Deborah 66
Declaration on the Question of the Admission of Women to the Ministerial Priesthood 2–5, 7, 8, 10–16, 18, 19, 22, 23–27, 29, 30, 39, 42, 45, 47–49, 51, 56–62, 64, 82, 88, 97, 104, 117, 118, 123, 145, 147
Decree on the Missionary Activity of the Church 134
diakoneo (nos) 40, 62, 63, 68, 86, 103, 133, 135, 136
Didaskalia 62
disciple 8, 33–39, 41, 43–46
discipleship 88, 114
discipleship of equals 1, 6, 54, 55, 122, 147
Donahue, John R. 8, 16
Dorca 67
The Double-Cross: Ordination, Abortion and Catholic Feminism 131
Doyle, Bishop James L. 73
Dulles, Avery 80, 81, 84, 128, 130, 134

The Effects of Women's Experience on Their Spirituality 138
ekklēsia 2, 142, 147
the Eleven 35
Ephesus 61
Eucharist 5, 9, 13, 19, 20, 22, 23, 38, 48, 55, 65–67, 89, 109, 110, 133, 142, 146
Eusebius 66
Eve 23, 126
The Exclusion of Women from the Priesthood: Divine Law or Sex Discrimination 17
Exodus 46
Ezekiel 46
Ezra 46

Farley, Margaret 16, 17
Father imagery 15, 18, 20–23, 31, 36, 75, 107, 111, 121, 124
Faxon, Alicia Craig 38, 40
Fessio, Father Joseph 106–109, 110–112, 114, 115
Flahiff, Cardinal George B. 98
Forest, Jean 98, 110
Fortna, Robert 37

Galatians 21, 25, 58
Galilee 35, 40, 45
Galileo 123
Gaudium et Spes 115, 129
Genesis 113
Gentiles 12, 57, 87
Gillman, Florence 12, 57
God Calls: Man Chooses—A Study of Women in Ministry 99
Good News 88, 119, 132
gospel 4, 10, 30, 33–35, 37, 40, 42, 46, 72, 76, 111, 125, 128, 141, 145
Gottwald, N. 46
Gryson, Roger 68
Günther, Heinz 45–49, 127

Haight, Roger 77
Hamelin, Archbishop 83, 106, 112–114
Hardesty, Nancy 30, 62
Haughton, Rosemary 76
Hayes, Archbishop 83

Hebrews 9-10, 15
Heine, Suzanne 63
Hermaniuk, Archbishop 82
hierarchy 19, 23, 36, 39, 56, 72-76, 81, 87, 88, 90, 93, 96, 100, 102, 105, 116, 121-123, 131, 132, 135-137, 140, 142, 146, 147
Holy Bible (N.C.E.) 37
Holy Spirit 10, 12, 18, 34, 35, 46, 54, 66, 82, 90, 94, 135, 147; *see also* Spirit
Hopko, Thomas 17, 18
house Church 66, 67, 125, 126
Hubert, Bishop Bernard 75, 101
Huels, John 79
Huldah 66
Humanae Vitae 115, 136

incarnation 15, 20, 24, 55, 107, 109, 118, 124
Interpreter's Bible 67
Isaiah 66
Israel 46, 47, 87, 130

James 4, 13, 45
Jeremiah 23
Jerusalem: Bible 15; Church 13; town 40, 86
Jewett, Robert 63, 64
Joanna 40
John 4, 33, 34, 36, 37, 39
John XXIII, Pope 131-132
John Paul II, Pope 15, 22, 29, 32, 112, 116, 117
Joses 40
Judaism 9, 15, 17, 30, 31, 35, 36, 39, 43, 47, 49, 52, 53, 58, 86, 87, 118
Judas 3, 4, 39, 45, 64
Junia(s) 4, 14, 65, 66

Karris, Robert 59
Kilmartin, Edward J.S.J. 12

King, Martin Luther, Jr. 131
Klauck 63
Komonchak, Joseph A. 20, 21, 22, 25
Kroeger, Catherine 63, 65, 67, 68

Lacelle, Elisabeth J. 116
lalein 59
laos 72
Lardner-Carmody, Denise 129, 131, 132, 134, 141
Last Supper 4, 5, 8, 9, 13, 38, 46, 146
Lay-Ministries Formation Program 98-99
Lazarus 3, 33, 37
Lebel, Bishop 104
Leckey, Dolores 103, 104
liberation theology *see* theology of liberation
Lineamenta 74, 81, 82
Luke 9, 34-36, 40-42, 64, 67, 119, 124, 125
Lydia of Thyatria 67

McAteer, Michael 84
McBrien, Richard 85, 88
MacHaffie, Barbara J. 36
McKenna, Sister Mary 67
Maione, Romeo 84
maleness 11, 15-22, 24-26, 30, 31, 44-48, 55, 56, 58, 100, 107, 118-119, 121, 124-127, 138-140
Malone, Mary 97
Mark 8, 32, 33, 35, 38-40, 48, 49, 135
Martha 3, 33, 34, 36, 37, 39
Martin, John 78, 80
Mary Magdalene 3, 40-45, 48, 118, 145
Mary of Bethany 36-39, 41
Mary of Nazareth 3, 15, 40, 42-44, 108, 117, 119, 120, 124, 139
Massey, Lesly F. 66-68
Matthew 2, 20, 35, 38, 41, 130
Matthews, Mary 73, 93

Matthias 45
metanoïa 128, 147
Ministry: Leadership in the Community of Jesus Christ 89
The Ministry of Women in the Early Church 68
Ministry to Word and Sacraments 129
Miriam 66
Models of the Church 128
Molinari, Mary Ann 84
Mollenkott, Virginia 52
Moltmann-Wendel, Elisabeth 32, 37
Morris, Joan 58
Morrisey, Rev. Francis 106
Mosaic law 118
Mother Teresa of Calcutta 131

National Conference of Catholic Bishops 96
New Code of Canon Law 74, 78, 80, 90, 104, 105, 111, 112, 116
New Testament 2, 7-10, 13, 20, 22, 25, 26, 29, 31-33, 36, 37, 40, 45, 49, 52, 58, 60, 64-66, 68, 86, 88, 98, 125, 130
Noadiah 66
Norris, R.A., Jr. 19, 25
Nympha of Laodicea 67

Oddie, William 54-55
Old Testament 8-10, 15, 31, 39, 46, 52, 66, 87, 122, 130, 131
On the Dignity and Vocation of Women on the Occasion of the Marian Year 9, 22, 117, 123

Pacem in Terris 115
Palestine 46, 87
Parvey, Constance F. 34
Paschal Mystery 119
patriarchy 17, 19, 21, 23, 29-33, 36, 52-54, 96, 100, 101, 114, 116, 117, 121-123, 127, 132, 140-142

Paul 4, 8, 14, 15, 21, 22, 33, 41, 45, 51-53, 56-68, 87, 98, 126, 145
Paul VI, Pope 2, 74
Pentecost 47
People of God 11, 74, 78, 81, 82, 84, 85, 90, 94, 134, 142
Peter 3, 4, 36, 37, 39, 41, 42, 44, 45, 67
Peterson, Randy 58
Philemon 52
Philip 40
Phoebe 4, 62-64
Platt, Elizabeth E. 38
Pontifical Biblical Commission 2, 7, 8, 10, 25-26, 48, 65, 89, 125
Prisca 57, 60, 65-67
prostasis 63

Quitslund, Sonya A. 15
Qumran 46

Radford Ruether, Rosemary 1, 10-12, 15-17, 20, 21, 39, 42-44, 55, 101, 121-122, 141-142
Raming, Ida 17
Rausch, Thomas P. 8
Reasons Given Against Women Acolytes and Lectors 106
resurrection 33, 41, 42, 45, 47, 64, 66, 131
revelation 17, 55, 66, 108, 118, 121, 124-127, 139, 140, 146
Roman law 110
Romans 4, 14, 25, 57, 60, 62-64, 100, 108
Rome 107
Rossi, Mary Ann 127, 146

Sacred Congregation for Divine Worship 106
Sacred Congregation for the Doctrine of the Faith 7, 29
St. Paul University 106

Salome 40
salvation 1, 2, 6, 19, 25, 55, 72, 75, 81, 82, 102, 107–109, 117, 119, 121, 124, 130, 142, 146
Samaritan 47
Scanzoni, Letha 30, 62
Schillebeeckx, Edward 72, 86, 88, 89, 129, 131, 133, 134, 141
Schneiders, Sandra M. 13, 47, 48, 52, 125, 138–140
Scholer, David 61
Schüssler-Fiorenza, Elisabeth 1, 31, 33, 37–39, 41, 43, 45–47, 51, 53–57, 59–63, 65, 66, 100, 101, 119, 141, 142, 147
scripture 7, 36, 37, 47–49, 51, 52, 58, 103, 118, 124–126, 129, 139, 145
seminary 95, 96, 101, 116
service 2, 8, 34, 36, 38, 40, 43, 59, 60, 64, 71, 76, 80, 85, 88–90, 93, 94, 96, 98, 100, 109, 111, 114, 116, 120, 122, 123, 127–134, 138, 139, 141, 143
sexism 74, 104, 121, 132, 140
Sexism and God-Talk 55
Sheehan, Mary Ellen 95
Sherlock, Bishop 84
Sirach 46
Spain 63, 64
Spirit 55, 75, 86, 108, 119, 129, 132, 135–137, 143; *see also* Holy Spirit
Stagg, Evelyn 33–35, 40, 47
Stagg, Frank 33–35, 40, 47
Statute of Apostles 67
Stephen 40
Susanna 40
Swidler, Arlene 58, 95
Swidler, Leonard 40
synagogue 63

Tambasco, Anthony 43–44
Testament of Our Lord Jesus Christ 68

Tetlow, Elisabeth 35, 36, 39–41, 47, 49, 87
theology of liberation 117, 123, 140, 141
Thessalonians 21, 63
Timothy 8, 57, 60, 61, 67
Titus 61
Torah 30, 39
tradition 4, 7, 8, 10–12, 17, 23, 26 39–45, 47, 49, 51, 53–56, 59, 62, 87, 90, 101, 104, 105, 109, 121, 122, 125–127, 130, 145, 146
Trinity 18
the Twelve 3, 4, 8, 9–10, 12–15, 18, 20, 22, 23, 24–26, 32, 33, 38–40, 45–49, 64–68, 86–87, 96, 118, 119, 124, 125, 127, 145

United Nations 102

Vachon, Archbishop 102, 115
Vatican 97, 101, 104, 106, 110, 111
Vatican II 11, 51, 73–78, 80, 81, 94, 97, 107, 112, 128, 129, 132, 134, 141
virginity 5, 44, 120, 134
vocation 5, 76, 82, 100, 109, 116, 117, 120, 123, 128, 129, 134–137
Vogel, Arthur A. 21, 25

Weakland, Archbishop 97, 101, 113, 114
What Will Happen to God? 54
widow 67, 68
Witherington, Ben 32, 34, 35, 38
witness 8, 42, 45, 64, 66, 86, 87
women-church 2, 142